NEGOTIATION IN SOCIAL CONFLICT

MAPPING SOCIAL PSYCHOLOGY SERIES
Series Editor: Tony Manstead

Current titles:

Icek Ajzen: Attitudes, Personality, and Behavior
Robert S. Baron, Norbert L. Kerr, and Norman Miller: Group Process,
　　Group Decision, Group Action
Steve Duck: Relating to Others
J. Richard Eiser: Social Judgment
Russell G. Geen: Human Aggression
Howard Giles and Nikolas Coupland: Language: Contexts and
　　Consequences
Dean G. Pruitt and Peter J. Carnevale: Negotiation in Social Conflict
John C. Turner: Social Influence
Leslie A. Zebrowitz: Social Perception

Forthcoming titles:

Marilynn B. Brewer and Norman Miller: Intergroup Relations
Miles Hewstone and Neil Macrae: Stereotyping and Social Cognition
Richard Petty and John Cacioppo: Attitude Change
Wolfgang Stroebe and Margaret Stroebe: Social Psychology and Health

NEGOTIATION IN SOCIAL CONFLICT

Dean G. Pruitt
Peter J. Carnevale

BROOKS/COLE PUBLISHING COMPANY
PACIFIC GROVE, CALIFORNIA

University Press
Court
moor
gham MK18 1XW

First Published 1993

This U.S. edition published in 1993 by
Brooks/Cole Publishing Company
A Division of Wadsworth, Inc.
511 Forest Lodge Road
Pacific Grove, CA 93950

Library of Congress Cataloging-in-Publication Data

Pruitt, Dean G.
      Negotiation in social conflict / Dean G. Pruitt and Peter J.
Carnevale.
            p.   cm. — (Mapping social psychology series)
      Includes bibliographical references and index.
      ISBN 0-534-20689-1
      1. Negotiation   2. Social conflict.   I. Carnevale, Peter J.
II. Title.   III. Series.
BF637.N4P79   1993   93-16972
158'.5—dc20   ·   CIP

Typeset by Graphicraft Typesetters Limited, Hong Kong
Printed and bound in the United States by
Malloy Lithographing, Inc.
Ann Arbor, Michigan

We dedicate this book to our spouses and
  parents:
France J. Pruitt and Andrea B. Hollingshead,
Frances M. Carnevale and Hubert A. Carnevale,
and the memory of
Grace G. Pruitt and Dudley M. Pruitt

CONTENTS

FOREWORD

There has long been a need for a carefully tailored series of reasonably short and inexpensive books on major topics in social psychology, written primarily for students by authors who enjoy a reputation for the excellence of their research and their ability to communicate clearly and comprehensibly their knowledge of, and enthusiasm for, the discipline. My hope is that the *Mapping Social Psychology* series will meet that need.

The rationale for this series is twofold. First, conventional textbooks are too low-level and uninformative for use with senior undergraduates or graduate students. Books in this series address this problem partly by dealing with topics at book length, rather than chapter length, and partly by the excellence of the scholarship and clarity of the writing. Each volume is written by an acknowledged authority on the topic in question, and offers the reader a concise and up-to-date overview of the principal concepts, theories, methods and findings relating to that topic. Although the intention has been to produce books that will be used by senior level undergraduates and graduate students, the fact that the books are written in a straightforward style should make them accessible to students with relatively little previous experience of social psychology. At the same time, the books are sufficiently informative to earn the respect of researchers and instructors.

A second problem with traditional textbooks is that they are too dependent on research conducted in or examples drawn from North American society. This fosters the mistaken impression that social psychology is a uniquely North American discipline and can also be baffling for readers unfamiliar with North American culture.

To combat this problem, authors of books in this series have been encouraged to adopt a broader perspective, giving examples or citing research from outside North America wherever this helps to make a point. Our aim has been to produce books for a world market, introducing readers to an international discipline.

In this volume, Dean Pruitt and Peter Carnevale provide a thorough yet highly readable introduction to the social psychological literature on negotiation and mediation as means of resolving social conflict. We hardly need to be reminded that conflict is an all-too-common feature of social life. Indeed, conflict seems to be endemic to social relationships, be they personal, professional, industrial, organizational, or international. Understanding how conflict can most effectively be resolved is clearly a key task for social psychologists, and the authors of this book provide us with an overview of the current state of knowledge. The focus of the book is on understanding what happens when people try to negotiate their way out of social conflict. The authors draw primarily on what they call the behavioral tradition in the study of negotiation, in which investigators try to develop and test theories about the impact of different circumstances on how negotiators behave, and on the outcomes achieved by parties to the negotiation. For example, does it make a difference to negotiator behavior or to outcomes if the negotiators are representatives of the disputants, rather than the disputants themselves? In addressing questions such as this, the authors refer mainly to experimental research, much of it conducted in laboratory settings. The objective of this type of research is to accumulate a stock of theoretical knowledge about the processes involved in negotiation; because these processes are thought to be involved in most if not all types of negotiation, the findings from such studies should be generalizable to different settings. Where appropriate, the authors also cite parallel findings from field research conducted in "natural" settings.

In Chapters 1 through 5 of this book, the authors introduce us to the concepts, methods and key findings that have emerged from what they refer to as the "dominant paradigm" underlying behavioral approaches to negotiation research. In this approach the parties to the negotiation are seen as unitary decision-makers, without a past or future relationship, who have a divergence of interest that they wish to resolve by reaching some verbal agreement. It is assumed that each party wishes to maximize his or her self-interest. In the second half of the book, the authors broaden the scope of research issues beyond those raised by this traditional approach. Thus they take account of the possibility that negotiators may have motivations other than the maximization of self-interest, and they address issues such as the social context of negotiation (e.g. the impact of social norms, relationships, group processes), the time course of negotiation (e.g. what happens before and after the negotiation), and why disputants choose to negotiate rather than, say, go to arbitration. Because these issues have not been addressed within the traditional approach to negotiation, the authors draw quite extensively on literature from neighboring fields of inquiry, such as group dynamics and procedural justice and thereby achieve a more complete picture of the processes involved in negotiation.

Readers who have not specialized in the study of conflict management should find this an excellent introduction to the field. It is written in a highly accessible style and the text is liberally supported with examples and illustrations. No background knowledge is assumed, and concepts and methods are carefully explained. The book should also be of considerable interest to specialists in this area, for it covers the whole field of conflict management, including third-party intervention, provides a comprehensive overview of the findings of past and contemporary research, and successfully integrates contemporary topics in dispute resolution.

Tony Manstead
Series Editor

PREFACE

Negotiation, the main topic of this book, can be defined as a discussion between two or more parties aimed at resolving incompatible goals. The parties involved may be individuals, groups, organizations, or political units such as countries or the UN Security Council. When there are incompatible goals, a state of social conflict exists. Hence, negotiation is a way of dealing with social conflict.

Social conflict, the secondary topic of this book, is an ever growing phenomenon. The menace of nuclear annihilation may have receded in the past few years; but the weakness or disintegration of several authoritarian regimes has unleashed a series of inter-ethnic conflicts that threaten people in many parts of the world. Negotiation, and its close cousin mediation, are the best way to solve most conflicts including these, because they are the main route to win–win solutions. Hence a theory of negotiation speaks to some of the largest problems faced by mankind.

Another reason for studying negotiation is that it presides over much of the change that occurs in human society. Conflict often results from dissatisfaction with the status quo, and it often leads to negotiation about how to do things differently. The agreements achieved in negotiation may involve new divisions of resources, new rules of behavior, new people hired, new departments organized. Hence, negotiation is at the root of many of the norms and social structures that govern society. Society usually prospers if negotiation goes well and the agreements reached are mutually satisfying to the parties involved. Conversely, society is often harmed when negotiation goes poorly and fails to produce a mutually satisfying outcome.

Scholarly writing on negotiation can be roughly divided into "prescriptive" and "descriptive" categories. The prescriptive literature provides practical advice – how to go about negotiation. The descriptive literature characterizes negotiation and examines the forces that determine its course and outcome. This book is primarily in the latter category. Its main aim is to present and critique research findings and scientific theory about how negotiation works. It is based on a solid body of knowledge that has been developed over the past 40 years. Yet at the same time, the book has considerable practical value, because the research and theory that exist today are rich enough to serve as a basis for deriving sound advice. Practical suggestions are provided at many points in the book, and others can be easily derived from the material presented.

We, the authors of this book, were trained in social psychology, and this intellectual orientation is apparent throughout. However, research on negotiation is very interdisciplinary; hence, the book is based on material from a large number of fields. Besides social psychology, these include organizational behavior, communication, economics, game theory, sociology, anthropology, law, industrial relations, international relations, and others.

In keeping with the broader series, this book is a suitable text for advanced undergraduate and graduate courses. We also view it as a contribution to the scholarly literature on negotiation. The first seven chapters summarize and integrate this literature, and a later chapter does the same for mediation, which can be defined as negotiation assisted by a third party. We also critique this literature, pointing out limitations in the theoretical paradigm that underlies most research on negotiation, including our own.

By "theoretical paradigm," we mean the basic picture researchers have of a phenomenon under study and the fundamental assumptions they make about this phenomenon. The standard paradigm in negotiation research makes the oversimplified assumptions that there are only two negotiating parties and that these parties (even if they are organizations or nations) are unitary intelligences whose aim is to maximize self-interest. The paradigm focuses attention on psychological states that affect negotiation and seeks the antecedents of these states in the situation at the time of negotiation. This means that little attention is paid to broader contexts in which negotiation takes place, including the past history of the issues, relationships between the negotiators, and prevailing social norms.

The paradigm also ignores the question of how and why people choose negotiation for dealing with conflict, instead of other procedures such as arbitration or struggle.

The standard paradigm has been very useful for generating new research and theory. But it has come under increasing attack as providing too limited a view of negotiation. One of its deficiencies, the assumption that negotiators are only motivated by self-interest and take no interest in the other party's welfare, has been recently remedied by theoretical and empirical developments discussed in Chapter 7. We have tried to remedy other deficiencies in four later chapters that examine the choices people make among the procedures for dealing with conflict and the impact of social norms, relationships, and group behavior on negotiation. These chapters rely heavily on research outside the realm of negotiation and are more speculative than the earlier chapters.

Researchers studying social conflict have sometimes placed subjects in "games of moves" where negotiation is not permitted. Examples for such games are the prisoner's dilemma, the game of chicken, and various resource (social) dilemmas. These games and most forms of negotiation can be viewed as "mixed-motive" settings, where there are incentives for both cooperation and competition. Many of the findings on these games are similar to those on negotiation. These parallels are noted throughout the book, and we also sometimes extrapolate speculatively from other findings on these games to aspects of negotiation that have not been researched. This means that some sections of the book can be viewed as discussions of behavior in mixed-motive settings in general.

We are very much indebted to three colleagues who read an earlier version of this book and gave us many useful comments: Linda Putnam of Purdue University, Evert van de Vliert of the University of Groningen, and our series editor, Tony Manstead. We are also very grateful to Susan Brodt and Josh Arnold who gave their time to provide many useful comments on one or more chapter drafts. Finally, the encouragement and support of our spouses and parents has meant much to each of us and it is to them that this book is dedicated.

Dean G. Pruitt
Peter J. Carnevale

1 / INTRODUCTION

Sales and Production are at it again! Dan, the Director of Sales, has just lined up two orders for a total of 15,000 men's suits. Together, they will gross over a million dollars, with a fine profit for the company. The only problem is that Dora, the Director of Production, insists that it will take four months to make the suits, and Dan's customers want a two-month turnaround. Dan and Dora are discussing this issue and, so far, have accomplished little more than making each other angry. What will happen next? Can they resolve their differences? If so, how?

Charles is trying to buy a 1992 Mazda. The dealer, Barbara, has mentioned a price of $10,750, and Charles has countered with $9,500. What can be done to bridge this gap? Can both parties succeed in their goals, Charles to get a decent bargain and Barbara to turn a reasonable profit?

Jane and John were married but it didn't work out, and they are trying to divide up the furnishings in their apartment. Both of them think they put more money than the other into the furnishings, and there is some disagreement about who gave what to whom. What approach should each of them take, with what effect? Can they settle their problems amicably?

Mary, a lawyer, has been hired by a school board to negotiate a three-year contract with Rod, the chief negotiator from the teachers' association. There are nineteen issues, including how much is to be paid into the health insurance fund and the wording of rules on personal leave. They have talked and talked, but no agreement has been reached. Finally, a state mediator, Chuck, is called in to help them resolve the impasse. What tactics will this mediator follow, and with what effect? All four of these examples involve negotiation, the latter with the help of a third party or mediator. Our aim in this book is to present a behavioral analysis of this phenomenon – detailing the conditions that determine the way negotiators behave and the effects of this behavior. We will also devote a chapter to mediation, which can be thought of as assisted negotiation.

We will discuss, among other topics, what happens if an executive like Dora publicly commits herself to a negotiation position when she states, to a large group of co-workers, "We will deliver the suits in four months and not a day sooner." We will examine the kinds of ploys a dealer like Barbara might adopt, and the strategies Charles should use to counter them. We will also look at ways in which people like Jane and John can find a mutually acceptable agreement that allows them both to succeed. We will examine the kinds of proposals that are available to mediators like Chuck and the impact of such proposals.

Unlike most other books on negotiation, this is not a cookbook – it is not a collection of recipes or remedies. Rather, it is a research-based analysis that helps us to understand what happens in negotiation. Hence, it provides a solid basis for people like Dora, Charles, Jane, and Chuck, to grasp the situations they are in, to predict how others will behave, and to choose a proper strategy. The past few years have witnessed a rapid growth of scientific knowledge about these topics. This means that we have moved beyond the era of cookbooks.

The nature and importance of negotiation

Negotiation is a discussion between two or more parties with the apparent aim of resolving a divergence of interest and thus escaping social conflict. The parties (also called "disputants") may be individuals, groups, organizations, or political units such as nations. Divergence of interest means that the parties have incompatible preferences among a set of available options. Negotiators are usually seriously interested in reaching agreement; but they occasionally use negotiation as a delaying tactic, to buy time while building the capacity to beat the opponent in some other way (Ikle 1964).

Divergence of interest is found in all social arenas, from relations between children on the playground to international relations. Hence, a theory of negotiation is essential for understanding topics as diverse as marital decision making, industrial relations, inter-office coordination, corporate mergers, intra-group decision making, and international relations.

The arenas just named differ, to some extent, with respect to the way negotiation works. But, in our view, there are more similarities than differences among them, making it possible to develop a general theory of negotiation. This outlook allows us to learn things in one arena that apply to others – for example, to generalize from negotiation between neighbors to negotiation between nations. The theory that is emerging from this enterprise does draw some distinctions between types of settings. For example, it is clear that negotiations between representatives differ in some respects from negotiations between individuals who are acting on their own behalf (see Chapters 4 and 10). Furthermore, negotiators who are concerned about both parties' interests behave rather differently from those who are only concerned about their own interests (see Chapters 4, 5, 6, and 7). Such differences are more fundamental, in our view, than the differences between the arenas in which negotiation takes place.

Strategies in negotiation

It is possible to distinguish five broad strategies that can be used in negotiation. A strategy is a plan of action, specifying broad objectives and the general approach that should be taken to achieve them. Some of these strategies must be translated into more specific tactics in order to be used. The strategies are:

1 *Concession making* – reducing one's goals, demands, or offers.
2 *Contending* – trying to persuade the other party to concede or trying to resist similar efforts by the other party. There are many tactics that can be used to implement this strategy, including threats (messages indicating that one will punish the other party if the other fails to conform) and positional commitments (messages indicating that one will not move from a particular position).
3 *Problem solving* – trying to locate and adopt options that satisfy both parties' goals. There are a host of problem solving

tactics, including active listening and providing information about one's own priorities among the issues under discussion.

4 *Inaction* – doing nothing or as little as possible; for example, putting off meetings, talking around the issues, etc.

5 *Withdrawal* – dropping out of the negotiation.

The first three strategies in this list can be thought of as "coping strategies," because they are alternative ways of moving toward agreement. Assuming that agreement is sought, if conditions reduce the likelihood of using one of the coping strategies, the other two become more likely. If two of these strategies are problematic, the third will be given especially heavy consideration.

Alternatives to negotiation

Negotiation is one of several procedures for dealing with divergence of interest in social conflict. Three broad classes of procedures can be distinguished:

1 *Joint decision making*, which includes negotiation and mediation. Mediation is like negotiation except that a third party helps the disputants reach agreement (see Chapter 11).

2 *Third-party decision making*, which includes adjudication (going to court), arbitration, and decision making by legitimate authorities within an organization.

3 *Separate action*, in which the parties make independent decisions.

Three types of separate action can be distinguished, each with a parallel among the strategies that are available to negotiators.

(a) *Retreat*, in which one of the parties yields to the other's requirements. Retreat has the same effect as concession making in negotiation.

(b) *Struggle*, which can take the form of physical combat (military battles, strikes), wars of words (shouting matches, accusations to the press), political contests (vying for allies), or taking unilateral advantage (e.g. theft, slipping out of the house unobserved by one's spouse). Struggle is analogous to contending in negotiation.

(c) *Tacit coordination* (also called "tacit bargaining"), in which the parties accommodate to each other without a discussion

(Schelling 1960). An example of tacit coordination is the pattern of alternation that often develops when two lines of cars are entering the same single lane. Tacit coordination often follows a period of struggle. For instance, two students seated side by side may elbow each other for a period of time before settling down to a nonverbal agreement in which one uses the front and the other the back of the arm rest between them. Tacit coordination can be thought of as a nonverbal form of problem solving.

Arguments for joint decision making

Decisions among the procedures just mentioned involve a weighing of pros and cons. The joint decision procedures – negotiation and mediation – have a number of advantages over third-party decision making and separate action. Third-party decision making can be quite expensive: going to court costs money, bosses usually do not like to be troubled by disagreements between their employees, etc. Furthermore, third-party decision makers often do not understand the parties' interests well enough to locate "win–win" agreements that are mutually beneficial, and they may not regard such agreements as their aim. (See the next chapter for a full discussion of types of outcome in negotiation.)

In addition, joint decision making is usually less costly and dangerous than struggle, the most common form of separate action. Struggle often requires heavy expenditure of resources (e.g. bombs, loss of customers in a strike, frayed nerves) and endangers the relationship between the parties (Ury et al. 1988). Negotiation and mediation tend to be much more benign. Indeed, involvement in joint decision making usually protects the parties against more costly struggles, because initiating struggle tactics during negotiation or mediation is usually seen as illegitimate.

Joint decision making is also better than tacit coordination for locating mutually beneficial agreements. Discussions are flexible and subtle, allowing joint projection into the future, while tacit coordination is often a clumsy procedure. This advantage of joint decision making is revealed by the finding that communication encourages cooperation in games of moves, such as the prisoner's dilemma (Voissem and Sistrunk 1971; Wichman 1972) and the resource dilemmas (Edney and Harper 1978). (Games of moves will be discussed in the next chapter.)

Arguments against joint decision making

Given these points in favor of joint decision making, why are third-party decision making and separate action so popular? Sometimes joint decision procedures are at a disadvantage. Communication may be difficult, because the parties cannot meet or do not understand each other when they do. Trust may be so low that they dare not enter into an explicit agreement with each other. One party may be too proud to concede or too hostile to agree to anything that favors the other's welfare. Both parties may be so angry at each other that their discussion degenerates into arguments and name calling (Deutsch 1973); or their values may be so different that contacts between them lead to a sense of shock and outrage (Druckman and Zechmeister 1973; Rubin 1980).

In addition, it is very common for one or both parties to believe that they can achieve more through struggle or third-party decision than through joint decision. One's power may seem greater than that of the other party, encouraging an effort to exploit the other. One's case may seem stronger than that of the other party, encouraging appeal to an arbitrator or judge. There may be no continuing relationship to worry about or no apparent common ground.

Another disadvantage of negotiation and mediation is that it is usually necessary for *both* parties to agree to enter into them. By contrast, the other party can often be forced to submit to third-party decision making, and struggle is always the default option.

Moving from struggle to joint decision making

Some of the points made above help to explain why a period of struggle often precedes negotiation or mediation. Boys fight and then work out their differences. Unions go on strike and then talk it over. Nations threaten each other and then negotiate. What usually happens is that struggle seems initially advantageous to one or both parties, but its defects become more apparent over time. The costs of struggle often increase to the point where they become prohibitive. Experience shows that the other party cannot be exploited or pushed around; or the other concedes for a while and then becomes resistant to further pressure. The parties enter what Touval and Zartman (1985) call a *hurting stalemate*.

As struggle loses its allure, other forms of separate action may be considered, but they also have their problems; for example, tacit coordination cannot produce the kind of fine-tuned agreement that is needed to end the controversy. Finally, the parties turn to negotiation or mediation.

The study of negotiation

There are three main traditions in the study of negotiation. The first consists of books and manuals providing *advice* (e.g. Fisher and Ury 1981; Moore 1986). The second consists of *mathematical models* of rational behavior developed by economists and game theorists (see Luce and Raiffa 1957; Young 1975). These models are ordinarily limited to a narrow set of tactics, such as concession making or third-party recommendations for particular agreements. These two traditions are sometimes combined by theorists who use the tools of rational analysis to examine the wide range of tactics used by most negotiators and third parties (e.g. Raiffa 1982; Schelling 1960). The third, *behavioral*, tradition seeks to develop and test predictive theory about the impact of environmental conditions on negotiator (and mediator) behavior and the impact of these conditions and behaviors on outcomes (see Dupont 1982; Morley and Stephenson 1977; Pruitt 1981; Rubin and Brown 1975; Walton and McKersie 1965). This last tradition, which leans heavily on the first two traditions for inspiration, is the focus of our book.

Any number of parties may be involved in negotiation; however, theory and research have mostly examined the two-party case. Hence, the main subject of our book will be negotiation between two parties.

The dominant theoretical paradigm

There is a traditional, dominant theoretical paradigm or model of thought underlying most behavioral approaches to theory and research on negotiation. In this paradigm, there are only two parties who, whether they are individuals or groups, are treated as unitary decision makers. They are brought together by a desire to resolve a divergence of interest by reaching a verbal agreement.

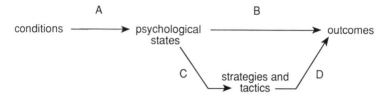

Figure 1.1 Causal sequence in the theoretical paradigm that dominates behavioral research on negotiation

Their aim is to maximize self-interest, though they may not be very good at doing so. They are not usually viewed as having a past history or future involvement with each other but to be responding to here-and-now circumstances.

This paradigm is shown schematically in Figure 1.1. Conditions that prevail at the time of negotiation are assumed to have an impact on psychological states, such as motives, perceptions, and cognitions (path A in Figure 1.1). These states, in turn, have either a direct impact on outcomes (path B), or an impact that is mediated by the strategies and tactics chosen by the parties (paths C and D).

The origins of this paradigm can be traced to two early bodies of literature: (a) mathematical models of rational decision making in negotiation that were developed by economists and game theorists (see Luce and Raiffa 1957; Roth 1985; Young 1975), and (b) theories about the origins and impact of negotiator tactics that were developed by an economist (Schelling 1960) and industrial relations specialists (Stevens 1963; Walton and McKersie 1965).

The traditional, dominant paradigm has been a good starting point for the development of theory and research. We will use this model of thought to organize the first half of our book, which will present the bulk of the research findings on negotiation. Nevertheless, the dominant paradigm is overly simplistic. It relies too much on the assumption that negotiators are always trying to maximize self-interest. It ignores the social context of negotiation, overlooking such important phenomena as social norms, relationships between negotiators, group decision processes, and the behavior of third parties. It lacks a time dimension, failing to come to grips with the stages of negotiation and the events that occur before negotiation starts and after it is over. It also provides no information about why people choose negotiation rather than arbitration, struggle, or some other approach to conflict. The second half of our book will be largely devoted to expanding the field of vision beyond this traditional paradigm. A fair amount of the literature cited there will be drawn from related fields, such as group dynamics and procedural justice.

Methodology

Research in the behavioral tradition has been conducted in both the laboratory and the field. Field research often involves in-depth interviews with professional negotiators or mediators (Kressel 1972), case studies of actual instances (Touval and Zartman 1985), and questionnaire surveys where professional negotiators or mediators are the respondents (Kochan and Jick 1978).

Since laboratory methodology may not be familiar to the reader, we will describe it briefly here. The subjects in laboratory experiments are usually undergraduate volunteers. Two or more true subjects may deal with each other, or a single subject may (without knowing it) deal with a confederate or a computer program. Communication is sometimes face-to-face, sometimes by means of note passing, and sometimes between two computer terminals.

The tasks used in experiments on negotiation usually involve stripped-down simulations of real-life negotiation. Two kinds of task are most common. The first involves negotiation about a single issue; for example, the price of a used car (e.g. Yukl 1974a). The second involves negotiation about two or more issues, such as the price of a car and the accessories to be mounted on it (e.g. Kelley 1966; Pruitt and Lewis 1975; Siegel and Fouraker 1960). Only the second kind of task allows the development of win–win agreements, in which both parties accomplish their major goals.

An example of the second kind of negotiation task, drawn from Pruitt (1981), is shown in Table 1.1. The subjects play the roles of buyer and seller in a wholesale market. The buyer is said to represent a large department store and the seller a manufacturer. The buyer and seller are required to reach agreement on prices for three appliances: television sets, vacuum cleaners, and typewriters. The buyer is given the profit schedule shown on the left of Table 1.1 and the seller is given the profit schedule shown on the right. These schedules list nine prices, represented schematically by the letters A to I. Next to each price on the sellers' sheet is the profit made by their company for selling each appliance at that price.

Table 1.1 Buyer and seller profit sheets employed in some studies of negotiation

Buyer

Television sets		Vacuum cleaners		Typewriters	
Price	Profit	Price	Profit	Price	Profit
A	$2000	A	$1200	A	$800
B	$1750	B	$1050	B	$700
C	$1500	C	$900	C	$600
D	$1250	D	$750	D	$500
E	$1000	E	$600	E	$400
F	$750	F	$450	F	$300
G	$500	G	$300	G	$200
H	$250	H	$150	H	$100
I	$000	I	$000	I	$000

Seller

Television sets		Vacuum cleaners		Typewriters	
Price	Profit	Price	Profit	Price	Profit
A	$000	A	$000	A	$000
B	$100	B	$150	B	$250
C	$200	C	$300	C	$500
D	$300	D	$450	D	$750
E	$400	E	$600	E	$1000
F	$500	F	$750	F	$1250
G	$600	G	$900	G	$1500
H	$700	H	$1050	H	$1750
I	$800	I	$1200	I	$2000

Source: Pruitt (1981)

Next to each price on the buyers' sheet is the profit made by their company for reselling the same appliance if it is purchased at that price. Buyers and sellers see only their own profit schedules. They can say anything they want during the negotiation but cannot show each other their profit schedules. Their offers, statements and outcomes are recorded and then submitted to statistical analysis.

Virtues and shortcomings of laboratory experiments

Much of the literature cited in this book is based on laboratory experiments involving simulated negotiation and mediation. This methodology has three virtues in contrast to most studies of negotiation in natural settings:

1 Causal hypotheses can be tested by manipulating one variable and observing its effect on others.
2 Extraneous conditions can be controlled, permitting the isolation of particular effects of interest.
3 Perceptual, motivational and decision processes can often be examined as they unfold, permitting the tracking of complex sequences of events that are hard to observe in other settings.

However, the experimental method also has two shortcomings. One is that it does not reveal the relative importance of different variables as they influence negotiation. It only tells us what effects can occur (Mook 1983). The other shortcoming is that there are often difficulties in generalizing results from laboratory settings to natural settings. This problem is shared with field research, since natural settings differ from one another. But it can be more acute with laboratory research since the latter tends to be done in simplified settings.

There are two solutions to the latter generality issue. One is to do laboratory research that tests hypotheses derived from theory. The results of such research can then be generalized, not because the procedures for collecting data correspond to natural settings but because the theoretical processes on which they are based also occur in natural settings. The second solution is to do parallel research in laboratory and natural settings. Such studies complement each other. The laboratory research helps to clarify causal mechanisms, while the natural research establishes the relevance of these mechanisms to real-life negotiation. Parallel results of this kind are cited at various points in this book.

Overview of the chapters

In Chapter 2, we will take a look at the issues under discussion in negotiation and the possible outcomes of negotiation. This will lead into a discussion of several other settings that involve a divergence of interest, including the prisoner's dilemma and various resource dilemmas. These "games of moves" are sufficiently similar to negotiation in basic structure that research on them contributes to an understanding of negotiation. Chapter 3 will present a detailed discussion of the five basic negotiation strategies and their impact on the outcomes of negotiation.

The following three chapters will report theory and research that is compatible with the traditional paradigm mentioned above. Two of these chapters will examine the determinants of negotiator demands, concessions and contentious tactics, with Chapter 4 focusing on environmental conditions, and Chapter 5 on the effect of the other party's strategies. Most of the effects described in these chapters will be explained in terms of motivational states; for example, goals, limits, and orientations. Chapter 6 will be devoted to a different kind of psychological state, negotiator cognitions, reporting on some very recent developments in this part of the field.

The remaining chapters will discuss variables and processes that are outside the scope of the traditional paradigm, but are nevertheless important for understanding negotiation. There will be somewhat more speculation in this part of the book, because of the smaller amount of research available.

Chapter 7 will examine the determinants of problem solving behavior in the context of a systematic theory of motivation – the dual concern model – which challenges the assumption that negotiators are always trying to maximize self-interest. According to this model, two motivational states must be assessed to understand negotiation: the strength of self-interest and the strength of other-interest, i.e. interest in the other party's welfare.

The next four chapters are related in that they examine aspects of the social context of negotiation. Chapter 8 examines the impact of social norms. Norms are shared beliefs about how people should behave. They often determine how negotiators behave and the agreements they reach. Fairness norms (e.g. equal outcomes, equal concessions) are particularly important in negotiation. Chapter 9 looks at the effects of relationships between negotiators.

Chapter 10 presents an analysis of negotiation by groups and organizations. This discussion moves us well beyond the traditional picture of the negotiating party as a unitary decision maker. Chapter 11 deals with mediation, examining mediator strategies and their effects, and the sources of mediator behavior. Chapter 12 broadens the scope of our inquiry once more to look at disputant preferences among various procedures for addressing conflict – including negotiation, mediation, arbitration, and struggle. The chapter will also examine the organization of dispute resolution systems that encourage optimal mixes of these procedures. Conclusions are presented in Chapter 13.

Suggestions for further reading

Deutsch, M. (1973). *The resolution of conflict: Constructive and destructive processes.* New Haven, CT, and London: Yale University Press.

Druckman, D. (ed.) (1977). *Negotiation: Social-psychological perspectives.* Beverly Hills, CA, and London: Sage Publications.

Kremenyuk, V. A. (ed.) (1991). *International negotiation: Analysis, approaches, issues.* San Francisco: Jossey-Bass.

Morley, I. E. and Stephenson, J. M. (1977). *The social psychology of bargaining.* London: Allen and Unwin.

Pruitt, D. G. (1981). *Negotiation behavior.* New York: Academic Press.

Rubin, J. Z. and Brown, B. R. (1975). *The social psychology of bargaining and negotiation.* New York: Academic Press.

Walton, R. E. and McKersie, R. B. (1965). *A behavioral theory of labor negotiations.* New York: McGraw-Hill.

2 / ISSUES AND OUTCOMES IN NEGOTIATION AND RELATED SETTINGS

This chapter will examine the reward structures that are found in negotiation and related settings. By reward structure is meant the configuration of options and outcomes under consideration – in other words, the alternatives people must choose among and the possible results of these choices. The chapter is more technical than any other in the book, but this is necessary in order to introduce the reader to the basic concepts in the field.

Issues, options and divergence of interest

The topics under consideration in negotiation can usually be divided into one or more *issues* requiring separate decisions by the parties. Each issue entails two or more options (also called "alternatives"). Consider the car buying example mentioned at the beginning of Chapter 1. The main issue is how much Charles must pay for the car. The options under consideration might be all possible prices between $9,000 and $11,000. A secondary issue might be whether a particular package of accessories will be installed in the car. The options would be installation and non-installation.

When several issues are related, they are often discussed together as an *issue group*, involving various combinations of the options being considered. For example, the dealer might try to link the price of the car to whether or not the package of accessories will be installed. The options in such a group would include the following: $10,500 with the accessory package, $11,000 with the accessory package, $11,000 without the accessory package, etc. As will be shown in the next chapter, the way issues are combined and uncombined ("unbundled") has a lot to do with the way negotiation turns out.

Issues often change as negotiation goes along. Some of this change results from the combining and uncombining just described. Other changes result from an effort to find interests, values, and needs that underlie the positions initially stated by the parties (Burton 1984; Fisher and Ury 1981). For example, negotiation between two divisions in a firm about who is to make certain repairs may reflect a broader controversy about business philosophy or relative status in the organization. If they come to realize this, the parties are likely to begin discussing these broader issues. Seeking underlying issues of this kind is one aspect of problem solving (see Chapter 3).

Divergence of interest between two negotiating parties can be precisely understood in terms of the joint utility space shown in Figure 2.1 (see Raiffa 1982). The points in this space correspond to the options available for settling an issue or issue group. The filled points refer to options that are currently under consideration and the open points to options that can be devised with some creative thinking. The axes give the utility (i.e. the subjective value) to each party of the options shown.

Figure 2.1 represents our car buying example at the beginning of negotiation, when only the price of the car is under discussion. Options 1 through 5 are possible prices between $9,000 and $11,000 (space limitations in the figure do not permit us to show finer gradations of price, though these are possible). These options are arranged in the space so that higher prices have greater utility to the dealer and less utility to the customer than lower prices. This is what is meant by divergence of interest: that the parties differ in their utility ordering for at least some of the options under consideration.

Options 6 to 8 are mutually beneficial options, where the dealer throws in accessories that cost her less than they are worth to the customer. They are shown as open points because they have not yet been devised at the beginning of negotiation. There is also a divergence of interest among these three options, but they have the advantage of being better for *both parties* than some of the options that do not include the accessory package.

Figure 2.1   Joint utility space in car buying example

The following options are shown: NA = no agreement; 1 = $9,000;
2 = $9,500; 3 = $10,000; 4 = $10,500; 5 = $11,000; 6 = $10,000
plus accessory package (a.p); 7 = $10,500 plus a.p; 8 = $11,000 plus a.p.

The situation portrayed in this figure is said to have *integrative potential*, because of the existence of these mutually beneficial options. This term is used because these options are capable of integrating the interests of the two parties.

Outcomes in negotiation

Negotiation can end with one of four kinds of outcomes:

(1) *Victory* for one of the parties; for example, agreement on option 1 or 5 in Figure 2.1.

(2) A simple *compromise*; for example, agreement on option 2, 3 or 4. A compromise is defined as some middle ground on an obvious dimension connecting the parties' initial offers.

(3) A *win–win agreement* (also called an "integrative agreement");

for example, agreement on one of the mutually beneficial options 6, 7 or 8. In win–win agreements, the parties achieve higher joint benefit (collective utility) than they could with a compromise (Follett 1940). Win–win agreements are generally believed to have a number of advantages over compromises (Lax and Sebenius 1986; Pruitt 1981; Ury et al. 1988): they (a) are more popular with the parties; (b) are more likely to be complied with; (c) are more beneficial to the relationship between the parties; and (d) contribute to organizational effectiveness if the parties are sub-units of the same organization, such as departments in a firm that have differing goals because of their particular missions. In addition, (e) when the parties have ambitious goals, it is sometimes impossible for them to reach agreement unless win–win options can be identified. These points make sense, and the first and fifth advantages have been supported by research (Pruitt and Lewis 1975; Zubek et al. 1992). However, an effort to test the second and third advantages found no relationship between joint benefit and either compliance or improved relationships between the disputants (Pruitt et al. 1992b). This suggests that the impact of win–win agreements needs further study.

(4) *Failure to reach agreement*, whose value to the parties is shown by the point marked "NA" (no agreement). Unlike the other options, which require joint approval, either party can drop out of negotiation, producing a failure to reach agreement. Logically, the value of this outcome should be the utility of what Fisher and Ury (1981) call the "best alternative to a negotiated agreement" or BATNA. For example, in our car buying story, Charles would have a BATNA at the level of the $10,000 option if he knew that another dealer was willing to sell the same car at that price. BATNA is usually identical with the status quo; that is, the situation that would have obtained if negotiation had never taken place. In actual practice, other less rational considerations also influence the value of no agreement. For example, negotiators who pride themselves on always reaching agreement will place a low value on no agreement.

In Figure 2.1, no agreement is shown as a poor outcome for both parties. But this is not always the case. For example, one party may be very much advantaged by the status quo, making no agreement identical with a victory for that party (e.g. NA could be at point 1 or point 5 in Figure 2.1). No agreement can even be tantamount to a compromise or a win–win agreement.

Negotiation in mixed-motive settings

Most negotiations take place in *mixed-motive* settings. A setting is said to involve "mixed motives" if it evokes both competitive and cooperative motives in the parties involved (Schelling 1960). The competitive motive arises because the players have opposing preferences (i.e. a divergence of interest) for some pairs of options. Thus in the car buying example shown in Figure 2.1, the buyer prefers option 1 over option 2 and option 6 over option 8, while the seller has the opposite preferences. The cooperative motive arises because the players have similar preferences for other pairs of options. Thus both of them prefer option 7 (one of the win–win options) to option 3 (the equal outcome compromise), and options 2, 3 and 4 to no agreement (NA).

The mixed-motive nature of negotiation creates a *dilemma* for negotiators (Kelley 1966; Lax and Sebenius 1986; Walton and McKersie 1965). The competitive motive encourages them to be contentious and to try to push the other party while defending themselves. But the cooperative motive encourages them to make concessions and engaging in problem solving. As a result, they must forever face paradoxical questions, such as: Shall we hold firm or concede? Shall we commit ourselves not to move from our proposal, or try to devise a new proposal? Shall we protect ourselves by withholding information about our priorities among the issues, or provide this information in the interest of problem solving?

Dilemmas such as these are commonly solved by isolating competitive and cooperative strategies from each other in various ways (Pruitt 1991; Putnam 1990). These include rapid sequencing (e.g. concede–contend–concede–contend), moving through stages (e.g. contending followed by problem solving), arena shielding (e.g. contending at the negotiation table while problem solving in unofficial meetings on the side), personnel shielding (e.g. the bad guy/good guy routine, in which one team member takes a contentious approach while the other engages in problem solving), and issue shielding (e.g. holding firm on some issues while problem solving on others).

Games of moves

As mentioned in Chapter 1, negotiation is not the only procedure available for dealing with divergence of interest. Sometimes the parties employ separate actions that affect one another's outcomes, each trying to achieve its goals without coordinating with the other. An example would be a strategic interaction – involving public announcements, messages to allies, and military maneuvers – between two countries who are trying to gain control of a disputed territory. Such a procedure can be called a *game of moves*, in contrast to negotiation, which is a *game of agreement*.

The term "game" is a technical one in this context, referring to a situation that has the following components: a set of options that are available to two or more parties (the "players"), rules for making decisions among these options, and utility values associated with the possible outcomes of these decisions. This term derives from a branch of mathematics called the "theory of games," which prescribes rational strategies for various classes of games on the basis of an analysis of the impact of all possible combinations of strategies (see Luce and Raiffa 1957).

Negotiation is related to games of moves in two ways. One is that games of moves are sometimes solved through negotiation. The parties change the decision rules and start talking in an effort to reach agreement about their differences. The other is that the tactics employed in negotiation – for example, concession making, positional commitment, and the provision of information – can be viewed as actions in a game of moves. Negotiation is a game of agreement with respect to *final outcomes*, because consensus is required to achieve all of them except no agreement. But it is a vast game of moves with respect to *tactics*, because decisions about tactics are made by the parties separately. It follows that research on games of moves can tell us something about negotiation.

Three simple types of games of moves have been extensively researched in the laboratory: the prisoner's dilemma, the game of chicken, and the resource dilemmas. Each has its distinctive reward structure, and all are mixed-motive settings. (Many other games of moves have been described by Kelley and Thibaut (1978) and by Rapoport and Guyer (1966).)

The prisoner's dilemma

In its simplest version, the prisoner's dilemma involves only two parties, each with two options (see Pruitt and Kimmel 1977; Rapoport and Chammah 1965). An abstract example can be seen

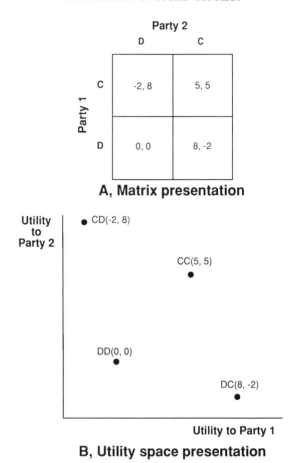

Figure 2.2   Prisoner's dilemma shown in matrix and utility space presentations

in the matrix shown in Figure 2.2A. Party 1's options are represented by rows C and D, and Party 2's options by columns C and D. Each party's C option can be thought of as a cooperative choice and its D option as a noncooperative choice. The outcomes associated with the four possible pairs of choices are shown in the cell defined by that pair, with Party 1's outcomes shown first and Party 2's outcomes shown second. For example, if Party 1 chooses C and Party 2 chooses D, the outcome is found in the CD cell:

-2 units of value (dollars, happiness, etc.) for Party 1 and 8 units for Party 2. There are many possible sets of numbers that fit the prisoner's dilemma, but all have the following feature in common: for each party, exploitation of the other party (DC) provides greater utility than mutual cooperation (CC), which provides greater utility than mutual noncooperation (DD), which provides greater utility than being exploited by the other (CD).

The reward structure of the prisoner's dilemma makes non-cooperation (D) the rational choice for each party, since this option produces a larger outcome than cooperation (C), regardless of what the other party does. However, the prisoner's dilemma is paradoxical because if both parties fail to cooperate (DD), they will both be worse off than if they both cooperate (CC). In short, behavior that is rational for each party separately (choosing D) is irrational for the parties collectively. The prisoner's dilemma can also be defined for more than two parties and more than two options (see, for example, Bonacich 1972; Pruitt 1967), with similar characteristics.

Areas of life that involve the potential for cooperation or competition often turn out to be prisoner's dilemmas. Examples of potential cooperation include lending and other helping practices in the relationship between neighbors or colleagues. I am better off not lending you my books (option D) than lending them to you (option C), because you might lose or damage them or not be around when I need them. Likewise, you are better off not lending me your books. But collectively, if we are close colleagues, we are both better off lending books to each other (CC) than not doing so (DD). In the realm of competition, it often seems rational for a country to arm (option D) against its neighbor and for the neighbor to do likewise; but the countries are better off if neither arms (CC) than if they both arm (DD). As can be inferred from these examples, the prisoner's dilemma is at the root of many moral and practical paradoxes.

In Figure 2.2B, the prisoner's dilemma shown in the matrix is presented in two-dimensional utility space. This illustrates the mixed-motive nature of the prisoner's dilemma. There is a divergence of interest, in that each party is motivated to try to exploit the other (to achieve CD or DC); but there are also compatible interests, in that the parties prefer mutual cooperation (CC) to mutual noncooperation (DD). Hence the prisoner's dilemma embodies a dilemma similar to those faced in negotiation.

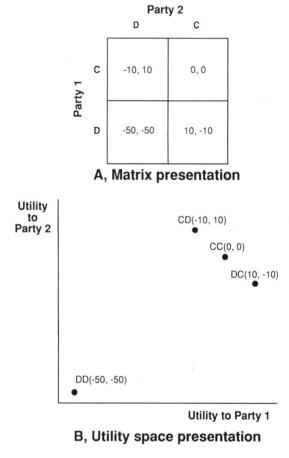

A, Matrix presentation

B, Utility space presentation

Figure 2.3 Game of chicken shown in matrix and utility space presentations

The game of chicken

The game of chicken, shown in Figure 2.3A, is similar to the prisoner's dilemma except that mutual noncooperation is the worst possible outcome for both parties. The name "chicken" comes from an often fatal automobile game that was once played by some young men in our society. They drive toward each other at great speed, and the first one to swerve off this course of destruction is the loser. The matrix shown in Figure 2.3A is the reward structure at the last minute in this contest. If I swerve (C) and you do not (D), you win and I lose (CD); and the opposite is true if you swerve and I do not (DC). If we both swerve (CC), we may be a little embarrassed, but this is much better for both of us than if neither of us swerves (DD). Chicken is different from the prisoner's dilemma in that commitment to noncooperation (D) is a potentially winning strategy. If I can make you believe that I will not cooperate, it becomes rational for you to cooperate (C), because unilateral cooperation (CD) is better for you than mutual noncooperation (DD). A commitment strategy can be implemented in the automobile game by talking tough before the game, looking resolute as one barrels down the road, or even removing one's steering wheel and visibly throwing it out the window (Schelling 1960).

The mixed-motive nature of chicken can be seen in Figure 2.3B. As with the other games discussed in this chapter, chicken poses a dilemma for each party.

Resource dilemmas

Resource dilemmas involve a common pool of resources which either can be exploited by the parties (in the case of *harvesting dilemmas*) or must be renewed by the parties (in the case of *contributions dilemmas*) (see Messick and Brewer 1983). Resource dilemmas can be defined in the two-party case, but they ordinarily involve larger groups. An example of a harvesting dilemma is the famous commons dilemma (Hardin 1968), in which all farmers have the option of allowing their animals to graze on the village green (the "commons"). An example of a contributions dilemma is paying dues to a club.

Resource dilemmas have features of both the prisoner's dilemma and the game of chicken. As with the prisoner's dilemma, each party is tempted to behave noncooperatively: to exploit the common resource (use the village green) or fail to renew it (fail to pay dues). But if all behave noncooperatively, the resource will be destroyed and all will suffer more than if they had all behaved cooperatively. For example, if all the farmers put their animals on the village green, the grass there will die and all of them will suffer; if all members of a club fail to pay dues, the club will fall apart, hurting them all. As with the game of chicken, failure to

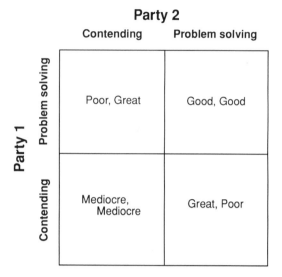

Figure 2.4   Negotiation as a prisoner's dilemma – the so-called "negotiator's dilemma." The adjectives refer to the outcomes of each pair of choices. Based on Lax and Sebenius (1986: 39)

cooperate by some of the parties (analogous to failure to swerve) encourages the other parties to cooperate in order to preserve the resource.

Negotiation as prisoner's dilemma and chicken

We said earlier that the choice of tactics in negotiation can be conceptualized as a game of moves. Taking this perspective, it turns out that negotiation, like the resource dilemmas, has features of both the prisoner's dilemma and the game of chicken.

The prisoner's dilemma aspect of negotiation has been called the "negotiator's dilemma" by Lax and Sebenius (1986: 39). Both negotiators face a choice between contending (which they call "claiming value") and problem solving (which they call "creating value"); hence, there are four possible outcomes, as shown in Figure 2.4. The values associated with these outcomes makes the situation a prisoner's dilemma. If one negotiator chooses contending and the other chooses problem solving, the contest becomes

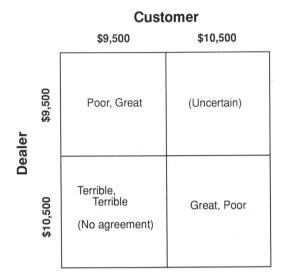

Figure 2.5 Negotiation as a game of chicken

If the dealer can commit herself to $10,500, the customer will concede from $9,500 to $10,500, because the alternative (no agreement) is terrible rather than just poor.

uneven, and the contender is likely to achieve a significant victory (a "great" outcome) while the problem solver suffers a significant loss (a "poor" outcome). (The problem solver in such a situation will usually want to change his or her strategy to contending.) If both of them are contentious, they are likely to argue with each other over a period of time and eventually end up with a noncreative compromise, a "mediocre" outcome for both of them. They would be better off if they both engage in problem solving, which will usually produce "good" (though not great) outcomes for both of them. This is clearly a prisoner's dilemma.

The chicken aspect of negotiation is revealed by the fact that positional commitments are often a winning tactic. An example of a positional commitment would be for the dealer in our car buying story to convince Charles that her boss will never allow a price below $10,500. This situation is illustrated in Figure 2.5, which makes the assumption that Charles finds this price excessive (a "poor" outcome) but is willing to pay it rather than not get the car (a "terrible" outcome). Quite clearly, the dealer will win and

Charles will lose if the dealer uses this tactic. The figure also suggests that Charles will win if he makes a credible commitment to $9,500 before the dealer gets a chance to commit herself, provided that the dealer is capable of making this concession. More will be said about positional commitments in the next chapter, but it is clear from this brief discussion that this aspect of negotiation is a game of chicken.

The fact that negotiation and the resource dilemmas are similar in structure to the prisoner's dilemma and chicken suggests that research on any of these games can help us to understand the others.

Summary and implications

This chapter has mainly been devoted to definitions and the linking of various concepts that are essential for understanding negotiation. We have defined issues and options and shown how issues often change as negotiation goes along. We have also described the various possible outcomes of negotiation: victory for one party, compromise, win–win agreement, and no agreement. Options and outcomes are best understood in the context of the joint utility space, such as shown in Figure 2.1. Diagramming them in this space makes clear the mixed-motive nature of negotiation, with incentives for both competition and cooperation. We also discussed three mixed-motive games of moves, in which the parties take separate actions that affect one another's outcomes: the prisoner's dilemma, chicken and the resource dilemmas. There are similarities between these games and negotiation, which make it possible to learn something about negotiation from research on these games, and vice versa.

The next chapter provides a detailed discussion of the strategies and tactics used by negotiators and their relationship to the outcomes of negotiation.

Suggestions for further reading

Lax, D. A. and Sebenius, J. K. (1986). *The manager as negotiator: Bargaining for cooperation and competitive gain.* New York: The Free Press.
Luce, R. D. and Raiffa, H. (1957). *Games and decisions: Introduction and critical survey.* New York: John Wiley & Sons.

Messick, D. M. and Brewer, M. B. (1983). Solving social dilemmas: a review. *Review of Personality and Social Psychology*, 4, 11–44.

Pruitt, D. G. and Kimmel, M. J. (1977). Twenty years of experimental gaming: critique, synthesis, and suggestions for the future. *Annual Review of Psychology*, 28, 363–92.

Raiffa, H. (1982). *The art and science of negotiation*. Cambridge, MA: Harvard University Press.

3 / STRATEGIES AND TACTICS IN NEGOTIATION

Sales and Production are still at it! Dan, the Director of Sales, is trying to arrange for production of his two new orders, one for 10,000 and the other for 5,000 men's suits. Dora, the Director of Production, is arguing that the job will take four months, instead of the two months desired by Dan's customers. Dan and Dora are negotiating, whether they call it by that name or not. Hence, they have a choice between the five basic strategies mentioned in Chapter 1: concession making, contending, problem solving, inaction and withdrawal. We will take up these strategies, one at a time, and examine their nature and their impact on negotiation outcomes.

Concession making

Concessions involve a reduction in demands – changing one's proposal so that it provides less benefit to oneself. Negotiators usually assume that their concessions provide greater benefit to the other party, thereby moving the negotiation toward agreement. However, this assumption is not always valid, since the other party's values are not always clear. Reductions in demands usually involve reductions in the goals underlying these demands, which are also sometimes called concessions.

There are three interrelated findings concerning the impact of concession making on negotiation outcomes. One is that if agreement is reached, firmer negotiators will usually achieve larger outcomes (Bartos 1974; Benton *et al.* 1972; Donohue 1981; Siegel and Fouraker 1960). A firm negotiator is one with high goals, who makes large initial demands and resists concession making. This is not a surprising finding for settings without integrative potential, where my gain is your loss. If I concede less, you must concede more in order to reach agreement; hence my outcome will be larger. It is more surprising to learn that this finding also holds up in settings with integrative potential (Weingart *et al.* 1990). This is because soft negotiators who give up easily are not likely to explore the integrative potential, and hence are not likely to find the win–win options. As a result, they often achieve poor agreements.

The second finding is that firmness tends to lengthen negotiation and make agreement less likely (Bartos 1974; Benton *et al.* 1972; Hamner 1974). In other words, the more negotiators demand at first and the slower they concede, the harder it will be to reach agreement. This unsurprising finding is true over most of the range of firmness, but there is a strange reversal at the low (very soft) end of this dimension. If negotiators make really low initial demands or concede really quickly, agreement is less likely and tends to take longer to reach than if they had been a little more ambitious (Bartos 1974; Hamner 1974). This is probably because very fast movement signals extreme weakness, leading the adversary to stop conceding altogether. This makes it harder to reach agreement.

The third finding can be derived from the other two. If reaching agreement has any value to a negotiator, there is likely to be an inverted U-shaped relationship between firmness and negotiation outcome (Benton *et al.* 1972; Hamner 1974; Weingart *et al.* 1990). Negotiators who demand too much will fail to reach agreement and thereby do poorly. Those who demand too little will usually reach agreement but achieve low profits. The most successful negotiators will be those who are moderately firm and hence are between these two extremes. As an example, take Dan from Sales, for whom it is important to reach agreement. If he is overly firm and keeps on demanding a two-month schedule, negotiation may break down, leaving him in the lurch. But if he is overly soft and concedes a lot, Dora will win and he will lose his customers. His best bet is a strategy of moderate firmness.

The inverted U-shaped relationship holds for negotiators as individuals and for two negotiators collectively, when there is integrative potential in their situation. If both negotiators are very firm and make few concessions, agreement will not be reached. If both are very soft and make deep bilateral concessions, the result will be a compromise with mediocre benefits to both sides. The largest joint benefit will be obtained if both of them are moderately firm and also engage in some form of problem solving (Pruitt and Lewis 1975). They should reduce their goals sufficiently to bring them into a realistic range, where there is some possibility of discovering new options; but further concessions should be avoided.

Such a balancing act might seem hard to accomplish. How can one concede just "far enough"? Fortunately, this is not as hard as it sounds. In our example, the best way to find hidden options that will benefit both Sales and Production is for Dan and Dora to stick to their goals and search for new ideas by means of problem solving. If they are not successful in this initial search, they should reduce their goals somewhat and then renew the search, repeating this cycle until a mutually acceptable option is found. The point is to concede slowly enough for all possible options to be explored (Putnam and Wilson 1989).

Contending

Unlike concession making, contending takes a large variety of forms, which are called tactics. Among these tactics are threats, harassment, positional commitments, and persuasive arguments. All have the aim of persuading the other party to make concessions or of resisting similar efforts by the other. We will look at both the nature of contentious tactics and their impact on negotiation.

The nature of contentious tactics

Threats
Contending often takes the form of a threat; that is, a commitment to punish the other party if one's demands are not accepted. For example, Dan might threaten to complain to the President of the company if Dora does not alter her production plans to accommodate the new orders. In addition to trying to get the other to concede during negotiation, threats are sometimes used to push the other party into negotiation.

Threats are more effective the larger the penalty threatened

(Tedeschi *et al.* 1973) and the greater their credibility. By *credibility* is meant the perceived likelihood that a threat will be carried out. Threat size and credibility are additive in their effects (Horai and Tedeschi 1969). Hence, large threats can be effective even if they are not fully credible. If Dora is very unhappy about the prospect of Dan contacting the President, she may make concessions even if she is not sure that Dan will take this step.

Threat credibility goes up when threats have been regularly carried out in the past (Horai and Tedeschi 1969). Credibility goes down when fulfilling the threat is costly to the threatener as well as the target (Mogy and Pruitt 1974). Threats are also more credible when they come from people who have the resources to carry them out (Tedeschi and Bonoma 1977), from high status people (Faley and Tedeschi 1971), and from people who are viewed negatively (Schlenker *et al.* 1970). The latter finding suggests that threats from unpleasant individuals are especially likely to be believed.

Credible threats make no agreement seem less attractive to the other party. Hence, they are often successful at eliciting concessions; and they are sometimes the only way to get the other party to negotiate at all. However, threats have their down side because they tend to generate resentment and resistance. People are not happy when they are forced to take action. It diminishes their freedom of choice and violates their sense of justice, sometimes making them feel like suckers. As a result they often try to escape or to build some form of counterpower against the threatener, another form of contentious behavior. A common way to build counterpower is to seek allies (Freedman 1981); for example, the Director of Production might seek the support of the Director of Research in the face of threats from the Director of Sales. Threats also tend to be imitated, producing counter-threats (Deutsch and Krauss 1962; Hornstein 1965; Smith and Anderson 1975).

The resentment engendered by threats often leads to negative attitudes toward the threatener. In addition, respect for and a sense of obligation to the threatener diminish (Gaski 1986). This means that threateners may have less influence in the long run than if they had not used this tactic.

There are several ways for threateners to reduce the resentment and resistance against their tactics. They can be careful to employ only legitimate threats; for example, going to the President rather than sabotaging the production line. They can state their threats indirectly or diplomatically, so as to get their point across without seeming pushy. An example of diplomacy is to employ deterrent rather than compellent threats; that is, to say what you want the other *not to do* rather than what you want the other *to do* (Rubin and Lewicki 1973). Or threats can be combined with promises ("sweeteners") or with a clear concern about the other party's legitimate needs. However, none of these approaches is likely completely to counteract the down side of threats.

Harassment

Harassment involves annoying the other party, with the explicit or implicit promise to stop this action if the other complies. Harassment is like threat in that it involves punishment; but the punishment is immediate and inevitable, rather than delayed and contingent on the other's behavior. An example would be for Dan to make constant phone calls to Dora with respect to one or another aspect of the new contracts. Dora is likely to understand that this behavior will stop if she yields to Dan's demands.

Harassment has some advantages over threat. The punishment is more tangible and immediate, making it more motivating. Furthermore, the problems of credibility are solved – it is quite clear that the harasser can and will take action. However, there is another credibility problem, in that the target must have reason to believe that the harassment will stop if he or she complies. Otherwise there is no point complying.

The down side of harassment is similar to that of threat – resentment and resistance. But these problems are likely to be more severe than with threats, since the target's interests are actually being hurt. The result may be serious negative feelings and escalation of the conflict, making it very hard to solve the current issue and poisoning future relations between the parties. In short, harassment is usually the more risky tactic.

Positional commitments

Positional commitments (sometimes called "irrevocable commitments") are statements of a determination to hold firm at a particular offer – to make no further concessions. They are often combined with a threat to break off negotiation if the other party does not accept this offer. For example, after a period of negotiation, Dora might tell Dan that she is absolutely unable to make the suits in less than four months and that there is no point in talking any more about the issue. Positional commitments are only effective if failure to reach agreement is costly to the target. Hence, Dan may not find this tactic useful, since failure to reach agreement does not appear to hurt Dora.

As with threats, positional commitments must be credible to be effective. They are not very credible if it is clear that their user will be badly hurt by no agreement. Hence, a road to credibility is to demonstrate that one has a respectable BATNA, a credible alternative to negotiated agreement. For example, a car buyer who commits to a price of $10,500 could emphasize this commitment by showing that the same car is available from another dealer at the same (or a better) price. A second way to establish credibility is to attach a normative principle to one's commitment. For example, if a wholesaler is known to have paid $5,000 for a used car and a dealer to whom he is trying to sell the car can get $6,000 for it, the dealer might credibly commit to $5,500 on the grounds that equal profits are the only fair outcome.

A third way to establish credibility is to demonstrate that one will suffer costs if one concedes. The costs of concession become quite clear when one makes one's commitments public, especially if one has powerful, firm constituents (Wall 1977a). Thus Schelling (1960: 29) writes about international negotiation: "If national representatives can arrange to be charged with appeasement for every small concession, they place concession visibly beyond their own reach." Schelling points out further that the "weakness" of being unable to move without suffering cost is paradoxically a source of strength when combined with a positional commitment.

Positional commitments can be hazardous tactics. The danger is that they will lock the negotiator into a demand that is unworkable because it is beyond the other party's limit – the option that is minimally acceptable to the other party. There are two ways to diminish this danger. One is to *hedge* one's commitment, indicating that it is not completely firm (Shapiro and Bies 1991). This allows a graceful retreat from the commitment if the tactic does not work, but it has the defect of endangering credibility. The other approach is to *delay* making a positional commitment until one can determine the location of the other party's limit. That this is a useful approach is suggested by the finding that experienced negotiators, in comparison to novices, tend to delay positional commitments to the end of negotiation (Kelley 1966).

Persuasive arguments
Persuasive arguments have the aim of changing the target's attitude toward the issues under consideration. This can be done in two ways. One is to show that the target's interests are served by one's proposal. Thus Dan could argue that it is important to the company as a whole and hence to Dora to keep the goodwill of customers. Or he could argue that the added demand on Dora's production line would justify an expansion of this line, an investment that Dora has been advocating. The second is to show that one's own (the speaker's) interests are served by the proposal. Thus Dan might argue that getting these orders will be a feather in his cap and help him gain a promotion. This kind of argument will be persuasive to the extent that the other party places a value on the speaker's interests. It can also help to strengthen the credibility of a positional commitment made by the speaker.

The effectiveness of persuasive arguments has been a topic of extensive research by social psychologists (see, for example, Petty and Cacioppo 1981).

Other contentious tactics
There are many other kinds of contentious tactics. Indeed, most forces that influence concession making can be harnessed as tools to encourage the other party to concede. For example, time pressure encourages concession making (see Chapter 4); hence, putting time pressure on the other party can be a contentious tactic. It follows that many of the ideas presented in the rest of this book will have implications for contentious tactics.

The impact of contentious tactics

Not surprisingly, unequal use of contentious tactics has been shown to lead to an agreement favoring the heavier user (Williams and Lewis 1976). But such agreements can be Pyrrhic victories in situations with integrative potential, because contentious tactics often lead to low joint benefit and, when limits are high, to failure to reach agreement (Weingart *et al.* 1990; Zubek *et al.* 1992). This is partly because contentious tactics often wed their users to particular demands, making them unlikely to seek or discover new options (Roloff and Campion 1987). It is also because contending creates a rigidity of thought that is incompatible with creativity (Carnevale 1991).

Contentious tactics can be especially problematical when they are imitated by the other party – when threats elicit counterthreats or harassment is reciprocated. A number of studies have shown that such imitation is associated with failure to reach agreement in negotiation and poor long-run relations between the parties (Putnam and Jones 1982; Sillars 1981). One reason for this is that imitation often leads to escalatory spirals, with each party retaliating against the other party's most recent contentious tactic, leading to a growth in hostility between the parties.

Imitation of contentious tactics can be avoided; for example, Gottman (1979) has shown that in successful marriages, the partners tend to refrain at first from reciprocating unpleasant remarks. However, imitation is a common outcome of the use of contentious tactics, as was mentioned in the discussion of threats.

Despite their defects, contentious tactics are sometimes useful as precursors to, or in conjunction with, problem solving. They can bring a reluctant adversary into negotiation or reduce that party's goals to a realistic level that allows discovery of a solution. They can help to persuade adversaries that their own contentious tactics are not likely to succeed, encouraging them to shift to problem solving. Contentious tactics can sometimes contribute to the development of win–win agreements by sharpening understanding of their user's key concerns. This has been shown in the case of threats by Putnam and Wilson (1989). However, this is only likely to happen if escalatory spirals do not ensue and problem solving also takes place.

An illustration of the latter points is a threatening message sent to the Soviet Union by President John F. Kennedy during the Second Berlin Crisis in 1961. The message committed the United States to defend its key concern, continued Allied presence in West Berlin. The message was backed up by a military buildup. This threat was followed by successful negotiation with the Soviet Union, probably at least in part because it was coupled with a sweetener – the promise to remove "irritants" to the Soviets in exchange for their cooperation with the demands of the threat (Snyder and Diesing 1977). Promises and other problem solving tactics will be discussed in the next section.

Problem solving

Problem solving involves an effort to find a mutually acceptable agreement – a win–win solution. There are many problem solving tactics. Some involve joint problem solving, in which the two parties work together to try to find a mutually acceptable alternative. Others involve individual problem solving, in which one or both parties act on their own. Problem solving leads to win–win agreements, provided that there is integrative potential and the parties adopt ambitious, but at the same time realistic, goals.

In presenting and evaluating the tactics of problem solving, we will first describe the way win–win agreements are constructed, because several different routes can be traveled in search of these agreements. We will then examine the role of promises; ways to acquire information about the other party; and ways to structure the negotiation setting, approach the issues, and handle relations with the other party.

Constructing win–win agreements

There are three general ways to construct win–win agreements: expanding the pie, exchanging concessions, and solving underlying concerns. Each leads to a different kind of agreement and requires a different set of problem solving tactics (Pruitt 1981; Pruitt and Rubin 1986).

Expanding the pie

Some win–win agreements are constructed by increasing the available resources so that both sides can get what they want. This is called expanding the pie. Consider Sales and Production in our example. Their problem can be solved by finding a way to enlarge the suit manufacturing capacity. For example, another company might be found that has a lull in its own suit production and can make these new orders as a subcontractor. If so, Sales will get its product in two months, and Production will avoid disrupting its other pressing assignments.

Exchanging concessions

A second way to construct win–win agreements is to exchange concessions on different issues, with each party yielding on issues that are of low priority to itself and high priority to the other party. Such concession exchanges are sometimes called "tradeoffs." If the issues involved in the exchange are already on the negotiation agenda, the exchange is called *logrolling*. Suppose, for example, that it is higher priority for Sales to get fast action on the 500 suit order than the 1000 suit order, and that it is of higher priority for Production to *avoid* handling the 1000 suit order. These two departments have the makings of a logrolling deal, involving a two-month schedule for the 500 suit order and a four-month schedule for the 1000 suit order.

If only a single 1000 suit order were at issue, another kind of logrolling solution might be possible. If the order could be split into two parts, Production might be willing to accept a two-month schedule for the first 500 suits if Sales would accept a four-month schedule for the second 500 suits. This kind of logrolling requires a prior mental operation called *unbundling*, which "converts one issue into more than one" (Lax and Sebenius 1986: 108). In other words, somebody has to realize that the single order can be divided into two parts. Another name for unbundling is "unlinking" (Pruitt 1981).

If one of the issues is not on the agenda, such an exchange is called *nonspecific compensation*. In this form of win–win agreement, one party gets what it wants and the other is repaid on some unrelated issue. For example, Dora from Production might agree to fast movement of the suits in exchange for the right to attend future Sales Division meetings that are of interest to her. Nonspecific compensation is similar to logrolling except that the issue involved in the compensation is not part of the original negotiation and must be discovered in the broader relationship between the parties (Neale and Bazerman 1991).

Solving underlying concerns
The third way to construct win–win agreements is for somebody – one of the disputants or a third party – to examine the concerns that underlie the positions taken by one or more of the parties and to seek a way to achieve these concerns. As mentioned in Chapter 2, such concerns may involve goals, values or principles. For example, Dan may be pushing for quick production because he assumes that this is the best way to achieve his goal of keeping the customer. Dora may be resisting this demand because she fears that an overload will delay other pressing orders or because she

fears she will run out of certain materials needed for the suits, such as metal buttons. If these underlying concerns can be brought to the surface, it may be possible to find a way to resolve most or all of them (Fisher and Ury 1981). Indeed, conflicts sometimes evaporate when one gets down to underlying concerns.

Sometimes only *one* party's underlying concerns need to be examined, because that party will accept the other's demands if these concerns are met. For example, knowing that Dora is worried about depleting her stock of metal buttons, Dan may be able to persuade his customer to accept plastic buttons. This is called a solution by *cost cutting* – Dora's costs are cut to the point where she can agree to what Dan wants. Cost cutting need not come from the other party. A third party, or Dora herself, might find a way to restock metal buttons quickly, making it possible for Dora to accept Dan's proposal. Consider another example: knowing that Dan is putting pressure on Dora in order to gain a new customer, a mutual friend might introduce Dan to a retailer who would not require such quick delivery. This is called a solution by *specific compensation* – Dan would be repaid for agreeing to Dora's time schedule by receiving a benefit that serves the precise goal he was seeking.

At other times, win–win solutions are devised by an analysis of both parties' underlying concerns. For example, if the underlying issues are metal buttons and keeping the customer, it may be possible for Dora to find a source of imitation metal buttons that will allow her to make the suits in two months and for Dan to persuade the customer to accept this design alteration. Alternatives that solve both parties' underlying concerns are called *bridging* solutions. In bridging solutions, "neither side achieves its initially stated . . . position; instead, the parties search for creative (new) options" (Neale and Bazerman 1991: 38). Some bridging solutions are quite novel and may even be elegant, as in the case of two people who were fighting over an orange. The problem was completely solved when it was discovered that one wanted the pulp to make juice and the other wanted the peel to put in a cake.

Kinds of integrative potential

Situations differ in the methods available for constructing win–win solutions. Hence, we can speak of various kinds of integrative potential: logrolling potential, cost cutting potential, bridging potential, etc. Some situations have more than one kind of integrative potential, so that there is more than one possible route to mutual success. This is the case for Dan and Dora.

The nature of underlying concerns

The concerns underlying a negotiator's position may have to do with either the *issues* under discussion or the negotiation *process*. Dan's request for a two-month production schedule can be logically deduced from his desire to win a new customer and to be viewed as a success in his work. Hence, the latter are examples of issue-related concerns. Dan may also fear that if he concedes he will be seen as weak or as admitting that Dora is right and he is wrong. These are process-related concerns. Process-related concerns may seem irrational, but they are often powerful determinants of negotiator behavior.

In searching for underlying concerns, one should keep in mind that the same issue may have different meanings to the two parties. For example, one side may be concerned about substance while the other is concerned about appearance. Thus the mediator in an international dispute gave one side actual control of a road so as to stop military shipments and the other side apparent control so that its government would not be embarrassed in the eyes of its citizens (Pruitt and Rubin 1986). The parties may also differ in their forecasts about the future or their time preferences. There are standard solutions to each of these kinds of differences that can help in developing win–win solutions (see Lax and Sebenius 1986, Chapter 5).

There are often several layers of underlying concerns, with some concerns providing the rationale for others, in a *hierarchical* pattern. For example, Dan's demands may be based on his desire to keep his customer, which may derive from a belief that he gains recognition in his company by landing steady customers.

Burton (1984) has argued that basic human needs like recognition and security lie at the base of all concern hierarchies and that conflicts cannot be fully resolved unless these needs are brought to the surface. Once brought to the surface, such concerns can often be easily reconciled. For example, a territorial dispute may seem intractable until it is discovered that the territory stands for security to one side and national integrity to the other. It may then be possible to demilitarize the territory (solving the former side's security problem) and give it to the latter side (solving their national integrity issue). Such a solution was successful in resolving the dispute over the Sinai Peninsula between Egypt and Israel. Such a procedure should not be regarded as a universal formula or panacea for resolving all conflicts. Underlying concerns are sometimes no more amenable to settlement than surface issues. If an orange is the only item of food around, two people who are fighting over it will not be helped by knowing that they are both motivated by the basic human need of hunger. Furthermore, there are types of win–win solutions that do not require analysis of underlying concerns; for example, expanding the pie (e.g. finding another orange) and logrolling (which only requires an understanding of the parties' priorities among two or more surface issues).

Sometimes several *parallel* (nonhierarchical) concerns underlie one party's (or both parties') demands. In such cases, it may be necessary to drop some concerns in order to achieve the others. This requires unbundling concerns that were previously linked and seeking priorities among them. If this is done by both parties, a process akin to logrolling may take place, at the level of concerns rather than demands. Take, for example, a married couple who are seeking a vacation spot. The husband wants to go to the mountains to serve the goals of hunting, fishing, and viewing mountain vistas. The wife wants to go the sea shore because of her interest in swimming, boating, and smelling the sea air. If the goals of mountain vistas and sea air can be unbundled from the other concerns and dropped, it should be possible to locate an inland lake that is acceptable to both parties. This would be a bridging solution involving a logrolling-like exchange of concessions in the realm of underlying concerns.

Refocusing questions

The various methods of constructing win–win agreements just mentioned can serve as a checklist for negotiators and mediators who are trying to find ways to resolve a conflict. Connected with each method is a set of refocusing questions, which are useful for identifying the win–win options (Pruitt and Rubin 1986).

- For *expanding the pie*: How can both parties get what they are demanding? Is there a resource shortage? How can the critical resource be expanded?

- For *logrolling*: What issues are of higher and lower priority to myself? What issues are of higher and lower priority to the other party? Are some of my high-priority issues of low priority to the other and vice versa? Are several separable issues bundled together for myself or the other party?
- For *nonspecific compensation*: What are the other party's goals and values? What can I do to satisfy them?
- For *cost cutting*: What risks and costs does my proposal pose for the other party? How can these risks and costs be mitigated?
- For *specific compensation*: What goals and values are served by the other party's proposal? Can these goals and values be served in some other way?
- For *bridging*: What underlying concerns are served by the other party's proposal? What underlying concerns are served by my proposal? What are the two parties' priorities among these underlying concerns? How can both parties' high priority concerns be served?

The questions listed for expanding the pie show that this kind of solution can be achieved with no knowledge about the other party except his or her demands. It turns out that this is also sometimes true of logrolling solutions, where only the first question, about one's own priorities, is absolutely essential. If the first question is answered, logrolling solutions can sometimes be achieved by means of *systematic concession making* (Kelley and Schenitzki 1972; Pruitt 1981; but see also Weingart *et al.* 1990). This involves starting with high goals and proposing all the combinations of options one can think of that serve these goals. If none of these combinations is accepted by the other party, one relaxes or drops one's lower priority goals and again proposes all possible combinations, continuing this cycle until the other party accepts a proposal. Although this is a possible route to logrolling solutions, these solutions can usually be achieved more efficiently if the other party's priorities are also known.

The other routes to win–win agreements require some knowledge about the other party, and the knowledge requirements become greater as one goes down the list. Bridging, at the bottom of the list, requires detailed and intimate information about the other's underlying concerns and the priorities among these concerns. This implies that it will be harder to reach agreement in settings that require solutions that are farther down this list (Quirk 1989).

Acquiring information about the other party's concerns

How can negotiators acquire information about the other party's goals, values and priorities? *Empathy* is of great value for this purpose. Negotiators benefit if they can take the other party's perspective – imagining themselves in the other's shoes and sensing what the other is feeling. This requires that they not be hostile to the other or defensive about the other's attitude toward themselves. These emotions tend to produce stereotypic thinking and to block empathy. Negotiators who are suffering from these emotions should consult other people who are familiar with the adversary and have a clearer mind. Some negotiators are better at empathy than others, and they have been shown to achieve more win–win agreements (Neale and Bazerman 1983).

Information gathering is assisted by engaging in *active listening* (also called "reflective listening"). This means paying attention to what the other is saying, asking questions when the other's meaning is unclear, and periodically checking on one's understanding by rephrasing the other's position (Katz and Lawyer 1985; Rapoport 1960). Johnson (1967, 1971) has shown that active listening is effective as a means of gathering information. His studies show that it also improves the other's attitude toward oneself and increases the other's willingness to concede. However, if active listening is done too warmly, it runs the risk of signaling weakness and thus diminishing the other's willingness to concede (Johnson 1971).

Sometimes the other party is willing to speak directly about his or her goals, priorities and concerns, a phenomenon called *information exchange*. Information exchange is a crucial element of *joint problem solving* – a process in which the negotiators view their separate interests as a common problem and brainstorm about various possible alternatives for solving it.

Both laboratory and field studies have confirmed that information exchange and joint problem solving are useful ways to achieve win–win agreements (Thompson 1991a; Weingart *et al.* 1990; Zubek *et al.* 1992). There is also some evidence that joint problem solving encourages longer-lasting agreements (Pruitt *et al.* 1992b). Kremenyuk (1991) has argued that joint problem solving is the best approach in international negotiation, combatting the rigidities and delays that are inevitable when the parties develop their proposals before coming to the negotiation table.

Unfortunately, information exchange and joint problem solving require a high level of trust in the other party, which is often not available in negotiation. Without trust, negotiators tend to fear that the other party will misuse the information provided; hence they give little of it (Kimmel *et al.* 1980). This raises an important question: how can negotiators who do not trust each other get the information that is usually needed to develop win–win solutions? Neale and Bazerman (1991: 30–32) have three answers to this question:

1 *Ask lots of questions.* Negotiators who ask for information about underlying concerns often get it (Roloff and Campion 1987; Thompson 1991a). If this does not work, they can ask the other party for an opinion about the most objectionable parts of their proposal. Answers to the latter kind of question can help identify the other party's priorities.
2 *Give away some information.* Negotiators tend to reciprocate most forms of behavior, including the provision of information (Thompson 1991a). Hence, it may be possible to start a cycle of information exchange by giving the other party a little innocuous information.
3 *Ask for preferences among proposals*, with the understanding that neither party is bound by the answer given. Two studies have shown that negotiators can decode the answers to such questions into information about the other party's priorities (Kimmel *et al.* 1980; Pruitt *et al.* 1978).

Promises

Promises are often employed in constructing win–win agreements that involve exchanging concessions, cost cutting, or specific compensation. For example, Dan might promise to invite Dora to future sales meetings that discuss production if she pushes his order through quickly – a solution by specific compensation. Hence, promises can be considered problem solving tactics. Promises are the mirror image of threats; they commit one to reward the other for compliance to one's demands instead of punishing the other for noncompliance. Credibility is an issue with promises as with threats. The main findings are that the credibility of promises is enhanced by past consistency (Schlenker *et al.* 1973) and by past accommodative behavior (Tedeschi *et al.* 1973).

Promises have few of the deficiencies associated with threats. If they work, they tend to build credit rather than resentment. Liking and respect tend to go up, making the party using them more influential in the future (Gaski 1986). Promises also evoke less resistance than threats, and one study found that there was more compliance to a promise of giving a certain amount of money than to a threat of taking away the same amount of money (Freedman 1981). Promises are also more flexible in the face of failure. If a promise does not work, negotiators can try another tactic. But a threat commits its user to take retaliatory action if it does not work, tying the user's hands. This means that negotiators contemplating the use of threats need to be more certain of success than those contemplating the use of promises.

If promises have all of these advantages, why are threats so common? The main reason is probably that they are cheaper if they work. "An effective promise costs Party whatever reward was promised. By contrast, a threat that works as intended costs Party nothing" (Pruitt and Rubin 1986: 54). Another reason is that threats are more psychologically consistent with the negative feelings toward the adversary that so often develop during conflict.

Combinations of threats and promises are commonly used in negotiation and other forms of social conflict. The two types of tactics often serve different aims. Threats are used to emphasize boundaries: to signal the limits below which we refuse to concede and to bolster the restrictions that we wish to place on the other party's behavior. The cost issue is probably paramount in the choice of threats for this purpose, since people would be quickly bankrupted if they tried to repay people for observing all of the boundaries they had to place on them. Promises are used to encourage cooperation within the confines of these boundaries: to encourage settlement on our terms or to inspire cooperative, rather than simply correct, behavior. An example of such a combination is Kennedy's message to the Soviet Union, which was cited above.

Other guidelines for problem solving

Good problem solving requires a proper *setting*. Fisher and Ury (1981) have suggested that it is best to meet the other party in private, because public sessions discourage information exchange and encourage the making of positional commitments, especially when there are powerful constituents in the audience. Research supports this observation but suggests that male audiences are more problematical than female audiences (Pruitt *et al.* 1986). Indeed female audiences sometimes contribute to problem solving, because people usually assume that women stand for reconciliation and hence will be unhappy if they witness heavy contentious action. Effective problem solving is also encouraged by settings that produce good moods, such as those involving interpersonal warmth, the exchange of presents, good food, pleasant music, and recent success of any kind (see Chapter 6). Additional advice on settings will be encountered in Chapter 7, where we discuss the antecedents of problem solving.

The way negotiators *approach the issues* is also important. In discussions of conflict, there is a powerful tendency to dwell on the past, hashing and rehashing memories of past unpleasantness for which the other is held accountable. This is often a necessary ventilation process, which must be permitted in the early stages of negotiation to avoid a sense of injustice (Lind and Tyler 1988). Such ventilation can also help to sharpen up the issues if each party does not take too much offense at what the other says. But the parties must eventually focus on the future, because changes can only be made in that realm.

Once they focus on the future, it is useful to make an agenda of issues to be discussed (Zubek *et al.* 1992). This should allow some initial success, so as to improve moods and give people faith in the negotiation process (Huber *et al.* 1986), though this success should not involve issues that could later enter into a logrolling solution. A policy of withholding the final decision until all issues have been discussed is also useful (Pruitt 1981). This makes it possible to discover logrolling potential (i.e. pairs of issues that can be traded off) that might otherwise go unnoticed. In discussions of issues, negotiators should pose problems before coming up with solutions and state their proposed solutions in a tentative fashion. Otherwise there is a tendency for the discussions to deteriorate into a defense and rebuttal of demands. They should also try to generate as many options as possible, in the hope of finding one that will appeal to both parties.

In addition, it is important for negotiators to develop and maintain *good interpersonal relations*. Otherwise the tensions produced by the divergence of interest tend to undermine problem solving.

Relations between negotiators will be discussed in considerable detail in Chapter 9.

The most successful problem solving involves a *firm but concerned and flexible stance* (Pruitt and Rubin 1986). Firmness, in this context, means resistance to yielding on one's basic goals. Firmness is needed, because one's basic goals must be represented in a viable solution to the problem. This point was mentioned earlier in our discussion of concession making. Being firm does not mean being bullheaded. We are talking about moderate firmness, in which goals are re-examined after a period of time if they seem unobtainable. In addition to being firm, it is important to be concerned about the other party's welfare and flexible about the means to achieve one's goals, so that the other party's perspectives can be brought into the final solution.

A firm but concerned and flexible stance has two advantages. The first is that it allows one to devise win–win solutions. The second is that it encourages the other party to take a similar approach. Firmness discourages contending by the other party, and concern and flexibility should enhance the other party's conviction that problem solving will pay off. Like courtesy, problem solving is catching.

Inaction and withdrawal

We end with inaction and withdrawal because they are fundamentally different from the other strategies in that they do not move the negotiation toward agreement. Withdrawal means breaking off negotiation, which results in no agreement, with the effects discussed in Chapter 2, including success for parties who are advantaged by the status quo. Inaction can take a number of forms, such as not showing up for discussions or talking around the issues. Inaction is usually a way-station in negotiation, a pause before the adoption of some other strategy. But if it goes on indefinitely, it is tantamount to withdrawal. This is one reason why people who are advantaged by the status quo tend to opt for inaction (Peirce *et al.* 1991). In our example, Production is such a party, since Sales is trying to get Production to change its usual schedule. Hence Production is more likely to favor inaction.

Summary and implications

This chapter has examined the nature of five basic strategies used by negotiators and the outcomes associated with these strategies. Concession making, inaction, and withdrawal are relatively simple strategies involving lowering goals and demands, doing nothing, or leaving the negotiation. But contending and problem solving are very complex because of the many possible tactics associated with them. Contending is any effort to persuade the other party to concede. It involves – among other tactics – threats, harassment, positional commitments, and persuasive arguments that buttress negotiator positions. Problem solving is any effort to find a win–win solution. To understand problem solving, we must grasp the three ways in which win–win solutions are constructed: expanding the pie, exchanging concessions on different issues, and solving underlying concerns. Among the tactics that can be used in problem solving are asking refocusing questions, acquiring information about the other's party concerns, and making promises to compensate the other or cut the other's costs for making concessions. The settings in which negotiation takes place and the way in which negotiators approach their task are also important for successful problem solving.

With respect to outcomes, an inverted U-shaped relationship has been found between the extent of concession making and the degree of success. If negotiators are too firm, they will fail to reach agreement; and if they are too soft, the agreements they reach will provide them little benefit. Hence, a moderate rate of concession is usually the most effective approach. Provided there is integrative potential, moderate concession making combined with active problem solving is likely to lead to win–win solutions that provide good benefit to both sides. One or the other side can sometimes achieve more profit than this by employing contentious tactics instead of problem solving. However, contentious tactics are often imitated by the other side in a defensive or retaliatory reaction, leading to an escalatory spiral. The most common result of such a spiral is failure to reach agreement, or agreement on an obvious compromise that provides less benefit to both parties than would be achieved in a win–win agreement. Although they are often counterproductive, contentious tactics can sometimes contribute to the development of win–win agreements by bringing reluctant parties to the negotiation table or providing information about the needs and priorities of the users of these tactics. However, problem solving must also take place for this effect to be achieved.

Suggestions for further reading

Chatman, J. A., Putnam, L. L. and Sondak, H. (1992). Integrating communication and negotiation research. In *Research on negotiation in organizations, Volume 3. Handbook of negotiations research.* Greenwich, CT: JAI Press, pp. 139–64.

Fisher, R. and Ury, W. (1981). *Getting to Yes: Negotiating agreement without giving in.* Boston: Houghton Mifflin.

Glasl, F. (1982). The process of conflict escalation and roles of third parties. In G. B. J. Bomers and R. B. Peterson (eds), *Industrial relations and conflict management.* Boston: Kluwer-Nijhoff.

Pruitt, D. G. and Rubin, J. Z. (1986). *Social conflict: Escalation, stalemate, and settlement.* New York: McGraw-Hill.

Tedeschi, J. T., Schlenker, B. R. and Bonoma, T. V. (1973). *Conflict, power, and games: The experimental study of interpersonal relations.* Chicago: Aldine Publishing.

4

DETERMINANTS OF DEMANDS, CONCESSIONS AND CONTENTIOUS BEHAVIOR

Charles decided to buy a new 1992 Mazda at the beginning of the 1993 season. The model he wanted had sold at $12,000 during the 1992 season, but his past experience led him to believe that he could get it for $1,000 less at the end of the season, so his initial goal was to pay $11,000. He certainly could not spend more than $11,500, since that was how much he had in the bank. Hence, Charles was happy when Barbara, his local Mazda dealer, told him that there were still a lot of 1992s on the lot and that she was asking $10,750 for the car. Barbara's limit, unknown to Charles, was $10,100, which was determined by her supervisor at the car dealership: "Barbara, we cannot sell any car for less than $10,100." Based on learning Barbara's asking price of $10,750 for the car, Charles revised his initial goal. He reasoned that if Barbara started with such a low demand, she might be willing to take even less. So he developed a revised goal of paying only $10,000 and made an opening offer of $9,500 to give himself a little bargaining room. Barbara conceded to $10,500 and Charles reciprocated by conceding to $9,900. Then Barbara said that she could not make another concession and that $10,500 was as low as she could go. This was a take-it-or-leave-it offer. Charles replied that he could take his business elsewhere. But he wasn't sure that it was a good idea to walk out because her demand was so close to his goal and he had already spent so much of the day at the dealership. He also remembered that he had originally been willing to pay as much as $11,000, so he agreed to accept her demand. Barbara wrote out the contract at $10,500 and Charles signed.

This everyday sequence of events illustrates many of the features of negotiation discussed in this chapter. Charles was reacting to several environmental conditions: past experience with prices at the end of the season, Barbara's remarks about the state of the inventory, Barbara's demands, Barbara's positional commitment (the take-it-or-leave-it offer), the lateness of the day. These conditions affected several aspects of his *motivation*: his goals, the limits to how far he will concede, and his desire to avoid no agreement. The result was a series of tactics: a set of demands and concessions (including acceptance of the other's demand) and a contentious statement (the threat to take his business elsewhere).

The heyday of research on the determinants of demands, concessions and contentious behavior was in the 1960s and 1970s. Most of the research in that period was in the laboratory and employed single-issue tasks, such as dividing nine points (Kelley *et al.* 1967) or establishing the price of a car (Yukl 1974a, b). Experimental research on the prisoner's dilemma was ongoing at the same time, eventually evolving into studies of the resource dilemmas. The subjects in all of these studies were usually instructed to be concerned about self-interest, to try to maximize their own outcomes. In other words, they were given an *individualistic orientation*.

Goals, limits and demands

Most negotiators have goals, because otherwise they would blunder along not knowing what direction to take. In addition, there are almost always limits to how far they will concede. However, like Charles, they are sometimes not aware of these limits at first, which means that from a psychological viewpoint these limits do not yet exist.

Demands are usually more ambitious than goals, which are more ambitious than limits (Yukl 1974a, b). These points are illustrated for a one-dimensional issue by Figure 4.1, which is based on the car buying story presented at the beginning of this chapter. The point in time illustrated is just before Charles and Barbara made reciprocal concessions. Charles was demanding $9,500, his goal was $10,000 and his limit was $11,500. Barbara was demanding $10,750, and we can speculate that her goal was $10,500 and her limit was $10,100. Figure 4.1 is simply Figure 2.1 with the two parties' outcome axes overlapping in such a way that one is in the

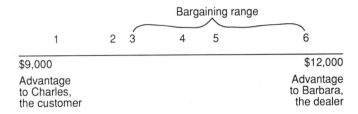

Figure 4.1 Location of options in a one-dimensional issue

1 = $9,500, Charles' demand; 2 = $10,000, Charles' goal;
3 = $10,100, Barbara's limit; 4 = $10,500, Barbara's goal;
5 = $10,750, Barbara's demand; 6 = $11,500, Charles' limit.
The bargaining range is positive.

opposite direction from the other. A figure like this is useful whenever negotiation involves only a single issue (see Raiffa 1982).

The distance between two parties' limits is called their *bargaining range* (Lax and Sebenius 1986). A bargaining range can be positive, in which case agreement is possible, or negative, in which case agreement is impossible unless the parties change their limits. There is a positive bargaining range in the car buying example shown in Figure 4.1. Barbara was willing to take as little as $10,100 and Charles was willing to pay as much as $11,500, so agreement was possible at all the prices between these limits. Agreement could not have been reached if there had been a negative bargaining range – for example, if Barbara's limit had been $11,750 instead of $10,100 – though the parties might have negotiated for a while hoping that an agreement was possible (Lax and Sebenius 1986).

The possible agreements within a positive bargaining range are called *viable options*. Research (Bazerman *et al.* 1985; Ben-Yoav and Pruitt 1984b; Pruitt and Lewis 1975) suggests that agreement is more likely and more rapid the larger the bargaining range, presumably because there are more viable options. The only exception to this generalization would appear to be the unusual circumstance where each party knows the other's limit. In this case, it may be better to have a single viable option rather than several, because this option is likely to become a prominent solution (see Chapter 8).

An experiment by Yukl (1974a) traced the location of demands, goals, and limits over time in an experiment where the subject

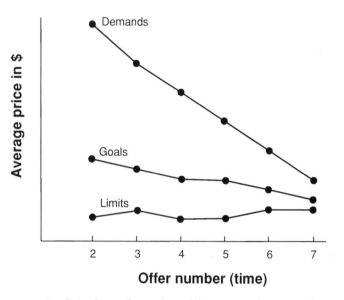

Figure 4.2　Dealer's demands, goals and limits as a function of time
Source: Yukl (1974a: 233)

played the role of the seller of a used car. The subject's goal was measured by asking, "What do you think is the best price that you can expect to get from the buyer?" The subject's limit was measured by asking, "What is the rock bottom lowest price that you would be willing to sell the car for?" The results are shown in Figure 4.2. They indicate that in the early stages of negotiation, demands are often far in advance of goals and limits. This is called *overbidding* or sham bargaining, and is presumably due to negotiator efforts to create an image of firmness. But as time goes on, overbidding diminishes, and demands are often close to or identical with goals at the end. Goals, in turn, tend to approach limits, as wishful thinking becomes eroded. The upshot of these trends is that limits are usually the most stable and demands the least stable of these three entities, as can be seen in Figure 4.2.

Goals and limits (when they exist) typically have a big impact on a negotiator's initial demand and subsequent concessions. Higher *limits* produce larger initial demands and greater resistance to concession making (Holmes *et al.* 1971; Kelley *et al.* 1967; Smith *et al.* 1982; Yukl 1974a, b). This leads to slower agreements and fewer agreements for the reasons given earlier (Bazerman *et al.*

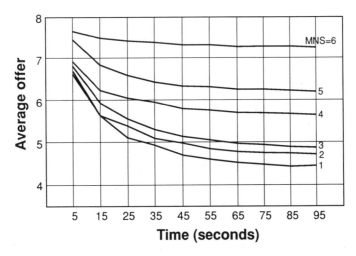

Figure 4.3 Demand level at each time point for negotiators with
different sizes of limit (MNS values)
Source: Kelley *et al.* (1967: 372)

1985; Ben-Yoav and Pruitt 1984b; Pruitt and Lewis 1975). If
agreement is reached, parties with higher limits tend to achieve
more (Ben-Yoav and Pruitt 1984b; Kelley *et al.* 1967).

One qualification on these findings is that a negotiator's limit
has a greater impact on that negotiator's demand the closer it is
to the demand. Thus, in our example, an increase in Barbara's
limit from $10,100 to $11,100 would have more impact on her
demand if that demand were in the $11,500 range than if it were
in the $13,000 range.[1] This means that limits have a larger impact
on demands at later stages of negotiation, when overbidding is
sufficiently reduced to bring demands into the range of limits
(Holmes *et al.* 1971; Kelley *et al.* 1967; Yukl 1974b).

This point can be seen in the data shown in Figure 4.3, which
are from an experiment done by Kelley *et al.* (1967). Two subjects
negotiated with each other by holding up black cards with numbers
between 1 and 8, which constituted their demands. Agreement
was reached when the numbers on the two cards summed to 9.
Each subject had a break-even point (or MNS as it was called), in
the form of a red card between 1 and 6. If agreement was reached,
the subject's outcome was the value of the last black card held up
minus the value of the red card. It seems reasonable to view these

break-even points as limits, since the subjects made negative points if their demands (their black cards) were lower than their break-even points. Figure 4.3 shows the average value of the demands at ten-second intervals as a function of the value of these limits. It will be seen that the limits had a larger impact on the demands the more time had elapsed.

The findings on *goals* are similar to those on limits. Higher goals produce higher demands (Hamner and Harnett 1975; Holmes *et al.* 1971; Yukl 1974a, b), smaller concessions (Hamner and Harnett 1975), and slower agreements (Kahan 1968). Because higher goals produce higher demands, they lead to larger profits if agreement is reached (Holmes *et al.* 1971; Siegel and Fouraker 1960).

Determinants of goals and limits

As was pointed out in Chapter 2, it is rational for negotiators to limit their concessions to what Fisher and Ury (1981) call the "best alternative to a negotiated agreement" or BATNA. Charles, the hero of our little parable, would have a BATNA of $10,000 if he knew that another dealer were willing to sell the model he wanted at that price. It would be rational for him to set his limit at this figure, and he could also make a good argument for this limit by quoting the other dealer's price.

There is evidence that negotiator limits are indeed influenced by their BATNAs. Bacharach and Lawler (1981) have shown that concession making is greater and agreements are less rewarding when BATNAs are less favorable. It follows that negotiators can increase their chances of success by surveying the options that are available to them outside negotiation in search of a favorable BATNA. Another tactic is to claim a favorable BATNA even if one does not have it, but this may not be as credible and runs the risk of undermining long-term trust between the parties (Shapiro and Bies 1991).

Limits are also sometimes set at the break-even point (the point of zero gain) if this is known, as in the example shown in Figure 4.3, because it is hard for people to accept a loss. If Charles were buying his car to resell it to a friend in another country, he might set his limit at the amount he could get from the friend, because he would incur a loss below that price.

Positional commitments are another source of limits. Thus

Barbara's take-it-or-leave-it offer of $10,500 might well have raised her psychological limit to this figure because of the embarrassment she would suffer if she made any further concessions. The wider the audience for such commitments, the more effect they are likely to have.

It also seems reasonable to assume that limits will be lower, and hence negotiators will be more willing to concede, the greater is the perceived cost of failing to reach agreement. Negotiators are willing to take risks by failing to concede if there is little perceived penalty for no agreement. This attitude tends to vanish if it is important to reach agreement.

Negotiator goals are never lower than their limits and hence are influenced by all the determinants of limits. In addition, they are affected by what seems *feasible*. This means that they will be heavily influenced by expectations about how far the other party will concede (as is implied by the method used to measure goals in the data shown in Figure 4.2). The further the other is expected to concede, the more ambitious will be a negotiator's goals, and hence his or her demands. This has been called the principle of *tracking* (Pruitt 1981), the tracker adjusting his or her behavior to what the other is expected to do. Tracking can be seen in the results of a study by Chertkoff and Baird (1971), in which information about the other party's limits was found to structure goals and demands. Given this finding, it is no surprise that negotiators usually conceal their limits unless these limits are quite elevated (Kelley *et al.* 1967). If Charles knew that Barbara was willing to sell the car for as low as $10,100 (her limit), it is likely he would have offered $10,100.

Principles – that is, convictions about what is proper or fair – are an additional source of both goals and limits. This is usually because people aspire to, and are unwilling to concede beyond, benefits to which they feel entitled. When principles are involved, goals, limits and demands are often identical. Suppose that Charles thought he was entitled to a price of $9,750, because Barbara had given that price to one of his friends. He would very likely have set both his goal and his limit at that price. He might also have demanded $9,750, because of a belief that a principled argument would prevail.

The introduction of principles often rigidifies negotiation, making it hard or impossible for parties to make concessions (Dupont and Faure 1991). This is in part because demands tend to be identical with limits when principles are at stake. It is also because principles tend to be deeply felt, making it difficult for people to rethink limits that are based on them (Touzard 1977). All of this suggests that negotiators will be well advised to try to prevent their opponents from linking principles to the issues under consideration and to try to undo such linkages if they are made. Methods for undoing linkages will be discussed in Chapter 8.

Other determinants of demands and concessions

Representation

Negotiators often represent other people, who can be called their "constituents." Imagine that Charles, in our car buying story, was buying the car for his sports car club. As a representative of the club membership, Charles wanted to please his constituents (Enzle *et al.* 1992; Gruder and Rosen 1971; Wall 1975). Hence, if he believes that his constituents wanted to make a killing on a car deal, he will tend to make high demands and few concessions. But he will tend to make concessions if he believes that the club membership favors cooperation with the dealership and agreement (Benton and Druckman 1974; Tjosvold 1977).

Representatives are motivated to make a positive and avoid making a negative impression on their constituents (Gruder and Rosen 1971; Wall 1975). Evidence supporting this generalization was seen in a study by Adelberg and Batson (1978). Negotiators representing a simulated helping agency were more likely to use an allocation rule they thought would please their constituents than a rule that would provide the most effective help to these constituents.

The desire to please constituents means that representatives will tend to make high demands and be unwilling to concede to the extent that they believe that their constituents are anxious to win. In the absence of information about constituent preferences, representatives tend to view their constituents as more anxious to win than themselves (Gruder 1971), a belief that is often quite accurate (Walton and McKersie 1965). Hence, representatives are usually less yielding and take longer to reach agreement than negotiators acting on their own behalf (Benton 1972; Benton and Druckman 1973, 1974; Druckman *et al.* 1972). Occasionally representatives come to believe that their constituents are more interested in cooperation and reaching agreement than in winning. In such cases they respond with concession making (Benton and Druckman 1974; Tjosvold 1977).

Several studies indicate that representatives are especially eager to please their constituents when they are *accountable* to these constituents. Accountability is the extent to which negotiators can be rewarded or punished by their constituents for their performance. It is produced by giving the constituents power over negotiators' outcomes (Bartunek *et al.* 1975; Ben-Yoav and Pruitt 1984a; Neale 1984), or by making it clear that the constituents will receive information about the outcome of the negotiation (Gruder 1971; Klimoski 1972; Klimoski and Ash 1974). In these studies, accountability has usually been found to slow concession making and enhance contending, making it harder to reach agreement.

In addition, there is evidence that the relationship between the negotiator and constituent is an important determinant of the negotiator's behavior. Studies by Klimoski (1972) and Breaugh and Klimoski (1977) suggest that accountable representatives take longer to reach agreement only when they have some attraction to the group they represent. Druckman and Zechmeister (1973) found that negotiators who spent time with their constituents before negotiation were more likely to view negotiation as a win–lose, competitive enterprise than were negotiators who spent time with members of the other party before negotiation.

Representatives are also especially eager to please their constituents when they feel *insecure* about their standing in the group. Negotiators are insecure when they have low status in their organization, or when they feel distrusted by their constituents. Representatives who have higher status in their group are not so tied to their constituents' views and thus are freer to make concessions than those with lower status (Hermann and Kogan 1968; Kogan *et al.* 1972). For example, it is much less likely that the manager of a car dealership will have to seek approval before selling a car at a reduced price than will one of the floor salespersons. Several studies suggest that negotiators who are distrusted by their constituents are more likely to make tough initial first offers and reach fewer agreements (Frey and Adams 1972; Wall 1975). Klimoski and Ash (1974) and Haccoun and Klimoski (1975) found that this was also true for representatives who were selected at random as opposed to elected (election presumably leads to greater trust). Apparently, distrusted representatives, like low-status representatives, feel a need to ingratiate themselves with their constituents and thus try especially hard to gain good outcomes for them. These findings suggest a paradox: even though distrusted group representatives aspire to improve their relationship with their group, they often undermine their group's interests by failing to reach agreement.

A practical implication of these findings is that in inter-group or inter-organizational negotiation one should usually try to persuade the other side to send a trusted, high-status representative who can make concessions without fearing that they will undermine his or her support back home. In practice, it is hard to persuade the other side to send a representative who is higher in status than one's own representative. Hence, the most common request is for a representative who is equal in status to one's own.

Constituent *surveillance* of the negotiation also tends to reinforce perceived constituent preferences. In part this is because constituents are an audience, and Brown (1968) has found that negotiators are highly sensitive to the image held of them by an audience. If negotiators think that their constituents favor conciliation, surveillance will push them toward concession making (Organ 1971; Pruitt et al. 1986). But surveillance is more likely to enhance negotiator toughness (Benton 1975; Carnevale et al. 1979; Druckman et al. 1972; Klimoski and Ash 1974), especially under conditions of high negotiator accountability (Sharma et al. 1991). Indeed, with constituents (or journalists reporting to them) in the room, there is a strong tendency for heroic grandstanding. Hence, to reach agreement, it is often necessary to move into executive session with only the chief negotiators in attendance.

Hostility

Negotiators sometimes feel hostility toward the adversary, as for example when the adversary has been unpleasant or is perceived to have acted unfairly. There are mixed findings with respect to the impact of such hostility on demands and concessions. Some studies suggest that hostile feelings make negotiators reluctant to concede (Gruder 1971; Michener et al. 1975; Zubek et al. 1992). This may be because concession making is seen as an endorsement of the opponent or the opponent's behavior. However, in two other studies, subjects made larger concessions in negotiation (Baron 1988b) and cooperated more fully in the prisoner's dilemma (Schlenker *et al.* 1970) when faced with an unpleasant opponent. The key to this mystery may lie in a particular feature of the latter two studies: the opponent employed heavily contentious tactics, either making minimal concessions or issuing threats. The credibility of these tactics may have been enhanced by the opponent's unpleasant behavior.

If our interpretation of these conflicting results is right, they imply that negotiators should usually try to build good will and avoid antagonizing their adversaries if they can do so without forsaking their demands. Such tactics are likely to encourage concession making by the adversary. However, if negotiators expect to use heavily contentious tactics, an unpleasant demeanor may have the offsetting advantage of enhancing the credibility of these tactics.

Time pressure

Demands and concessions are also affected by time pressure. Many conditions lead to time pressure. In the words of Carnevale and Lawler (1986: 637):

> One factor is the costs of continued negotiation, such as time lost from other pursuits, or when the goods being negotiated are deteriorating (for instance, fruit beginning to spoil). Time pressure is also produced by the negotiator's nearness to a deadline, or the total amount of time available to negotiate. Some real-world examples of deadlines that produce time pressure include a contract that will expire at midnight, another buyer who will soon make an offer, and a foreseeable point at which open hostility will start. In addition, third parties often use deadlines as a tactic to facilitate compromise. . . . To some extent, all negotiations involve time away from other pursuits and time pressure almost always increases as negotiations proceed, especially as negotiators become fatigued or frustrated.

What effect does time pressure have on negotiation? Quite a few studies have shown that time pressure produces lower demands, faster concessions, and faster agreement (Hamner 1974;

Komorita and Barnes 1969; Pruitt and Drews 1969; Smith *et al.* 1982; Yukl 1974a). Yukl's (1974a) study shows that time pressure also produces less ambitious goals and that this may be the mechanism by which it reduces demand levels. Time pressure also interacts with limits, in that limits have a larger impact on demands under greater time pressure (Pruitt and Drews 1969). This is probably because under greater time pressure, limits and demands are closer to each other.

Kelley *et al.* (1967) have suggested that time pressure does not reduce, but acts in opposition to, resistance to concession. What this subtle distinction means is that under high time pressure, negotiators will be just as reluctant to concede as under low time pressure, but they will feel greater urgency about doing so. This will encourage reluctant concession making, accompanied by a great deal of ambivalence.

The relationships described in this section suggest that time pressure can be a useful contentious tactic if it is applied unilaterally on the other party. For example, negotiators who are dealing with out-of-town opponents may be able to delay agreement until Friday afternoon. This will put time pressure on all guests who wish to go home for the weekend, motivating them to make concessions they would not otherwise consider.

Determinants of contentious behavior

Many of the conditions that produce resistance to concession making also incline negotiators toward contending. This is true of high limits (Ben-Yoav and Pruitt 1984b; Kelley *et al.* 1967), hostility (Michener *et al.* 1975; Zubek *et al.* 1992), accountability to constituents (Ben-Yoav and Pruitt 1984a; Carnevale *et al.* 1981), and surveillance by male (though not by female) constituents (Pruitt *et al.* 1986). Given the opposite effects these conditions have on concession making and contending, it is not surprising to find a high negative correlation between these two forms of behavior (Kabanoff and van de Vliert 1990).

In addition, there is a tendency to prefer contending when one's own goals seem far removed from the other party's goals, giving the situation a win–lose character in which it seems that one or the other party must triumph (Deutsch 1973; Thompson and Hastie 1990).

Time pressure

Time pressure has a different effect from the variables just mentioned. There is evidence that it encourages both concession making (as was mentioned earlier) and *increased* use of contentious tactics (Carnevale and Lawler 1986). This is probably because the basic effect of time pressure is to reduce the feasibility of inaction, and thus to heighten the urgency of taking action to move toward agreement. Concession making is one form such action can take, contending is another; hence, time pressure can produce both reactions.

There is also evidence that time pressure reduces the likelihood of achieving win–win agreements (Carnevale and Lawler 1986; Yukl *et al.* 1976). There are two possible reasons for this. As indicated in Chapter 3, concession making and contending – two results of time pressure – both militate against the development of win–win agreements. In addition, it usually takes time to find novel solutions – information must be gathered and/or a variety of possible agreements must be tried out. Time pressure makes it hard to do these things.

Physical barriers

Putting a physical barrier between negotiators, so that they can hear but not see each other, tends to reduce contending under conditions that ordinarily produce such behavior (Carnevale and Isen 1986; Carnevale *et al.* 1981; Lewis and Fry 1977). As a result, win–win agreements are more often found with the barrier in place. This unusual but reliable effect is probably due to two nonverbal elements of contending, staring at the other party and moving into the other's territory (Lewis and Fry 1977). With the barrier in place, people cannot see their opponents doing these things and hence are less defensive.

Summary and implications

In this chapter, we have discussed many antecedents of demands, concessions, and contentious tactics, including the following. High goals and limits encourage high demands, resistance to concession, and the use of contentious tactics. High break-even points and favorable BATNAs, in turn, encourage high goals and limits. Hostility toward the other party and accountability to constituents also produce resistance to concession and contentious behavior. Time pressure, in contrast, encourages both concession making and contending.

The effects just described are compelling and consistent. But their generality must be questioned, because many of them seem to be specific to negotiators who are individualistically oriented – who are seeking to maximize their own interests. A number of studies have shown that these effects disappear when negotiators are cooperatively oriented – that is, concerned about the other party's welfare as well as their own. The tendency for *high limits* to induce rigidity and contending disappeared when the negotiators were married to each other (Schoeninger and Wood 1969) or expected to have to work together in the future (Ben-Yoav and Pruitt 1984b). *Time pressure* failed to encourage contending and failed to interfere with the development of win–win agreements when negotiators were instructed to "get the most" for themselves *and* the other party (Carnevale and Lawler 1986).

In addition, some circumstances appear to attenuate the effects of negotiator accountability. Accountability was not found to enhance rigidity and contending when: (a) a prominent solution existed (Benton and Druckman 1973); (b) a mediator suggested a solution or encouraged role-reversal behavior (Bartunek *et al.* 1975); (c) negotiators were unable to see one another and thus could not employ nonverbal dominance behaviors (Carnevale *et al.* 1981); or (d) the negotiators expected to have to work together in the future (Ben-Yoav and Pruitt 1984a). All of these circumstances can be understood as inhibiting competitive motivation or behavior.

All of this suggests the need for a broader theory of negotiation behavior that deals with the impact of concern about the other party's interests as well as one's own. Such a theory – the dual concern model – will be presented in Chapter 7. But first we must look at how negotiators react to one another's concession making and contending.

Note

1 From the viewpoint of the buyer, a *higher* limit, goal or demand involves a *lower* sum of money. Hence, an increase in Charles'

limit from \$11,000 to \$10,000 would have more impact on his demand if that demand were in the \$9,000 range than if it were in the \$6,000 range.

Suggestions for further reading

Carnevale, P. J. and Pruitt, D. G. (1992). Negotiation and mediation. *Annual Review of Psychology*, 43, 531–82.

Dupont, C. (1986). *La negociation*. Paris: Dalloz.

Kelley, H. H., Beckman, L. L. and Fischer, C. S. (1967). Negotiating the division of reward under incomplete information. *Journal of Experimental Social Psychology*, 3, 361–98.

Siegel, S. and Fouraker, L. E. (1960). *Bargaining and group decision making: Experiments in bilateral monopoly*. New York: McGraw-Hill.

Zartman, I. W. (ed.) (1978). *The negotiation process: Theories and applications*. Beverly Hills, CA: Sage.

5

REACTIONS TO THE OTHER PARTY'S BEHAVIOR

Negotiators are constantly reacting to one another's behavior. Many of these reactions can be described as *matching* and *mismatching*. In the realm of demands and concessions, matching means demanding more if the other's demands are larger, or conceding more rapidly the faster are the other's concessions. Mismatching means demanding more if the other's demands are smaller, or conceding more rapidly the slower are the other's concessions.

The negotiation cycle

Matching and mismatching tend to appear at different points in the negotiation cycle, depending on whether one is at the beginning, middle, or end of negotiation.

The beginning of negotiation

Mismatching is common at the beginning of negotiation, as a reaction to the other party's initial offer. People tend to respond with moderate demands when the other is initially firm and to demand a lot if the other is initially conciliatory (Liebert *et al.* 1968; Pruitt and Syna 1985; Yukl 1974b). This can be interpreted as *tracking*, an effort to place one's goals and demands at a reasonable distance from the best offer that can be expected from the other. In this interpretation, the other party's initial offer is assumed to provide information about where the other is likely to end up. The evidence for this interpretation is that this kind of mismatching disappears when sounder evidence is available about where the other is going, such as information about the other's limit or the existence of a prominent solution (Liebert *et al.* 1968; Pruitt and Syna 1985; Yukl 1974a).

Tracking was described in the car buying story in Chapter 4, in that Charles developed a more ambitious goal in response to Barbara's generous opening offer and the information that there was still a large inventory on the lot. Tracking occurs because negotiators want to take advantage of whatever opportunities for gain exist while not demanding so much that the other party will fail to take them seriously.

The middle of negotiation

Matching is common in the middle of negotiation, which is usually the longest period. Negotiators hold firm if the other holds firm and concede if the other concedes. For example, in our car buying story, Barbara's $250 concession to $10,500 prompted Charles' $200 concession to $9,900.

The evidence is clearest for matching the frequency of the other party's concessions (Bartos 1974; Esser and Komorita 1975; Hopmann and Smith 1977; Kelley *et al.* 1967; Yukl 1974b). Matching the other's concession size was also found in four experiments (Benton *et al.* 1972; Esser and Komorita 1975; Komorita and Esser 1975; Smith *et al.* 1982), though the phenomenon was always one of *undermatching*, with the subjects conceding considerably less than the other had just conceded. Matching did not appear at all in two other experiments (Pruitt and Drews 1969; Pruitt and Syna 1985).

A phenomenon similar to matching has also been found in three studies of real-life international negotiations (Beriker and Druckman 1991; Druckman and Harris 1990; Stoll and McAndrew 1986). Concessions tended to be made by the party who had conceded less in the prior time period and to be of a size that made up the difference.

To explain matching, we need to distinguish between matching the other's concessions (conceding when the other concedes) and matching the other's nonconcessions (failing to concede when the other fails to concede). Matching concessions (what Charles did in our example) is probably motivated by the social norm of reciprocity and a recognition that the other party is not likely to concede again unless one reciprocates. This phenomenon may also reflect a desire to reinforce the other for cooperative behavior. Matching the other's nonconcessions also serves the norm of reciprocity and probably derives, in addition, from a desire to prevent the other party from winning at one's expense. The latter reflects a fear of tangible loss, and of image loss – the fear of being seen as a sucker or weakling (Kerr 1986). Image loss of this kind can be a real danger in a predatory environment where "nice guys finish last."

The end of negotiation

Mismatching is often found again at the end of negotiation if time pressure becomes very high, as when a deadline is looming (Smith *et al.* 1982; Yukl 1974b; but see also Benton *et al.* 1972). Under high time pressure, firm opponents can often pull substantial concessions out of negotiators, because the latter are concerned about reaching agreement and will move to fill the gap. An example of this would be Barbara's success in persuading Charles to accept her last minute take-it-or-leave-it offer of $10,500, in our car buying story. However, negotiators will not move beyond their limits. Hence, problem solving in an effort to avoid no agreement is another common phenomenon at the end of negotiation (see Chapter 7).

Although mismatching is frequently found at the end of negotiation, the forces that push toward matching are still present. It follows that parties who face a firm opponent at the end will often experience severe *ambivalence*. They will be in conflict between an impulse to mismatch in order to fill the gap and an impulse to match in order to preserve reciprocity or avoid looking like a sucker. The result of this ambivalence is variability in response, with most negotiators mismatching but a few matching despite the risk of no agreement (Yukl 1974a).

Tactical implications

If mismatching is found at the beginning of negotiation and matching in the middle, a reasonable tactic for persuading the other party to concede should be to overbid at first (i.e. start with a high level of demand) and then concede regularly if the other concedes. Such a tactic has been shown to be more effective than one that starts with a moderate level of demand and makes few additional concessions (Bartos 1974; Benton *et al.* 1972; Hamner 1974). The latter tactic has two defects: it misleads the other party into setting unrealistically high goals and it fails to reciprocate the other's concessions. This helps to explain why so many negotiators engage in initial overbidding, a phenomenon that can be seen in Figure 4.2.

The fact that many negotiators mismatch as they approach a deadline might seem to support a tactic of holding firm at the end of negotiation, and thus forcing the other party to fill the gap. However, this is a risky tactic that should not be adopted lightly. It is a recipe for failure if one is holding firm at a point that is beyond the other's limit; hence, the tactic should only be used if there is insight into that limit. This tactic will also fail if the other party is so concerned about looking like a sucker that he or she is unwilling to fill the gap. Barbara used this tactic in our example, making a last minute take-it-or-leave-it offer of $10,500 that was actually higher than she was minimally willing to accept. Perhaps she had studied Charles long enough to realize that his limit was higher than this figure and that he was not likely to be concerned about looking like a sucker.

Matching of contending and problem solving

Matching of contending and problem solving are also found in negotiation. Druckman (1986) found that international negotiators tend to match the level of contentious rhetoric recently exhibited by the other party. Consistency between negotiators in the use of contentious tactics has also been found in several laboratory studies (Kimmel *et al.* 1980; Michener *et al.* 1975; Pruitt and Lewis 1975).

Inter-negotiator consistency has also been found in various measures of problem solving (Kabanoff and van de Vliert 1990; Kimmel *et al.* 1980; Pruitt and Lewis 1975). In an effort to discover whether these results involved actual matching, Thompson (1991a) manipulated the extent to which negotiators spoke about their priorities among the issues under discussion. The data showed that the other party partially matched the amount of information provided, but the results did not reach conventional levels of significance.

Matching and mismatching in games of moves

In Chapter 2, we discussed some games of moves that resemble negotiation in basic reward structure: the prisoner's dilemma, chicken, and two kinds of resource dilemmas (harvesting dilemmas and contributions dilemmas). Like negotiation, these involve mixed-motive settings in which the parties experience incentives for both cooperation and competition. There are instructive parallels between negotiation and these games in the way people react to the other party's behavior.

Matching

Matching is the dominant phenomenon in two-party prisoner's dilemma (Oskamp 1971) and resource dilemmas (Kerr 1983; Knapp 1989). Matching the behavior of the rest of one's group has also been found in a three-person prisoner's dilemma but not in a twelve-person prisoner's dilemma (Fox and Guyer 1977). Matching was also found in the early stages of a six-person resource dilemma (Messick *et al.* 1983), in which subjects tended to imitate the other members of their group in harvesting points from a limited pool. Two aspects of matching can be distinguished: matching the other's noncooperation and matching the other's cooperation.

Matching noncooperation
Most people match other people's noncooperation reliably – if you won't help me with my homework, I won't help you with yours. However, other people can sometimes get away with noncooperation *if they are not blamed for their behavior*. Thus, in a study of work, Kerr (1983) found that subjects reduced their level of effort (matched) when they thought they had a slacker as a partner. But this effect disappeared if it was clear that the partner lacked ability for the work. Kerr's explanation (Kerr 1986) is that the subjects felt less image loss – saw themselves less as suckers – when the partner could not be blamed for an inadequate performance. Hence, they were less likely to match their partner's poor

performance. The same may be true of negotiation: I may be more willing to concede unilaterally if I see you as un*able* to concede rather than un*willing* to do so.

Matching cooperation

Cooperation is also matched in prisoner's dilemma and resource dilemmas. However, there is a tendency toward undermatching here as in the middle period of negotiation. For example, Sermat (1967) found that a confederate who cooperated 100 percent in the prisoner's dilemma got only 40 percent cooperation in response. This was certainly higher than the 15 percent response achieved by a confederate who cooperated none of the time. But it was by no means proportional to the confederate's level of cooperation, and the subjects got much more reward than the confederates.

The perennial finding of undermatching suggests that people have a tendency to exploit consistent cooperation in mixed-motive settings. The norm of reciprocity is strong but by no means overwhelming. There is evidence that this exploitation increases over time as people discover that they can get away with it. Deutsch (1973) found this in a modified prisoner's dilemma, and Messick *et al.* (1983) found it in a six-person resource dilemma task if the other group members harvested at a reasonable rate. An initial tendency to match the others' harvesting rate was replaced by a tendency to overharvest. This was especially common when another group member started to overharvest. This suggests that taking advantage of another person's cooperation is more likely if one has a 'partner in crime' to serve as a model of poor citizenship. The latter phenomenon may be a variation of the so-called Asch effect. It is well known that a fellow deviant helps people escape from conformity to a social norm (Asch 1956). Messick's finding suggests that this escape can sometimes be in the direction of selfish exploitation of others, in violation of the norm of reciprocity.

Ambivalent mismatching

The phenomenon of ambivalent mismatching at the end of negotiation has its parallel in resource dilemmas during periods when people are faced by a resource shortage. When shortages arise, most people tend to remedy them. This means reduced harvesting in harvesting dilemmas such as the tragedy of the commons

(Samuelson *et al.* 1984). It also means increased contributions in contributions dilemmas, such as giving money to one's club when the dues collected are insufficient to cover costs. When the shortage can be attributed to one's fellow group members, remedial activity means mismatching their behavior – filling the gap left by their selfishness in order to preserve the common resource. Many people are willing to do this, but they are apparently ambivalent about it because mismatching violates the norm of reciprocity and makes them look like suckers (Rutte *et al.* 1987). Hence, as with negotiation at a deadline, some people resolve this conflict by matching their fellows – for example, following them into overharvesting – which further endangers the common resource (Brann and Foddy 1988; Messick *et al.* 1983).

Ambivalence about mismatching is also evident in the game of chicken in its final moments. To mention a common example of chicken, if your car and mine are barreling toward each other and you fail to swerve out of my way, it is rational for me to swerve, and most people will do so (Sermat 1964, 1967). But this violates reciprocity and makes me look like a sucker, as in negotiation and the resource dilemmas. Hence some people do not swerve, with deadly consequences.

Parallels between negotiation and resource dilemmas

The parallel findings just described suggest that negotiations at deadline and resource dilemmas in crisis have the same psychological reward structure as chicken in its final moments (a structure that was shown in Figure 2.3). Negotiation and the resource dilemmas may also have a common reward structure at earlier stages, but it is probably more like the prisoner's dilemma (Figure 2.4). This is suggested by the common finding of undermatching in these settings. By contrast, the tracking behavior that is so often found at the very beginning of negotiation appears to be unique to that setting.

Conditions that counteract undermatching

The tendency to undermatch the other party's cooperation, which is found in the mid-phase of negotiation and in most other mixed-motive settings, can probably be attributed to ordinary selfishness.

It is costly to cooperate in these settings, so one does as little as one can get away with.

There are two related conditions that combat undermatching and encourage full matching of the other party's cooperation. One is when the other party is perceived as *powerful*, the second is when the other party is perceived as *tough*.

Several studies have examined the impact of unequal coercive power (the capacity to punish the other), showing that the party with lesser power matches the other party's level of cooperation more fully than the party with greater power. Two of these studies examined the matching of concessions in negotiation (Michener *et al.* 1975; Tjosvold and Okun 1976), and two of them examined the matching of cooperation in the prisoner's dilemma (Komorita *et al.* 1968; Lindskold and Bennett 1973). A third prisoner's dilemma study showed the same effect for reward power (the capacity to reward the other). The other party's cooperation was more fully matched when the largest available rewards were controlled by the other party rather than oneself (Pruitt 1970).

Other parties are perceived as tough if they are seen as hard to push around and prone to noncooperative behavior. Perceived toughness can result from a prior episode in which the other failed to cooperate. Thus, in the prisoner's dilemma, a "reformed sinner" strategy, which shifts from noncooperation to cooperation, has been found to elicit more cooperation than a uniformly cooperative strategy (Bixenstine and Wilson 1963; Deutsch 1973; Harford and Solomon 1967). A related finding is that negotiators are more likely to reciprocate concessions from an opponent who has demonstrated resolve in a prior negotiation (Hilty and Carnevale 1992). Perceived toughness can also result from a perception that the other party has nonconciliatory constituents. Thus Wall (1977a) found that negotiators were more likely to match their adversary's concessions if that adversary was believed to have tough rather than soft constituents.

There are at least five reasons why people are especially prone to match cooperation from a powerful or tough other party. One is that this cooperation is unexpected and hence impressive, making them feel especially grateful. The second is that the other's cooperation is unlikely to be seen as a sign of weakness and hence unlikely to elicit an exploitative response that would block reciprocation. The third is that it makes sense to reward cooperation from such a party, because that party's failure to cooperate is so dangerous or so likely. The fourth is that failure to reciprocate may alienate the other party, with potentially disastrous consequences. The fifth, and probably the most interesting, is that collaboration becomes a goal because there seems little hope of exploiting the other; hence, one is ready to cooperate if the other cooperates.

The research cited above supports the common advice that negotiators should build power or a reputation for toughness before entering negotiation. However, this research also implies that power and toughness are most effective when they serve as a backdrop for cooperative behavior. In other words, the key to success is not so much negotiation from strength as *conciliation from strength*.

The tit-for-tat strategy

A common approach to all mixed-motive settings is to match (i.e. to reciprocate) the other's level of cooperation. One cooperates in response to the other's cooperation and fails to cooperate (i.e. retaliates) if the other fails to cooperate. Earlier we talked about conditions that produce or inhibit matching. In this section, we discuss matching as a strategy or tactic, which is commonly called the "tit-for-tat strategy" or simply "tit-for-tat." Research suggests that this strategy is very effective at eliciting concessions in negotiation (Komorita and Esser 1975; Wall 1977b) and cooperation in the two-party prisoner's dilemma (Deutsch 1973; Oskamp 1971). Use of the tit-for-tat strategy by a single party is less effective in the multi-party prisoner's dilemma. But there is evidence in the multi-party case that the larger the percentage of group members who use this strategy, the more likely are other group members to cooperate (Komorita *et al.* 1992).

Several studies have compared the effectiveness of tit-for-tat with that of a number of other strategies in the two-party prisoner's dilemma (Axelrod 1984; Bendor *et al.* 1991). These studies involved computer simulation of interpersonal interaction rather than actual interaction, because their object was to examine the pure effect of the strategies. They suggest that regardless of the strategy employed by the other party, tit-for-tat usually achieves high benefits for its user. This is not because tit-for-tat beats the other party: tit-for-tat never wins in this sense. Rather it is because tit-for-tat usually encourages the other party to cooperate.

Explanations for the success of the tit-for-tat strategy

There are three explanations for the success of the tit-for-tat strategy (Pruitt *et al.* 1987). The first postulates a noncognitive process of *behavior modification.* This process, if it occurs, enhances the strength of behavior that has been rewarded and diminishes the strength of behavior that has been punished. This explanation seems too simple in light of a finding by McGillicuddy *et al.* (1984) that watching one's opponent employ tit-for-tat with another negotiator had the same effect as directly experiencing tit-for-tat at the opponent's hands. This suggests that cognitive (perceptual) processes are involved rather than simple behavior modification.

The second explanation postulates a *cognitive learning mechanism.* Party A is assumed to learn from Party Z's tit-for-tat that Z will only cooperate if A cooperates first. A then cooperates if he or she views Z's cooperation as more valuable than the cost of eliciting it.

The third explanation (Pruitt and Kimmel 1977), which also postulates a cognitive process, presumes that tit-for-tat affects the *image of the strategist* in the target's eyes. By matching Party A's noncooperation, Party Z comes to be seen as *powerful* or *tough.* As a result, A realizes that there is no way to exploit Z and that trying to do so can only be self-defeating. Hence, collaboration with Z becomes a goal for A. But is it safe to collaborate, or will Z exploit A's collaborative initiatives? By matching cooperation, Z comes to be seen as *trustworthy* – as unlikely to try to take advantage of A. This allows A to cooperate further without fear of exploitation. A variant of this explanation holds that tit-for-tat produces an image of the strategist as "firm" but "fair" (Komorita and Esser 1975).

Evidence compatible with the third explanation comes from a negotiation study in which firm and soft strategies were contrasted with tit-for-tat (McGillicuddy *et al.* 1984). Opponents who followed a tit-for-tat strategy were rated as "stronger" than those who followed a soft strategy, and "fairer" than those who followed a firm strategy.

Enhancing the effectiveness of the tit-for-tat strategy

The tit-for-tat strategy is identical with the standard reinforcement paradigm, which has been employed very successfully in countless learning settings (Kazdin 1975). Hence, it is possible to gain some pointers about the success of this strategy by looking at that literature. Learning theorists have developed a number of guidelines for the successful use of tit-for-tat as an influence strategy. These embrace the use of both reward (e.g. concession or some other form of cooperation) and punishment (e.g. nonconcession, hostility, or contentious behavior). Some of these guidelines are also supported in research on negotiation and the prisoner's dilemma.

(1) *Immediacy.* Reward or punishment should follow the target's behavior as quickly as possible (Perin 1943). If they must be delayed, a symbol should be substituted; for example, a verbal promise to give a child candy after dinner in exchange for straightening his or her room.

(2) *Consistency.* Learning studies have shown that tit-for-tat is most effective if the target is rewarded or punished every time he or she makes the desired or the undesired response (Hulse *et al.* 1980). This effect has also been shown in research on negotiation. A regular pattern of reciprocating concessions elicits more concessions than an irregular pattern, even if the same overall amount is conceded in the irregular pattern (Esser and Komorita 1975).

Research on the prisoner's dilemma (Kuhlman and Marshello 1975; Oskamp 1971) and on bargaining (Komorita and Esser 1975) also suggests that it is more important to be 100 per cent consistent in rewarding cooperation than 100 per cent consistent in punishing (or failing to reward) noncooperation. A possible explanation for this effect is that reward and punishment tend to *be reciprocated* by the target as well as to reinforce the target's behavior. Hence, if the strategist is going to be inconsistent, it is better to be light on punishment (and thus diminish provocation of the other) than to be light on reward (and thus fail to build up positive credit with the other).

(3) *Size.* Larger rewards are more effective at strengthening cooperative behavior (Esser and Komorita 1975; Logan 1960). The case for large incentives is less clear for punishment. Research on laboratory animals shows a simple relationship between intensity of punishment and extent of learning (Church 1969). But punishing humans can produce side-effects such as resentment and withdrawal, which may interfere with learning (Kazdin 1975). Findings in mixed-motive settings (Lindskold *et al.* 1976) suggest that the most effective punishment is one that exactly "fits the crime," neither undermatching nor overmatching the other's level

of noncooperation. Such a penalty is as large as possible without seeming unfair.

(4) *Prior experience with a reward*. Rewards tend to be more effective if the other has experienced them in the past and hence come to value them. In addition to the evidence in the conditioning literature (Kazdin 1975), this point is supported by a prisoner's dilemma study in which tit-for-tat was preceded by a period of unconditional cooperation (Komorita and Mechling 1967). The more prior cooperation there had been (up to ten trials in the condition that went the longest), the more effective was tit-for-tat.

Prior punishment is a different story. Its advantages are often mitigated by the side-effects that were mentioned earlier: resentment and withdrawal. These may lead to obduracy, aggression, escalation, and loss of positive influence with the other, making it necessary to continue relying on punishment in the future (Deutsch 1973; Kazdin 1975). Hence punishment, if used, should be employed with finesse, making sure that it seems legitimate and that it is viewed in a context of overall concern for the other's interests (Pruitt and Rubin 1986).

These guidelines are useful if the goal of tit-for-tat is simply to *establish* a pattern of cooperation in the target. But the first three guidelines need to be radically revised if the goal is to *maintain* this pattern in the future after tit-for-tat ceases. Rewards should be immediate, consistent and sizable if one wants to establish a cooperative response. But they should be delayed (Mackintosh 1974), inconsistent (Skinner 1938), and small (Hulse *et al.* 1980) if maintenance is the goal.

These paradoxical findings pose a conundrum if one wishes both to establish and to maintain a pattern of cooperation. The usual solution to this conundrum is to start out with immediate, consistent and sizable rewards, in order to establish a cooperative response, and then gradually to diminish all three dimensions to increase the hardiness of this response (Kazdin 1975).

Defects in the tit-for-tat strategy

A major problem with the tit-for-tat strategy is that it sometimes produces and perpetuates mutual noncooperation. This can happen if the target fails to cooperate at the beginning of the interaction, because the target may never have an experience with the strategist's willingness to reciprocate cooperation, missing an essential part of the tit-for-tat message. Another way it can happen is if the target is also mainly following a tit-for-tat strategy and takes a noncooperative initiative even once. The strategist must then retaliate, encouraging further noncooperation by the target, and producing an escalatory spiral of retaliation and counter-retaliation.

There are three possible remedies for these defects. One is to adopt a variant of tit-for-tat. The second is to employ a "starting mechanism." The third is to communicate with the other party through an auxiliary channel. These options will be discussed below.

Variants of tit-for-tat

One useful variant of tit-for-tat is to precede this strategy with a period of unconditional cooperation. Komorita and Mechling (1967) have shown that this encourages the target to cooperate. Earlier we interpreted this effect as owing to the target's becoming aware of the value of the strategist's cooperation. It is also possible that the initial cooperation tends to be reciprocated by the target, allowing the target to be rewarded for cooperation. A third possible explanation is that this early cooperation gains the strategist idiosyncrasy credits (see Hollander 1958), which permit later punishment of the target, if warranted, without starting an escalatory spiral.

Another useful variant of tit-for-tat requires the strategist to be *slow to retaliate*, continuing to cooperate for a while if the other party switches to noncooperation. The advantage of this strategy is that escalatory spirals do not start in response to short episodes of noncooperation from the other party. In a computer study, Bendor *et al.* (1991) have shown that this strategy is superior to tit-for-tat in settings that involve occasional random episodes of noncooperation – as are so often found in real life.

There is a problem with a policy of slow retaliation if it is coupled with a policy of quick forgiveness – in other words, if after retaliating the strategist quickly switches back to cooperation in response to cooperation from the other. Such a "slow–quick" strategy leaves the strategist open to exploitation. The other party may learn that it is only necessary to cooperate periodically, on those occasions when the strategist has just retaliated; in other words, that the strategist will be open to exploitation most of the time if placated on the rare occasions when he or she protests. The solution to this problem is for the strategist to adopt a "slow–slow" strategy, being slow to retaliate and *slow to forgive*. In a prisoner's dilemma study involving human beings, the slow–slow strategy was found to be superior to a slow–quick strategy and to a quick–quick strategy which was identical to tit-for-tat as usually defined (Bixenstine and Gaebelein 1971).

Starting mechanisms

Various auxiliary tactics are available if the other party fails to cooperate from the start or if mutual noncooperation has set in. These "starting mechanisms" encourage a cooperative response that can then be reciprocated.

If the desired action is not in the other's repertoire, a *shaping* routine may be employed. This involves reinforcing a sequence of actions that look more and more like the behavior desired (Hulse *et al.* 1980). Verbal instruction or modeling may also be used to produce new responses. If the desired action is in the other's repertoire but rarely occurs, one can sometimes use *prompts* (Kazdin 1975), that is, stimuli that are known to elicit the response. For example, if one wants to reinforce smiling in an ordinarily dour person, one might show that person cartoons and follow each smile with a reward. One must then gradually fade the prompt out, to avoid continued dependence on it (Kazdin 1975). It may also be useful to employ unilateral conciliatory initiatives that enhance the other party's trust to the point of being willing to try cooperative behavior. These are discussed in Chapter 9.

Supporting communication

If the tit-for-tat strategist can communicate with the other party, a very useful procedure is to inform the other of the desired behavior and to describe the tit-for-tat contingencies. Such communication has been shown to enhance cooperation greatly in the prisoner's dilemma (Deutsch 1973). However, hostility between the parties can reduce the effectiveness of communication (see Chapter 9).

Summary and implications

Matching is a universal phenomenon in mixed-motive settings. In negotiation, concessions usually elicit counter-concessions, and contending and problem solving are also often reciprocated. In games of moves, cooperation and noncooperation are often imitated. However, matching is seldom exact; and concessions and cooperation tend to be undermatched unless the actor is seen as powerful or tough. Mismatching is also found at times in these settings. Offers are often mismatched at the very beginning of negotiation, when there is a tendency to demand more if the other is conciliatory than if the other is firm. This is probably a manifestation of tracking. Mismatching is also common at the end of negotiation, as deadlines loom. At such times, firm opponents may be able to elicit substantial concessions from negotiators, because of the negotiators' fear that they will fail to reach agreement. However, mismatching at deadline is an ambivalent phenomenon, and there are some negotiators who would rather fail to reach agreement than suffer the image loss involved in yielding to a firm opponent. Ambivalent mismatching is also found in the final moments of the game of chicken and when shortages develop in resource dilemmas.

A tit-for-tat strategy is often quite effective in mixed-motive settings. This involves matching both cooperation and noncooperation from the other party. This strategy tends to encourage the other party to cooperate, especially if the matching is both immediate and consistent. However, the success of this strategy depends on the other party cooperating enough to learn the contingencies and not responding to retaliation with further retaliation. Modified forms of tit-for-tat are probably better than the pure form at achieving these aims.

At the end of Chapter 4, we mentioned that there were limitations to the generality of several findings about the antecedents of demands and concessions. These findings were obtained when the negotiators were individualistically oriented but disappeared when they were cooperatively oriented.

Similar limitations of generality are found in some of the material presented in this chapter. For example, the *matching of noncooperation* is less common and less immediate to the extent that there is a positive concern for the other party's welfare. Thus, Gottman (1979) reports that in sound marriages (which presumably involve a cooperative orientation), harsh words from the spouse tend to be ignored or to be dealt with creatively unless they become a pattern. But in distressed marriages (which are more likely to involve an individualistic orientation), harsh words tend to provoke immediate retaliation. Sillars (1981) reports similar results for roommate pairs. Pruitt (1970) also found that immediate retaliation was less likely when people seemed dependent on the other party than when they seemed to control their own welfare.

Undermatching of cooperation also appears to be specific to the individualistic orientation. In a prisoner's dilemma study that measured individual differences in orientation, Kuhlman and Marshello (1975) found undermatching for subjects who were only concerned about their own welfare. But subjects who were concerned about both parties' welfare were fully cooperative if the other was fully cooperative. In addition, the *tit-for-tat strategy*, which was highly effective when dealing with individualistically oriented subjects, was no more successful than a fully cooperative strategy when dealing with the cooperatively oriented subjects. There is even evidence that, in intimate relationships, heavy use of the tit-for-tat strategy is resented (Clark and Mills 1979). This may be because the norms for these relationships prescribe generosity rather than an exchange of favors.

It appears that a broader model, which embraces both individualistic and cooperative motivation, is needed. Such a model is presented in Chapter 7; but before turning to it, we must discuss the impact of cognitions on negotiation. It will be recalled that "psychological states" were the second component of the paradigm shown in Figure 1.1. The psychological states we have discussed so far are mainly motivational, e.g. limits, time pressure, fear of being a sucker. But behavior is also heavily dependent on cognition, in other words, on how people see the world. Negotiation is no exception, and there has been a great deal of recent research interest in this topic.

Suggestions for further reading

Axelrod, R. (1984). *The evolution of cooperation.* New York: Basic Books.
Bartos, O. J. (1974). *Process and outcome in negotiation.* New York: Columbia University Press.

Kuhlman, D. M. and Marshello, A. F. J. (1975). Individual differences in game motivation as moderators of preprogrammed strategy effects in prisoner's dilemma. *Journal of Personality and Social Psychology*, 32, 922–31.

Wall, J. A. Jr. (1985). *Negotiation: Theory and practice.* Glenview, IL: Scott, Foresman.

Wilke, H. A. M., Messick, D. M. and Rutte, C. G. (eds). (1986). *Experimental social dilemmas.* Frankfurt am Main: Verlag Peter Lang.

6 / COGNITIVE AND DECISION PROCESSES IN NEGOTIATION

Negotiators routinely make difficult, complex decisions and inferences: which issues are most important, what offer to make and when to make it, how to interpret and respond to an opposing negotiator's offers and statements, and so on. Though previous chapters have stressed motivational processes, a few cognitive processes have also been described as important antecedents of negotiation tactics and outcomes. For example, in Chapter 5 we saw that attributions of responsibility were an important determinant of cooperation: Kerr (1983) found that workers were more likely to cooperate with a partner when the partner's poor performance was attributed to a lack of ability rather than to a lack of effort. Also in Chapter 5, cognitive learning mechanisms and perceptions of firmness and trustworthiness were seen to be important explanations of the success of the tit-for-tat strategy. In the present chapter we continue this theme, and focus on the individual negotiator as a *decision maker and information processor*.

An individual negotiator's decisions and inferences are often made in the context of complex social, organizational, and cultural systems that have legal constraints and historical underpinnings. A prime example is negotiation that occurs between public-sector workers (e.g. teachers, firefighters) and management (school boards, city councils) in the United States. In the public sector, management is often obligated to bargain with employees over salary, hours, fringe benefits, grievances, and other issues pertinent to the terms of employment.[1] Consider the following contract negotiation between a teachers' association and a school board.

There were two teams of individuals who met face-to-face to try to reach agreement on nineteen distinct issues. On one side of the table were several teachers and Rod, their hired chief negotiator from the State Education Association. The other side of the table had several school board members, the school superintendent, and Mary, a lawyer, the school board's hired professional negotiator. In the first session of the negotiation, Mary and Rod stated the two sides' positions on the nineteen issues. Some of the issues involved money; for example, a medical insurance issue (which in the US private system typically involves an employer contribution to the premium as a benefit of employment). Rod stated that the teachers wanted the school board to increase its payment on the insurance plan from $110 to $145. Mary replied that the school board's position was to keep it at $110. Other issues involved contract "language." For example, on the issue of personal leave during the first two weeks and last two weeks of the school year, the school board wanted the contract to read ". . . [it] shall not be granted except under extenuating circumstances as determined by the Superintendent." The teachers' association wanted the contract to read ". . . [it] shall not be used except when necessary."

The list of issues went on. There were so many, in fact, that organizing them required considerable cognitive and analytic effort. In negotiation, it can be cognitively taxing to come up with offers, combine issues, and make complex tradeoffs that satisfy both parties' interests. Such activities can strain the reasoning abilities of even the most seasoned and intelligent negotiator. The more issues and interested parties there are, the greater the strain.

Even a simple negotiation involving a single issue such as the price of a car may involve complex cognitive and decision processes. But many negotiations are quite complicated; for example, Rod and Mary's negotiation involved nineteen issues and had direct significance for many people. Hence, the cognitive problem in negotiation is usually quite formidable (Morley 1982). One can easily imagine the complexities involved in an international treaty negotiation, involving a number of nations and issues as detailed and technical as the control of nuclear and chemical weapons. It sometimes requires months or even years to sort out the issues requiring negotiation (Druckman 1986).

The rational negotiator

Researchers in the cognitive tradition have been heavily influenced by the criterion of "efficient" negotiated outcomes; that is, whether or not an agreement is *Pareto optimal* (Raiffa 1982). An agreement is said to be Pareto optimal when the parties achieve the maximum joint gain possible, and neither party can do better in an alternative agreement unless the other does worse. The win-win agreement in the negotiation task shown in Table 1.1 ("AEI") is Pareto optimal. Researchers in the cognitive tradition argue that negotiators often achieve Pareto inferior outcomes due to limitations of human reasoning and information processing. For example, if my conception of negotiation issues is that each issue should always be compromised 50/50, and I convince you of this, our agreement in the negotiation task described in Chapter 1 (see Table 1.1) is likely to be "EEE," which is Pareto inferior. Since we are better off, collectively and individually, if we had agreed to "AEI," we have made an *error* in negotiating, and have failed to realize the full potential of benefit from the negotiation (Lax and Sebenius 1986; Neale and Bazerman 1991).

The main question, in the cognitive approach to negotiation, is *What information and decision processes are important in negotiator reasoning about issues, concessions, tradeoffs, and strategy?* Usually this question is targeted at the processes that lead negotiators to arrive at suboptimal negotiation outcomes (see Hastie 1991). The recent emphasis is on the role of memory, the way information is processed, and the accuracy of judgment in negotiation (Carroll and Payne 1991; Thompson and Hastie 1990).

Cognitive effects and processes

Many researchers assume that the root of the problem of suboptimal outcomes in negotiation is that negotiators have limited attention, limited capacity to store and retrieve information from memory, and limited capacity to process information. In other words, negotiators are thought to be *cognitive misers*, a term coined by Fiske and Taylor (1991: 176) to characterize the general human tendency toward mental economy.

As a result of cognitive limitations, negotiators consciously or unconsciously rely on *heuristics* and *schemas*. Heuristics are mental shortcuts and simplifying strategies that people use to help to manage information (Tversky and Kahneman 1974). Schemas are cognitive structures that contain information about aspects of a particular situation (e.g. the school board negotiation in our example) or a general class of situations (e.g. negotiations in general). Schemas are thought to develop from prior observations of the phenomena to which they are relevant (Taylor and Crocker 1981), and they lead people to construe situations in specific ways (Markus and Zajonc 1985). Schemas tend to guide information processing, directing attention and memory, and thus cause some events to be noticed and remembered while others are ignored or forgotten. This means that schemas are self-perpetuating, since people tend to notice and remember evidence that supports their preconceptions (Grzelak 1982). This is a point that we will return to in Chapter 9 when we discuss relationships in negotiation.

Negotiation researchers who emphasize schematic information processing focus on how individual negotiators acquire and use knowledge in negotiation. The basic idea is that a person's construction of social reality – the perception of intentions, attitudes and beliefs about the other, the perception of the situation – determines negotiation behavior (see Abric 1982; Bar-Tal et al. 1989; Brodt 1990; Deutsch 1982; Ross and Nisbett 1991). The ordering and relevance of information in negotiation are determined by the way that the parties develop a cognitive interpretation of the context (Mather and Yngvesson 1981), the issues (Thompson and Hastie 1990), and the negotiation task (Carroll et al. 1988). For example, Pinkley (1990) has argued that disputants usually see the same conflict differently, and often in contradictory terms, as a result of differing schemas. Hammond and Grassia (1985) have developed an explanation of how people's judgments of the same circumstances can differ, leading to a quarrel. People may base their judgements on different features of the problem, or weight the same features differently and therefore reach opposing judgments. Similarly, Vallone et al. (1985) reported that both sides in a conflict tended to perceive that the news media were against them. And, in a prisoner's dilemma paradigm, Plous (1985) found that people were overly pessimistic about the other's willingness to cooperate. All of these effects suggest that perception and misperception of motives and intentions are an important part of negotiation (Jervis 1976).

In their effort to understand the role of cognition and decision making in negotiation, researchers have identified a litany of cognitive effects, and progress has been made in the important task of identifying the underlying processes responsible for these effects. The topics examined in this research include the fixed-pie assumption, illusory conflict, reactive devaluation, negotiation scripts, rigid thinking, overconfidence, availability, representativeness, anchoring, framing, and mood states. We will discuss these in turn and occasionally illustrate how each might play a role in the teacher–school board negotiation described earlier.

The fixed-pie assumption

An example of a schema that is often found in negotiation is the assumption that the two parties' interests are directly opposed, that "your win is my loss." This fixed-pie (also called zero-sum or win–lose) assumption makes problem solving seem infeasible and hence encourages contentious behavior (Follett 1940). For example, in multiple issue negotiation, the fixed-pie assumption implies that the other has the same priorities on the issues as the self (Pruitt 1981). This is a faulty judgement that can block the discovery of a win–win solution when the negotiation issues have logrolling potential (Thompson and Hastie 1991).

Consider Rod's and Mary's priorities with respect to the two issues of insurance and contract language. These priorities were complementary, in the sense that for Rod and the teachers' association the contract language was more important than the insurance, but for Mary and the school board the insurance issue was more important. However, the two parties did not recognize this complementarity, each thinking that the other's priorities were the same as their own; in other words, they made a fixed-pie assumption. As a result, they did not consider a *logrolling* agreement, in which the teachers' association would obtain a more favorable outcome on the contract language issue and the school board would obtain a more favorable outcome on the insurance issue.

The fixed-pie assumption is related to the social-psychological concept of *false consensus*, where people tend to believe that others have views or priorities that are similar to their own, i.e. where people overestimate the commonness of their own response (Dawes 1989). The fixed-pie assumption involves over- or underestimating another's actual preference. In a sense, it is an absolute error, rather than a relative error, in consensus estimation.

The same phenomenon can be seen in the laboratory negotiation tasks shown in Table 6.1 (see below). These tasks have logrolling potential because the disputants have different priorities among the issues. The negotiators' perceptions of the opposing negotiators' priorities were examined just after negotiation in several studies (Carnevale and Isen 1986; Kimmel *et al.* 1980; Lewis and Fry 1977; Pruitt and Lewis 1975). Negotiators who exhibited a fixed-pie assumption, believing that the two parties had the same priorities on the issues, tended to reach compromise agreements that split the difference on the three issues (e.g. "EEE") or failed to reach agreement. Negotiators who realized that the other negotiator had different priorities on the issues tended to achieve win–win agreements. Using a similar task and measure, Thompson (1990c) found that most of the negotiators entered a series of negotiations with a fixed-pie assumption but became more accurate in subsequent negotiations as they learned about tradeoffs. Accurate judgments about the other party's interests led to higher joint outcomes and higher individual profits.

There is evidence that negotiation schemas tend to persist from one negotiation to the next. Thompson (1990a) found that early experience with a negotiation task that had no integrative potential led negotiators to make a fixed-pie assumption about later negotiations. When the task was changed to one involving logrolling potential, these negotiators generally failed to find win–win agreements. Thompson (1991b) also showed that observers of the negotiation process were no more likely to have accurate perceptions of the different priorities in the task than were the negotiators. This suggests that persistence of the fixed-pie assumption was not linked to the role of the negotiator and hence was probably a perceptual effect.

While the fixed-pie assumption is undoubtedly harmful to negotiator outcomes, there is a danger in overestimating its frequency from one-shot laboratory studies with naive university students (Thompson 1990c). Neale and Northcraft (1986) showed that experienced negotiators (corporate real estate negotiators) were a good deal less susceptible to this assumption than the usual student subjects. Their experience had presumably taught them a more sophisticated schema that included the possibility that there was logrolling potential. It is also possible that labeling the task "negotiation" encouraged the fixed-pie assumption among the naive students in this study but not among the experienced negotiators. The usual stereotype of "negotiation" is of a heavily contentious interchange, whereas the reality often involves subtle problem solving. Had the students not been told they were involved in "negotiation," many of them might have escaped the fixed-pie assumption.

Illusory conflict

Sometimes disputes involve issues in which the parties want the same thing, but fail to realize it. Lax and Sebenius (1986) refer to these issues as "common value." To illustrate: Rod and Mary also faced a third issue that involved grievances. The issue had to do with the procedure that teachers would follow if they had a complaint against an administrator, such as a perception of unfair treatment or unjust disciplinary action. Rod, on behalf of the teachers, wanted to put a four-week time limit on how long it would take for any grievance action to be resolved. He assumed that the school board would want no time limit and that Mary would oppose his position. Hence he put forward what he believed to be a more acceptable proposal of a six-week limit on grievance deliberations. To his surprise, Mary agreed to that proposal without any discussion. Rod never learned that the school board also wanted to place a time limit on processing grievances, and would have accepted a four-week time limit if he had proposed it. In other words, Rod assumed conflict where none existed, and this belief led to a less than optimal outcome. Rod suffered from illusory conflict, the belief that there are opposing interests when none exist (Rubin *et al.* 1990).

Thompson and Hastie (1990) found a similar phenomenon in a study of behavior in a single negotiation involving a multiple-issue task that included issues on which the subjects had exactly the same preferences. Thompson (1990c) also found it when negotiators were given a sequence of seven negotiations. In the majority of the negotiation pairs, at least one negotiator failed to develop insight into the common value, and insight did not improve with experience. Hence, many of these negotiators, like Rod and Mary in our example, reached agreements that were less than optimal.

Lax and Sebenius (1986; see also Raiffa 1982) made an interesting observation regarding common value issues. If one negotiator perceives that there is a common value issue and that the opposing negotiator does not see it, the first negotiator can exploit this issue to extract concessions from the other negotiator on a different issue. For example, if Rod realized that Mary also wanted to place a time limit on processing grievances, he could say to her "I'll agree to let you have a four-week time limit on the grievance issue if you give us what we want on the contract language issue." If she agreed, Rod would get everything he wanted on both issues. This is called "strategic misrepresentation" (O'Connor and Carnevale 1992; Raiffa 1982).

Thompson (1990c) found evidence of strategic misrepresentation among experienced negotiators dealing with naive opponents. In the words of one of her subjects: "I tried to make it seem like I was doing a favor for her on some of the issues [the common value issues] even though I was getting all of the points in that category" (Thompson 1990c: 88). In a direct test of this, O'Connor and Carnevale (1992) found that negotiators were especially likely to be *passive* victims of strategic misrepresentation. Many negotiators unwittingly offered a concession on one issue in an effort to induce a concession on another issue, but did not realize that the other issue was common value. Imagine that Rod has not yet stated his position on the time limit issue (the common value issue). Mary says, "I'll give you what you want on that contract language issue, if you give me a six week limit on grievance deliberations." Rod, very pleased, says "OK." He was very happy to get what he wanted on both issues. Mary would think that she conceded on one issue and made gains on one. She passively fell into the trap of strategic misrepresentation, suffering from illusory conflict – not seeing the common value issue – and accepting a "concession" from Rod, when in reality none was made.

Reactive devaluation

Just before Mary entered the negotiation with Rod, she considered an alternative position on the contract language regarding the issue of personal leave. Instead of forbidding the teachers to take leave except under extenuating circumstances, she considered the possibility of having teachers complete a written explanation and justification for any proposed leave. These reports might later be used to establish guidelines for leaves. She decided to hold this alternative position in reserve as a possible concession if her first proposal was rejected. To Mary's horror, Rod made this proposal in response to her first proposal. Mary reasoned that if Rod offered this, and the teachers wanted it, it must be bad for the school board, and she rejected it outright. This reasoning has been called reactive devaluation by Stillinger et al. (1991).

Stillinger et al. (1991) found that proposals and offers suggested by the opposing negotiator tend to be devalued in negotiation, simply on the basis of knowledge that the adversary has offered them. In one study, some negotiators rated the value of an opposing negotiator's concession before it was actually made and others rated the concession after it was offered. The results indicated that negotiators tend to denigrate and misconstrue concessions offered by the opposing negotiator. Apparently, negotiators reason that whatever is good for the other must be bad for the self. This is the other side of the same coin as illusory conflict, which assumes that whatever is good for the self is bad for the other.

Negotiation scripts

People hold intuitive theories about the process of negotiation, much like they do about procedures in any situation. These are called "scripts" (Abelson 1981) or "event schemas" (Hastie 1981). Among other features, scripts usually include assumptions about the behavior that is fair or appropriate to expect from oneself and other parties. Consider, for example, an incident in which Rod agreed to the school board position on the insurance issue – that there would be no increase in how much the school board would pay – but then several hours later said "On reflection, we cannot accept that zero increase; we want at least a $20 increase." This made Mary angry because, in withdrawing a prior concession, Rod had violated an element of the standard negotiation script – a norm about the appropriate behavior in negotiation (see Pruitt 1981 for a discussion of this norm).

Negotiation scripts can have implications for attributions that negotiators make about one another's behavior. Attributions that a negotiator makes about the causes of the opposing negotiator's behavior are an important determinant of reactions to that behavior (Bar-Tal and Geva 1986; Hewstone 1988; Kelley and Stahelski 1970). In several studies, Baron (1985, 1988a) found that confrontational negotiation behaviors induced less retribution when they were attributed to sincerely held beliefs. Behaviors that suggested dishonesty were especially likely to elicit hostility. In Chapter 9, we will focus in some detail on the important role of attributional distortions and other information processes in perpetuating positive and negative relationships.

Rigid thinking

Social conflict can promote rigid thinking, which involves a tendency to dichotomize information, to assign extreme values to objects or items, and not to see relationships among concepts in memory (Deutsch 1969; Judd 1978; White 1984). Rigid thinking, in turn, tends to inhibit creativity and effective problem solving (Pruitt and Rubin 1986). Evidence of this can be seen in a study by Carnevale (1991) that compared subjects who expected to enter a hostile, competitive negotiation to subjects in another condition who expected to enter a cooperative negotiation. The subjects engaged in a categorization task that was unrelated to the negotiation. They were asked to rate the goodness of fit of several exemplars (such as "bus" and "camel") to general categories (such as "vehicle"). Subjects who expected to enter a hostile, competitive negotiation were less likely to see relationships among concepts, for example, were less likely to indicate that weak exemplars such as "camel" were good instances of the category "vehicle." These results suggest that even the anticipation of competitive interaction leads people to see the world in narrow, discrete categories that may inhibit creative thinking and hence make it harder for them to find a way out of their difficulties.

Overconfidence

Another cognitive source of suboptimal agreement in negotiation stems from the beliefs that negotiators have about their likelihood of success. Negotiators sometimes believe that the opposing negotiator will make greater concessions than they will (Kochan and Jick 1978; Stevens 1963). For example, in the negotiation between Rod and Mary described above, Mary was certain that Rod and the teachers' association would accept a zero increase on the insurance issue, thinking that Rod's position was only lipservice to a few teachers who wanted an increase. Mary was also sure that an arbitrator would agree with the school board's position on this issue, in the event that the negotiation did not produce agreement. Given these beliefs – mistaken as they might be – it was unlikely that Mary would consider making any concessions on the insurance issue.

Neale and Bazerman (1985) have reported a similar phenomenon in a laboratory experiment. They found that negotiators were overly optimistic about how well they would do in arbitration. Both parties believe that they have a greater than 50 per cent chance of prevailing in arbitration. If there is a possibility of arbitration, overoptimism of this kind tends to reduce concession making, making it harder to reach agreement in negotiation and mediation (Kochan and Jick 1978). In a related study, Peirce *et al.* (1991) found no overconfidence with respect to the outcome of arbitration, but found that disputants were overly confident about the success of struggle tactics involving the use of threats apart from negotiation. A study by Rothbart and Hallmark (1988) suggests that confidence in the latter effect may be more likely when negotiations are between people from different groups rather than the same group (see Chapter 10). In addition, overconfidence may be limited to situations where negotiators have low concern for one another's welfare. Carnevale and Keenan (1990) reported that negotiators thought that they had a much stronger case for winning in the negotiation than their opponents, when they had an individualistic motive; however, when they had a cooperative motive, they thought that their case and their opponents' case were equally strong.

Availability

Availability is the decision maker's use of the ease of recall of information as a cue for judgments about frequency or likelihood of occurrence (Tversky and Kahneman 1974). Consider this question: How many female astronauts are there in the US space program? To answer this question, you are likely to attempt to recall instances of female astronauts from your memory. Probably, not very many come to mind – and the number that you estimate is not likely to be very large. Imagine, however, that just yesterday you had lunch with several female astronauts, and today someone asks you to estimate the number of female astronauts. Reliance on the availability heuristic would lead you to overestimate this number. Female astronauts are easy to recall, so there must be a lot of them. The problem is that they are easy to recall because they are fresh in your memory, not because they are numerous. Tversky and Kahneman (1974) and others have argued that the availability heuristic can lead to biased judgment. Information that is more available in memory, more salient, or more concrete and vivid, may play a greater role in judgment than it should.

Several authors have argued that availability can lead negotiators to rely too much on salient information and therefore produce biased negotiator judgment (Neale and Bazerman 1991). In our example, Mary, the chief spokesperson for the school board, very readily recalled a recent incident where a teacher took a leave of absence, which was later regarded as unnecessary. Mary's memory of this incident influenced her estimate of the likely number of unnecessary leaves that would occur in the future – she thought there would be many, and this formed the basis of the school board's position that the superintendent should determine all personal leaves. By having the superintendent approve these requests, unnecessary leaves of absence would not occur. A different event was salient in Rod's thinking. Rod had a recent experience in another school district where a teacher's request for leave was unreasonably withheld by an autocratic school superintendent. His memory of this incident led him to oppose Mary's proposal. The likelihood that the school superintendent would act in an autocratic manner was just too high. Thus, the parties on either side developed and supported opposing positions because different information was easily accessible in their thinking.

In an experiment on availability, Neale (1984) has shown that negotiator behavior is affected by the salience of costs associated with failing to reach agreement. The more salient these costs are, the more likely negotiators are to reach agreement.

Representativeness

Representative thinking can also bias judgment. This involves making judgments solely on the basis of the most obvious features of the object being judged (Tversky and Kahneman 1974), and ignoring more subtle features that would permit a more balanced judgment. The object being judged may be the opposing negotiator, or it may include features of the negotiation context or issues.

An example of a more subtle feature that is usually ignored is *base-rate* information. Imagine that you are seated in the lobby of a large hotel where there is a national convention of used-car dealers. You strike up a conversation with someone sitting next to you, a person who is soft-spoken and somewhat shy, and who talks of an interest in reading and writing poetry. You ask yourself, what is this person's occupation? On the surface, this person has characteristics that are representative of a school teacher or librarian, so this is the conclusion you reach. You do not even consider the possibility that the person is a used-car salesman, because he or she does not have the characteristics you associate with that kind of person (loud, extroverted, not introspective). You make this judgment despite the very strong odds – given the number of car salesmen in the hotel – that the person is a used-car salesman. What you are doing is making inferences from the most obvious features of the person, his or her demeanor, and ignoring the more subtle base-rate information.

Some authors suggest that cognitive heuristics such as availability and representativeness might underlie the tendency for negotiators to rely too much on historical analogies. If a historical incident is highly memorable, or seems representative of a current situation, it may exert greater influence in the current decision than is warranted. Bazerman and Carroll (1987: 268) note this: "Thus, we tend to appreciate the power of analogy, such as when Afghanistan is called a 'Vietnam' for the Soviets. It seems much easier to reason comparatively from representative cases based on our existing knowledge structures than to reason absolutely." This may lead negotiators to miss other, possibly better, outcomes, or other approaches to the negotiation (Kramer 1991b). For example, in 1938 in Munich, negotiations between Neville Chamberlain and Adolf Hitler produced an agreement that resulted in British appeasement and unchecked Nazi aggression, with calamitous consequences. More than fifty years later, the statement, "If this aggression goes unchecked it will be another Munich," is sometimes used to justify the choice of struggle over negotiation. In this case, a historical negotiation is seen as representative of a current situation, when the current situation may in fact be quite different (see Gilovich 1981).

In addition to influencing the parties' choice of a negotiation position, availability and representativeness can affect their decisions about negotiation strategy. When it is easy for negotiators to recall previous instances where contentious tactics were employed, the use of these tactics is likely to increase. When the earlier use of problem solving is recalled, this becomes the more likely strategy. This is an argument for the point made in Chapter 5 that negotiation should begin with issues that are not too contentious. However, recall of disastrous consequences of contentious behavior in the past can create a desire in both sides to "never go back" to hostile times (Friedman 1989). Thus, easy recall of the consequences of the use of contentious tactics – hostile relations, nonagreement – can lessen their likelihood of occurrence.

Anchoring and insufficient adjustment

Anchoring and insufficient adjustment is a simplifying strategy in which an arbitrarily chosen reference point has too great an influence on judgment. A simple example was given by Tversky and Kahneman (1974). Subjects were asked to estimate the product of either $8 \times 7 \times 6 \times 5 \times 4 \times 3 \times 2 \times 1$ or $1 \times 2 \times 3 \times 4 \times 5 \times 6 \times 7 \times 8$. Tversky and Kahneman argued, from the literature on "primacy" in judgment, that the first number (either 8 or 1, given that students read from left to right) would serve as an anchor, and since students are not given enough time to work out the entire calculation they must extrapolate. In the descending version, they extrapolate from a higher number than do those who begin calculating the ascending version. Since 8 is larger than 1, the estimated product of the former string of numbers would be higher than that of the latter. Such was the case: the median estimate for the descending sequence was 2,250 in contrast to 512 for the ascending sequence. (Note that both estimates were too low; the true product is 40,320.)

As mentioned in Chapter 5, there is evidence that the other party's initial offer tends to have an especially large influence on demands and concessions. This may reflect use of the anchoring and adjustment heuristic (Neale and Bazerman 1991), if we assume that the first offer serves as an anchor. Use of this heuristic may explain why information about a prior price has a large impact on expert evaluation of an object (Northcraft and Neale 1987).

Perhaps the most common type of anchor is the status quo, the situation that exists at the time of negotiation. This often favors one side's position over the other's. An example of this is the school board's position that there should be no increase in its payment on the medical insurance issue. Rod, representing the teachers' association, had the uphill task of trying to change the status quo on this issue.

The inordinate influence of anchors may also help explain the large effect of salient, prominent solutions in negotiation (see Chapter 8). To continue our example, both Rod and Mary might be heavily influenced by an agreement for a $25 increase on the medical insurance issue that was recently reached by negotiators in a neighboring school district. Imagine also the heightened prominence of that option if a third party, such as a neutral mediator, mentioned that $25 was a reasonable settlement point.

Evidence that anchoring and adjustment can play an important role in negotiation was obtained by Fobian and Christensen-Szalanski (1992). These authors simulated a medical liability negotiation to examine the effects of ambiguity (high ambiguity meant uncertainty about the likelihood of winning in adjudication if there was no agreement in negotiation). They found that the use of an anchoring and adjustment heuristic was particularly likely to occur when negotiators experienced high ambiguity. Negotiators anchored on a probability estimate (e.g. a lawyer's best estimate of winning) and then "adjusted" the estimate by imagining other possible estimates. There was greater adjustment from the probability estimate under conditions of high ambiguity, which increased the chance of a negotiated settlement being reached. Thus, use of this heuristic under high ambiguity increased the likelihood of agreement and the parties' cooperativeness, and had a beneficial effect on negotiation.

Framing

The concept of "frame" refers to how decision makers formulate the issues and outcomes they are facing (Kahneman and Tversky 1979). The way decision makers behave is often heavily affected by the frames they employ. An example of this is whether the options under consideration are viewed as involving gain or loss. Options are usually evaluated against a neutral reference point such as the status quo; thus, a change in the status quo can affect whether an option is judged as involving gain or loss. If I am getting nothing for my work and you offer me $5,000, I will see it as a prospective gain. But if I am getting $10,000 and you offer me the same $5,000 for my work, I will view it as a prospective loss.

Tversky and Kahneman (1992) emphasize the importance of the gain and loss frame in terms of *loss aversion*, which refers to the greater impact that losses have on preferences than gains. For example, the negative reaction to losing $100 is stronger than the positive reaction to finding $100. Several lines of work suggest that people are motivated to minimize loss more than they are motivated to maximize gain (De Dreu *et al.* 1992; Kramer 1989; Taylor 1991). This implies that it is harder to concede when a concession means "loss" than when it means "failure to gain." Since a loss is perceived as more negative than an equivalent gain is perceived as positive, concessions made in the context of a loss frame should seem larger – and more difficult to make – than equivalent concessions made in the context of a gain frame (Kahneman 1992). As a result, negotiators with a loss frame should be more resistant to making concessions than negotiators with a gain frame. Loss framed negotiators should make fewer concessions and thus reach fewer agreements than gain framed negotiators.

Consider the medical insurance issue that was under discussion in the school board negotiation. Rod's position for the teachers' association was that the management contribution to the medical insurance should increase from $110 to $145. To Rod, this position represented a $35 gain; thus Rod had a gain frame. But Mary's position was for a zero increase, the status quo, and a $35 increase represented a loss to her; thus, Mary had a loss frame. Hence a $5 concession made by Mary (from $0 increase to $5 increase) should seem large to her, and more difficult to make, relative to how Rod should feel about making a $5 concession (from $35 to $30).

Bazerman *et al.* (1985) tested frame effects in a variant of the multiple issue, buyer–seller task described in Chapter 1 (Table 1.1). There were two conditions in the study, one involving a gain frame and the other involving a loss frame. For the gain frame, subjects were given the profit structure shown in Table 6.1A, in which the outcomes are defined as various levels of profit. In this profit structure, there is an implied status quo, or reference point

Table 6.1 Integrative bargaining task used in two conditions: A, positive frame and B, negative frame

A, Positive frame

Seller net profit schedule ($ 000)

	Delivery time	Discount terms	Financing terms
A	$ 000	$ 000	$ 000
B	200	300	500
C	400	600	1000
D	600	900	1500
E	800	1200	2000
F	1000	1500	2500
G	1200	1800	3000
H	1400	2100	3500
I	1600	2400	4000

Buyer net profit schedule

	Delivery time	Discount terms	Financing terms
A	$4000	$2400	$1600
B	3500	2100	1400
C	3000	1800	1200
D	2500	1500	1000
E	2000	1200	800
F	1500	900	600
G	1000	600	400
H	500	300	200
I	000	000	000

B, Negative frame

Seller expense schedule (gross profit = $8000)

	Delivery time	Discount terms	Financing terms
A	$-1600	$-2400	$-4000
B	-1400	-2100	-3500
C	-1200	-1800	-3000
D	-1000	-1500	-2500
E	-800	-1200	-2000
F	-600	-900	-1500
G	-400	-600	-1000
H	-200	-300	-500
I	000	000	000

Buyer expense schedule (gross profit = $8000)

	Delivery time	Discount terms	Financing terms
A	$ 000	$ 000	$ 000
B	-500	-300	-200
C	-1000	-600	-400
D	-1500	-900	-600
E	-2000	-1200	-800
F	-2500	-1500	-1000
G	-3000	-1800	-1200
H	-3500	-2100	-1400
I	-4000	-2400	-1600

The buyer and seller must agree on one letter for each of the three issues (e.g. ABF or HEC). A dollar value is associated with each letter for each issue. The profit to a party is the sum of the three dollar values defined by the agreement.
Source: Neale and Bazerman (1991: 46)

of $0, the baseline from which the profits are calculated. The loss frame condition involved exactly the same final profits but they were calculated in a different way. The subjects were given the chart shown in Table 6.1B and told that the numbers represented expenses that would have to be subtracted from a gross profit of $8,000 that they would definitely receive. Thus the status quo or reference point was $8,000 and the outcomes represented various levels of loss. (Look carefully and you will see that the final outcome in the two conditions is the same for every possible agreement: AEI, EHD, etc.) But the psychological meaning of the outcomes was quite different. In the gain frame condition, they were negotiating over profits; in the loss frame condition, they were negotiating over expenses.

Bazerman *et al.* (1985) showed that when the task was gain framed, subjects were more likely to reach agreement than when the task was loss framed. Neale and Bazerman (1991) speculate that loss aversion can explain why buyers tend to outperform sellers in laboratory studies of negotiation over a price (Bazerman *et al.* 1985; Neale *et al.* 1987). Buyers suffer a loss when they pay and hence have a loss frame with respect to price, while sellers incur a gain when they are paid and hence have a gain frame with respect to price. Bottom and Studt (1993) found a similar effect of frame, and also looked at a mixed framing condition in which one negotiator had a gain frame and the other had a loss frame. If loss framing produces resistance to concession, one can predict that in this condition the negotiator with the loss frame would do substantially better in an agreement than the negotiator with the gain frame. This is exactly what they found. These findings imply that a loss frame can be an asset if the opposing negotiator has a gain frame.

Carnevale and Keenan (1990) also found a frame effect similar to that mentioned above, but only when negotiators were individualistically oriented. When negotiators were cooperatively oriented, a loss frame had no effect on the likelihood of agreement. Instead, a loss frame produced an improvement in the likelihood of a win–win agreement. Neale *et al.* (1987) also reported that a loss frame led to an improvement in the likelihood of win-win agreements, but only in a condition where negotiators were given fictitious role labels ("buyer" and "seller" were replaced with "phrably" and "grizzat"). Taken together, these results suggest that a loss frame in negotiation is a two-edged sword, sometimes leading to poor outcomes and sometimes leading to improved negotiator outcomes.

Recent research has extended the concept of negotiator frame to negotiator communication processes (De Dreu and Carnevale 1992; De Dreu *et al.* 1992; Putnam and Holmes 1992). These studies suggest that negotiator language corresponds to the gain or loss frame of the issues in negotiation (as shown in Table 6.1), and that negotiators are influenced by the frame reflected in the opposing negotiator's language (e.g. "I cannot accept big losses and expenses" reflects a loss frame). De Dreu and his colleagues found that negotiators who started with a gain task frame were likely to switch to a loss frame in their language if the other negotiator communicated a loss frame; however, if negotiators started with a loss task frame, their language reflected a loss frame regardless of whether the other negotiator communicated a gain or a loss frame.

In addition, recent research has extended the frame concept to the effects of negotiator frame on a mediator's perceptions of the negotiation (Carnevale and Mead 1990). Subjects played the role of a mediator, and observed negotiators who had either a gain frame or a loss frame. Mediators who saw a negotiator make a concession that was framed as a loss viewed the negotiator as more cooperative than did mediators who saw a negotiator make a concession that was framed as a gain. This occurred despite the fact that the negotiators made the same size concession. Again, this can be explained on the assumption that it is harder for people to accept a loss than to fail to make a gain; hence, a third party will view concessions that increase loss as more significant – and reflecting greater cooperativeness – than concessions that decrease gain.

Mood states

Mood states, such as positive affect – pleasant feelings that are typically induced by commonplace events like reading a cartoon, hearing a joke, or getting a small gift or piece of candy – can have important effects in negotiation. Professional mediators know this when they tell humorous stories before and during negotiation in an effort to improve cooperation (Kressel and Pruitt 1989). Henry

Kissinger was well known for his use of humor as a diplomatic tool (Rubin 1981).

The evidence suggests that positive affect diminishes hostile and contentious behavior and makes problem solving behaviors more likely (Baron 1984, 1990; Baron and Ball 1974; Baron et al. 1990). Positive affect also enhances concession making. O'Quin and Aronoff (1981) found that attaching a humorous comment to an offer (following the offer with ". . . and I'll throw in my pet frog") produced large concessions. All of this is compatible with the finding that positive affect can encourage pro-social behavior (Isen and Levin 1972). Kramer et al. (1990) found that good mood led negotiators to set higher aspirations, and to be more confident that they would achieve their aspirations. Subjects in a good mood were also more trusting of others, and attained higher outcomes.

In addition to these effects, positive affect enhances cognitive functioning, including the capacity for creative problem solving (Isen et al. 1985). This has been seen in several studies of negotiation. Carnevale and Isen (1986) and Hollingshead and Carnevale (1990) found that positive affect enhanced the likelihood of adopting win–win agreements. In the Carnevale and Isen (1986) study, the subjects with positive affect were no more likely than the control subjects to exchange information during negotiation, but they were more likely to discover that the negotiators had complementary priorities among the issues and, hence, to discover the logrolling potential of the task. This was a sign of improved cognitive functioning.

Very few studies have examined the role of negative moods in negotiation. In a correlational study, Brodt (1991) found that affective extremes – strong positive or negative affect – were associated with lower individual and joint outcomes in face-to-face integrative bargaining. Clearly more work on the role of mood states in negotiation is needed.

A sad ending?

We end this chapter on a sad note. Rod and Mary, as representatives of the teachers' association and school board, were unsuccessful in their negotiation. They were unable to reach an agreement. Fortunately, however, the story does not end here. It will pick up again in Chapter 11 when we introduce a third party to the dispute:

Chuck, who is a mediator. As will be seen, Chuck will help Rod and Mary to reach an agreement.

Summary and implications

This chapter has examined the nature of cognitive processes in negotiation and their impact on negotiation behavior and outcome. Researchers in the cognitive tradition tend to focus on individual cognition in the negotiation setting, on information processes, and on the application of cognitive theory and method to negotiation.

A litany of cognitive effects and processes have been identified. These are related to schemas, organized knowledge structures that guide and potentially distort the acquisition, storage, recall and use of information (Fiske and Taylor 1991). They are also related to heuristics, mental shortcuts and simplifying strategies that people use to help to manage information (Tversky and Kahneman 1974). Ross and Nisbett (1991) propose the general thesis that heuristics and knowledge structures serve people well most of the time, but that there are certain prescribed situations in which they fail. In negotiation, research shows that these shortcuts sometimes lead to desired outcomes and sometimes to undesired outcomes. Simplifying strategies can have a positive impact on information handling and decision making in negotiation, as seen in studies by Fobian and Christensen-Szalanski (1992) on use of the anchoring and adjustment heuristic, and in studies by Bottom and Studt (1990) and Carnevale and Keenan (1990) on framing. In other cases, however, they produce suboptimal outcomes. The key in future research will be to specify the conditions under which particular heuristics or knowledge structures, and the ways people think about the social and nonsocial aspects of the negotiation context, will enhance, impede, or generally perturb the negotiation process (Brodt, personal communication).

There are several studies that suggest that learning and feedback play an important role in negotiation. Kelley (1966), for example, found that as negotiators gained experience, they learned to set their first offers higher, presumably to allow themselves more room to negotiate. Similar effects were reported by Thompson (1990c): not only did experienced negotiators set higher first offers, they offered fewer concessions.

There are important links between cognition, motivation, and affect (feelings or emotions) in negotiation. Some cognitive processes have strong motivational and affective components to affect behavior. Perception and memory are often selective, and attributions are often distorted. These processes will be taken up in Chapter 9, as they are particularly relevant to the persistence of attitudes and behavior in interpersonal relationships.

At the end of Chapters 4 and 5, we mentioned that there were limitations to the generality of several findings about the antecedents of demands and concessions. These findings were obtained when the negotiators were individualistically oriented but disappeared when they were cooperatively oriented. Similar limitations of generality are found in some of the material presented in this chapter. For example, *a loss frame of negotiator outcomes* was found to have a negative impact on the likelihood of agreement when negotiators had an individualistic motive, but a positive impact on the quality of offers when there was a positive concern for the other party's welfare. *Overconfidence in one's negotiation position* also appears to be specific to the individualistic motive.

Again, it appears that a broader model, which embraces both individualistic and cooperative motivation, is needed. We now turn to such a model.

Note

1 Outside of the United States, such as in the United Kingdom, there is no directly comparable process. In the UK, there are teachers' unions, but they negotiate on a national basis with the local authorities who are responsible for the delivery of public education.

Suggestions for further reading

Arkes, H. R. (1991). Costs and benefits of judgment errors: implications for debiasing. *Psychological Bulletin*, 110, 486–98.

Hastie, R. (1991). A review from a high place: the field of judgment and decision making as revealed in its current textbooks. *Psychological Science*, 2, 135–8.

Markus, H. and Zajonc, R. B. (1985). The cognitive perspective in social psychology. In G. Lindzey and E. Aronson (eds), *The handbook of social psychology*, volume 1, 3rd edn, New York: Random House, pp. 137–230.

Neale, M. A. and Bazerman, M. H. (1991). *Negotiator cognition and rationality*. New York: Free Press.

Payne, J. W., Bettman, J. R. and Johnson, E. J. (1992). Behavioral decision research: a constructive processing perspective. *Annual Review of Psychology*, 43, 87–131.

7 / THE DUAL CONCERN MODEL AND THE DETERMINANTS OF PROBLEM SOLVING

At the end of Chapters 4, 5, and 6 we discussed generality problems with some of the key findings on negotiation. These findings are quite strong when the negotiators are individualistically oriented, with concern only for their own outcomes; but the findings disappear when negotiators are cooperatively oriented, with concern for the other party's outcomes as well as their own. Concern for the other party is sometimes genuine and sometimes instrumental (strategic). Whatever its source, this concern appears to have a distinctive impact on negotiation behavior.

Most theories about negotiation have assumed an individualistic orientation. This seems one-sided in light of these generality problems. Negotiators are often concerned about the other party's outcomes (though this concern is seldom as strong as the concern about their own outcomes), and this concern must be worked into theory because it makes a difference. We present, in this chapter, a dual concern model that corrects for this one-sidedness.

The dual concern model turns out to be particularly useful for understanding the determinants of problem solving behavior, a topic we have not yet discussed. Other determinants of this behavior will also be discussed in this chapter.

The dual concern model (see Pruitt and Rubin 1986; Rahim 1986) is an extension of Blake and Mouton's (1964) conflict grid. Rather than viewing self-concern (concern about own interests) as a constant, as did earlier approaches, this model views it as a dimension running from weak to strong. When this concern is strong, one is willing to work hard for outcomes favorable to oneself; when it is weak, one is willing to let one's own interests

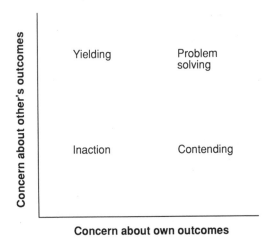

Figure 7.1   The dual concern model
Source: Pruitt and Rubin (1986: 29)

slip. Other-concern (concern about the other party's interests) is also seen as a dimension that runs from weak to strong. Self-concern and other-concern are regarded as independent dimensions, rather than as opposite ends of the same dimension (Thomas 1976).

The dual concern model is shown in Figure 7.1. It predicts preferences among four of the strategies described in Chapter 3 from various combinations of high and low self- and other-concern. High self-concern coupled with low other-concern is assumed to encourage contending. High other-concern and low self-concern is assumed to encourage concession making (yielding). High self-concern and high other-concern is assumed to encourage problem solving. Low self-concern and low other-concern is assumed to encourage inaction. These strategies have many other antecedents in addition to these two concerns; but the dual concern model is one basis for making predictions about strategic preference.

The dual concern model and conflict style

The earliest users of the dual concern model (Blake and Mouton 1964; Filley 1975; Rahim 1986; Thomas 1976) treated it mainly as a theory of *individual differences in conflict style*. Conflict style

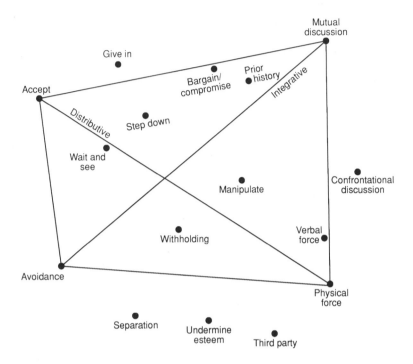

Figure 7.2 Multidimensional scaling of sixteen methods for handling interpersonal conflict

The two-dimensional solution obtained resembles the dual concern model, if we accept the following equivalences: avoidance = inaction, accept = yielding, force = contending, mutual discussion = problem solving.

Source: van de Vliert (1990: 75)

is the way a person most commonly deals with conflict. This outlook has produced a psychometric tradition of research, begun by Ruble and Thomas (1976), involving multidimensional scaling of the methods individuals use for dealing with conflict. A typical study asked forty subjects to rate the extent to which they used each of sixteen methods to handle particular conflicts in their lives (van de Vliert 1990). The results of the multidimensional scaling are shown in Figure 7.2. The sixteen methods are represented by points in the figure. When two methods are close together in the figure, it means they were used to the same extent (whether frequently or infrequently) by each person in the sample. When two methods are far apart in the figure, it means that a person who used one method tended not to use the other. Another way of stating this is that two methods that are close together represent a unitary conflict style, and two methods that are far apart represent opposing styles.

The methods at and near the four corners of this solution are close cousins of the strategies in the four quadrants of the dual concern model. As in the dual concern model, the largest distances were found between the extremes of contending (physical force) and concession making (accept situation), and the extremes of problem solving (mutual discussion) and inaction (avoid discussion). The placement of points in Figure 7.2 resembles that obtained on the average from twenty-seven earlier studies (van de Vliert and Prein 1989). The only consistent discrepancy from the dual concern model is that concession making and inaction are always closer to each other than expected.

It will be noted that we have not shown horizontal and vertical axes in Figure 7.2. This is because the multidimensional scaling method supplies no axes. However, the relative location of the points in the figure suggests that the axes and labels found in the dual concern model (Figure 7.1) are appropriate for these data. This suggests, in turn, that conflict style is a function of the strength of two nearly independent personality variables, concern about own interests and concern about other people's interests, the two dimensions in the dual concern model.

Studies like the one just described often include a "compromise" method, involving a search for a solution in which both parties make concessions. In Blake and Mouton's (1964) original formulation, compromise was in the middle of the figure, equidistant from the other four strategies. But multidimensional scaling usually locates it where it is shown in Figure 7.2, between concession making and problem solving at a considerable distance from contending and inaction (van de Vliert and Prein 1989). This suggests that a preference for compromise is the result of a strong conciliatory tendency coupled with a moderate concern about one's own interests.

Conditions that affect the dual concerns

In addition to being a theory about individual differences in conflict style, the dual concern model is a theory about the impact of changing conditions on strategic choice in negotiation. Some of these conditions affect concern about own interests; others affect concern about the interests of the party with whom one is currently negotiating. Combinations of these conditions predict the strategies that will be chosen in a particular circumstance.

In Chapter 4 we discussed several variables that produce resistance to concession: the height and rigidity of limits and goals, the strength of needs and principles that are linked to limits and goals, and accountability to constituents. These variables can be viewed as producing self-concern. Indeed, in the context of negotiation, it may be desirable to put "resistance to concession" rather than "self-concern" on the horizontal axis of the dual concern model.

Some degree of other-concern is almost always present in mixed-motive settings. This is shown by studies of the prisoner's dilemma (Kelley and Grzelak 1972) in which subjects tend to become more cooperative the more benefit the other party derives from this behavior. In addition, other-concern is especially strong under certain conditions. Some of these conditions produce a genuine concern, involving intrinsic interest in the other party's welfare. Others produce an instrumental concern, which is aimed at advancing one's own interests.

Genuine concern about the other party is enhanced by positive feelings toward and a perception of common group identity with that party. These conditions encourage helping behavior (Clark and Mills 1979; Hornstein 1976). They also foster cooperation in n-person prisoner's dilemmas (Grzelak 1988) and resource dilemmas (Kramer and Brewer 1984), and concession making in negotiation (Fry et al. 1983). The impact of positive feelings on concession making can be seen in a study of heterosexual couples done by Mullick and Lewis (1977). When there was unequal love between the two parties, the one who was more in love tended to get a lower outcome in negotiation, presumably because of making more concessions.

Genuine concern is also fostered by a positive mood, which has been shown to enhance cooperation in negotiation (Carnevale and Isen 1986; Pruitt et al. 1983). Carnevale and Isen (1986) explain their results (greater joint profit) as showing that a positive mood enhances creativity. Here, we suggest that positive mood may also strengthen other-concern given the evidence that a positive mood produces more concession making (Baron 1984; O'Quin and

Aronoff 1981) and enhances helpfulness (Isen 1970; Isen and Levin 1972); both are signs of strengthened other-concern.

In negotiation, other-concern more often arises from instrumental considerations, that is, informed self-interest. Such considerations arise when people expect to be dependent on the other party in the future and wish to make a good impression now. For example, they may want to establish a working relationship because they expect future interaction with the other party. Or they may fear an unfavorable report to additional parties with whom they expect to deal in the future. This state of mind has been shown to produce both concession making (Gruder 1971; Lamm and Kayser 1978) and problem solving (Ben-Yoav and Pruitt 1984a, b; Zubek *et al.* 1992) in negotiation and mediation. It also produces a preference for arbitration over adjudication (Sarat 1976), which suggests a readiness to reach a compromise settlement instead of seeking victory.

Experimental tests of the dual concern model

Support for the dual concern model comes in part from three experiments that independently manipulated self-concern and other-concern (Pruitt *et al.* 1983, Study 1; Ben-Yoav and Pruitt 1984a Study 2; Ben-Yoav and Pruitt 1984b, Study 3). All of them used an integrative bargaining task like that shown in Table 1.1, and all employed 2 × 2 designs. High self-concern was produced either by requiring the negotiators to achieve an ambitious profit target (Studies 1 and 3) or by making them accountable to powerful constituents, by telling them that their constituents would decide how much they would be paid and write a report about how well they had done (Study 2). High other-concern was produced either by giving the negotiators a gift and thus putting them in a positive mood (Study 1), or by telling them that they would have to cooperate with each other in a future laboratory session (Studies 2 and 3). In these studies, both negotiators were always in the same condition. However, the dual concern model applies to the behavior of individual parties and makes predictions about this behavior even if there are different conditions on the two sides of the negotiation table.

Similar results were achieved in all three studies; hence, only the results from Study 2 (Ben-Yoav and Pruitt 1984a) will be

Table 7.1 Joint benefit (top line in each cell) and use of contentious tactics (bottom line in each cell, expressed in standard scores) under two levels of own-concern (accountability) and two levels of other-concern (ECFI)

	ECFI		No ECFI	
	Hi ACC	*Lo ACC*	*Hi ACC*	*Lo ACC*
Joint benefit	9770	8600	8300	8840
Contentious tactics	−0.58	−0.72	2.52	−1.19

ECFI: expectation of cooperative future interaction.
Source: Ben-Yoav and Pruitt (1984a)

presented here. As can be seen in Table 7.1, win–win solutions (high joint benefit) were particularly likely to be achieved when there was high self-concern (high accountability to constituents) and high other-concern (the expectation of cooperative future inter- action with the other negotiator: ECFI), suggesting that some form of problem solving was prominent in that condition. Contentious tactics (threats, positional commitments, and strong arguments for one's own advantage) were especially likely to be used when there was high self-concern and low other-concern. Both results are implied by the dual concern model.

The form actually taken by problem solving was not apparent in these three studies. We measured the exchange of information about goals and priorities, but this was not elevated in the con- dition involving high self- and other-concern, probably because trust of the other party was not particularly high in this condition (see Kimmel *et al.* 1980). A later study (Carnevale and Isen 1986) suggests that the problem solving occurring in this condition takes the form of systematic trial and error. Subjects, who were placed in a good mood and thus encouraged to have high other-concern, proposed more new ideas, conceded more often on low-priority items, and more often asked the other party to react to their pro- posals than did those who were not in a good mood. The result was the discovery of win–win solutions without the exchange of information.

These three experiments show how the dual concern model can be used to resolve some of the problems of generality identified at the end of Chapters 5 and 6. Conditions such as high limits, high accountability to constituents, and strong principles can be viewed as inducing a strong concern about one's own outcomes. Hence, if they are combined with low concern about the other party's outcomes, these conditions should produce rigid, contentious behavior, undermatching, and difficulty in reaching agreement, as was found. But strong self-concern is a two-edged sword, according to the dual concern model, producing quite the opposite effects when coupled with high other-concern. Here it leads to efforts to *link* one's interests with those of the other party rather than to try to *force* one's interests on the other party. Hence, in the presence of high other-concern, we can expect the same conditions to produce problem solving and agreement, as was found in our studies.

Another way of looking at the dual concern model and the results of these experiments is that high other-concern leads to two contrasting types of cooperation, depending on the strength of self-concern: problem solving and concession making. When self-concern is strong, other-concern encourages problem solving, as suggested by the high outcome in the first column cell of Table 7.1. This implies that negotiators are likely to do their most creative thinking about the issues under circumstances that force them to try to reconcile both parties' interests. An example of such circumstances is when they are caught between a desire to please powerful constituents and a need to get along with the other negotiator in the future, as in the high accountability–ECFI condition of Study 2 (the first column of Table 7.1). This suggests that problem solving is encouraged when negotiators are well supervised but have a continuing working relationship.

When self-concern is weak, high other-concern produces concession making, as suggested by the low outcome in the second column of Table 7.1. With no strong concern about their own outcomes, subjects develop flimsy goals, which they easily abandon in the face of a strong desire to please the other party. Hence, they do not work at solving the puzzle of how to satisfy both parties' interests. This effect is shown most clearly in a study of negotiation in newly formed romantic couples (Fry *et al.* 1983). Afraid of antagonizing each other, the parties conceded so rapidly that they almost universally missed the readily available win–win solutions. Less rapid concessions and higher outcomes were achieved in negotiation between total strangers.

What all of this seems to suggest is that concern about other people's interests – whether due to altruism or informed self-interest – is usually quite desirable, but that it will lead to suboptimal results unless it is coupled with a healthy respect for one's own interests as well.

Additional sources of joint-concern and problem solving

The dual concern model asserts that problem solving results from the conjunction of two independent motives: high self-concern and high other-concern. Certain conditions produce the first of these motives, others produce the second. This perspective has generated some useful findings, but it is by no means an exhaustive account of the origins of problem solving behavior (Carnevale and Pruitt 1992; Thompson 1990b). There are a number of conditions that produce concern about both parties' interests *as a whole*, rather than as the sum of two parts. In discussing these conditions, we will often refer to concern about both parties' interests as *joint-concern*.

Team incentives

Joint-concern can result from team incentives, which give all parties an interest in the success of each individual. Such incentives arise whenever people are rewarded for the success of their group, an extremely common arrangement in such arenas as sports and business. Team incentives have been found to encourage information exchange and the development of win-win agreements in negotiation (Schulz and Pruitt 1978), and to enhance mutual cooperation in resource dilemmas (Kramer and Brewer 1984). In meta-analyses of studies in school (and a few other) settings, Johnson and his associates (1981, 1984) have shown that team incentives also encourage increased attraction between group members and improved scholastic performance. These findings support the co-operative learning movement in education.

Modified self-concern

Joint-concern can arise out of self-concern if negotiators conclude that it is not feasible to pursue a contentious path. In order to achieve one's goals in negotiation, it is necessary to persuade the other party to cooperate. According to the dual concern model, negotiators for whom self-concern is paramount will prefer to push the other into cooperating by using contentious tactics. But what happens if such pushing is unsuccessful and the other is unwilling to concede? The only way left for them to satisfy their goals is to try to *buy* the other's cooperation, in other words to seek a way in which both parties can be successful. Hence, joint-concern and problem solving develop as a matter of necessity.

This progression from self-concern to joint-concern probably underlies a sequence of *stages* that have often been observed in successful negotiations. Negotiators typically start with large demands backed up by contentious tactics (Stevens 1963). These tactics may be successful for a while, but a hurting stalemate often develops in the long run (Touval and Zartman 1985). Neither party is willing to make further concessions, and continued contending puts pressure on resources and runs the risk of failure to reach agreement followed by subsequent escalation. Out of this stalemate often comes an effort to find a win–win solution that will satisfy both parties' interests – in other words, problem solving. In Chapter 1, we indicated that a hurting stalemate can encourage a shift from struggle to negotiation; here we argue that a hurting stalemate, if it occurs during negotiation, can encourage a shift from contending to problem solving.

This two-part sequence of stages was observed in two studies of labor–management negotiation (Douglas 1962; Morley and Stephenson 1977). The evidence for it is that judges who were listening to the tape found it increasingly difficult as time elapsed to tell whether labor or management was speaking. At the end of negotiation, both parties seemed to be pursuing the same goals. Two-part sequences have also been observed in international negotiation (Snyder and Diesing 1977) and community mediation (McGillicuddy *et al.* 1987).[1]

A related sequence of stages can be seen in studies of the prisoner's dilemma (Rapoport and Chammah 1965). Plotting percentage of cooperation (choosing option C) over trials typically produces a U-shaped curve. First cooperation goes down and then it goes up. It seems reasonable to assume that cooperation declines at first because of efforts to exploit the other and defend oneself against exploitation – both self-concerned pursuits. However, this results in mutual noncooperation (the "DD trap") and a hurting stalemate. Cooperation then begins to rise because many subjects become aware that exploiting the other is infeasible and that it is necessary to entice the other party to cooperate by reciprocal cooperation. In other words, they develop a joint-concern. In the words of one of Terhune's subjects, "In the beginning I was trying to earn more and soon realized that we were both losing in the process. I then decided upon a small gain rather than a big loss and tried to get the other person to mark C's as I was doing" (Terhune 1974: 671). Watching other people who are experiencing mutual non-cooperation also encourages cooperation (Braver and Barnett 1976), presumably because it leads to an understanding of the need for reciprocal cooperation.

We are postulating that joint-concern and problem solving often develop as a result of insight into the fact that one is in a hurting stalemate. This suggests that taking a break in a contentious interchange should encourage cooperation by giving people time to think about their situation. This hypothesis is supported for the prisoner's dilemma by the finding that cooperation increases after a two-minute break and after within-team discussions when the parties are groups (Pilisuk *et al.* 1971). "Cooling off periods" are usually assumed to have the same impact in negotiation, though we know of no systematic evidence on this issue. Anything that stimulates careful analysis of the future should also encourage this kind of insight; hence there is greater cooperation in the prisoner's dilemma when the subjects get a chance to try out sequences of moves before making a binding decision (Pilisuk *et al.* 1965).

The perceived feasibility perspective

In explaining how problem solving can arise from modified self-concern, we have been employing a "perceived feasibility" perspective on strategic preference (Pruitt and Rubin 1986). According to this perspective, the dual concern model predicts a negotiator's *preferred* strategy. But if this strategy seems infeasible, he or she will shift to another strategy. Thus, high self-concern will lead to a preference for contending. But if contending seems infeasible, negotiators are likely to shift to problem solving as the next best approach to achieving their goals. Evidence that this is true can be seen in a prisoner's dilemma study, where the subjects became cooperative when it was impossible to exploit the other (Enzle *et al.* 1992).

Still other evidence supporting the perceived feasibility perspective was presented in the discussion of time pressure in Chapter 4. There it was postulated that time pressure reduces the feasibility of the strategy of *inaction*. This causes a shift to either concession making (Pruitt and Drews 1969; Yukl 1974a) or contending (Carnevale and Lawler 1986). Theoretically it can also cause a shift to problem solving, and there is some anecdotal evidence that this occasionally occurs (Pruitt 1981). But concession making and contending are closer to inaction in the dual concern model and hence constitute a less extreme leap, making them more probable replacements for inaction.

The perceived feasibility perspective also predicts that problem solving will be abandoned if it seems infeasible, even when there is high joint-concern. For problem solving to seem feasible, it is necessary for there to be *perceived integrative potential*; that is, some basis for believing that one can find a win–win solution. Pruitt and Rubin (1986) describe five conditions that encourage the perception of integrative potential and hence should encourage problem solving:

1 The two parties' goals seem flexible and not too ambitious.
2 Negotiators have faith in their own problem solving ability.
3 There has been prior success at resolving some other issues. Such success is sometimes said to have produced "momentum."
4 The other party is perceived as ready to participate in problem solving. This is important because joint problem solving is the most successful form.
5 A competent mediator is involved. Mediators often succeed in finding win–win solutions where the individual negotiators have failed. Hence, their presence should encourage problem solving – which will occur in discussions with the mediator.

Of these conditions, only momentum has been the subject of research. The task in this experiment (Huber *et al.* 1986) involved a sequence of three negotiations, the last of which had logrolling potential (see Table 1.1). Some sequences began with issues that were easily resolved because the parties had totally compatible goals – this established high momentum. Others began with issues that were hard to resolve and provoked a lot of conflict – this established low momentum. Win–win agreements were more likely to be achieved in the high momentum than the low momentum condition, suggesting that problem solving was a more prominent strategy. This study underlines the importance of having early confidence-building success in negotiation. It suggests that it is a good idea to place some easier items early in the agenda (see Neale and Bazerman 1991).

What strategy will be adopted if problem solving seems infeasible? The two closest neighbors in the dual concern model are contending (which serves one's own interests) and concession making (which serves the other party's interests). It seems reasonable to suppose that the choice between these possibilities is dictated by whether own interests or the other party's interests are more prominent in a negotiator's thinking.

What happens if both problem solving and contending seem infeasible? The perceived feasibility perspective suggests that negotiators will opt for concession making in this circumstance. After concessions have been made, both contending and problem solving may again seem feasible, because the parties' goals are closer together. Hence, one of these strategies may again be adopted.

It can be seen from this discussion that the perceived feasibility perspective provides an explanation for the shifts of strategy that are readily apparent in most negotiation. This corrects a limitation of the dual concern model, which is static in perspective. However, for the most part, the insights based on the perceived feasibility perspective have not been tested in research.

Summary and implications

The dual concern model presented in this chapter provides a broader motivational theory than was employed in earlier chapters. This model helps to clarify some of the findings reported in those chapters. In Chapter 4, we reported that high limits and accountability produce rigidity and contending when coupled with low other-concern; but they produce problem solving when coupled with high other-concern. This follows from the dual concern model if we assume that high limits and accountability are sources of self-concern.

In Chapter 5, we reported two kinds of findings that follow from the dual concern model if we assume the existence of high other-concern. One was the tendency to undermatch the other party's cooperation and match the other's noncooperation when other-concern is low. This suggests an exploitative outlook that is compatible with the contentious strategy. The other finding was the tendency to match cooperation fully and overlook non-cooperation when other-concern is high. This suggests an effort to achieve a mutually acceptable solution, in accordance with the problem solving strategy. In Chapter 6 we reported that a negative frame lessened the likelihood of agreement in negotiation when other-concern was low and that a negative frame enhanced problem solving when other-concern was high (Carnevale and Keenan 1990). These findings provide further support for the dual concern model if we assume that a negative frame increases resistance to making concessions and hence enhances concern for own interests. This is one more example where self-concern interacts with other-concern to predict behavior and outcome in negotiation.

Some limitations of the dual concern model are addressed by the perceived feasibility perspective. If a strategy seems infeasible, a negotiator will shift to another strategy. Although a simple and compelling idea, the perceived feasibility perspective has not been well tested.

Scholars have tended to derive their ideas from the traditional theoretical paradigm of negotiation (shown in Figure 1.1). This paradigm not only ignores other-interest in negotiation, but also ignores aspects of the social context of negotiation. The next four chapters are related in that they examine social context. We now turn to Chapter 8, which examines social norms and their impact on negotiation.

Note

1 It is not altogether clear how this two-part sequence is integrated with the mismatching–matching–mismatching negotiation cycle that was described in Chapter 5. These two pictures of the stages through which negotiation passes are based on different research.

Suggestions for further reading

Ben-Yoav, O. and Pruitt, D. G. (1984). Accountability to constituents: a two-edged sword. *Organizational Behavior and Human Performance*, 34, 283–95.

Carnevale, P. J. and Isen, A. M. (1986). The influence of positive affect and visual access on the discovery of integrative solutions in bilateral negotiation. *Organizational Behavior and Human Decision Processes*, 37, 1–13.

Rahim, M. A. (ed.) (1986). *Managing conflict in organizations*. New York: Praeger.

Thompson, L. L. (1990). Negotiation behavior and outcomes: empirical evidence and theoretical issues. *Psychological Bulletin*, 108, 515–32.

van de Vliert, E. and Prein, H. C. M. (1989). The difference in the meaning of forcing in the conflict management of actors and observers. In M. A. Rahim (ed.), *Managing conflict: An interdisciplinary approach*. New York: Praeger.

8 / SOCIAL NORMS AND THEIR IMPACT ON NEGOTIATION

Negotiation, like most human enterprises, is heavily affected by social norms. Norms are shared beliefs about how people should behave. They are social inventions designed to regulate what happens in a group or a society; and they contribute heavily to the scripts that people follow in their daily conduct. Norms are especially important in negotiation and other mixed-motive settings, because the regulation of social conflict is a major reason for norm formation (Thibaut and Kelley 1959).

Among the most important norms are principles of fairness (also called "distributive justice" norms), which govern the distribution of resources and obligations among people. These principles are very general in conception, and hence can be used to determine correct behavior in myriads of specific settings. There are three broad classes of fairness principles (Deutsch 1975; Leventhal 1976): the *equality* rule, which specifies that everybody benefits or contributes equally; the *equity* rule, which specifies that benefit should be proportional to contribution (e.g. that pay should be proportional to work done); and the *needs* rule, which specifies that benefit should be proportional to need (e.g. that sick people should be taken care of). Each of these classes embraces a number of more specific rules.

Some examples of norms that govern behavior in mixed-motive settings are:

For negotiation
1 The principle that both sides should make equal concessions as they move toward agreement. This reflects the reciprocity norm, which is an adaptation of the broader equality norm.

2 The common rule that concessions once made should not be retracted.

3 The usual arrangement in working relationships (a) to engage in problem solving if both parties have strong needs with respect to an issue *or* (b) to let the party with stronger needs win if problem solving fails or one party has much stronger needs than the other (see Chapter 9).

4 A "wage leadership" practice that involves awarding workers the same raise that was achieved earlier by other workers in the same industry. This practice is frequently found in labor–management negotiation.

For the prisoner's dilemma

5 A custom of lending books to other professors in one's department. It is advantageous to borrow but not lend books; but a department whose members take such a stance will end up with nobody lending books, which is in nobody's interest. Hence, a norm that everybody lends books is usually followed.

For resource dilemmas

6 The common practice that club members should pay equal dues. This is another adaptation of the equality norm.

Agreements reached in negotiation can also be viewed as norms. For example, an agreement to raise hourly wages by 75 cents if the workers discontinue their strike is a norm that identifies the actions expected from each party. Such norms are specific to the issues dealt with in the negotiation rather than being generally applicable. But they are nevertheless norms.

Norms and social conflict

Norms often curtail social conflict. This happens in three ways. The first is that norms sometimes *prevent conflict altogether* by making people's aspirations compatible with one another. For example, the principle of equal dues makes it unnecessary to debate the issue of whether some members should pay more than others. The fact that I could use your car and you could use my computer is not likely to put us into conflict, because of the norms of private property. Without such norms, social life would be an endless and ruinous round of conflict.

The second is that norms often regulate *the way conflict is conducted*. For example, Peirce *et al.* (1991) found that the norms governing conflict in ordinary interpersonal interaction prescribe that one should first talk to (i.e. negotiate with) one's adversary before turning to third parties or to struggle. There are also norms of fair fighting associated with every conflict procedure (van de Vliert 1990).

The third is that norms can help to resolve a dispute by *providing a solution once conflict arises* (Thibaut and Kelley 1959). For example, a dispute between mother and son about turning out lights may be resolved by the mother saying "everybody is trying to save energy these days." A dispute in which two friends are both trying to pay the entire restaurant bill may be solved by splitting the bill.

The solutions provided by norms are often of the win–win variety. For example, the custom of lending books to other professors means that all department members will have the books they need at the time they need them. The rule that provides victory to the party with the stronger needs on each issue means that the most important needs on both sides will be fulfilled in the long run.

Norms are not an infallible route to win–win solutions, however. For example, the equal concessions rule can encourage people to accept an obvious 50–50 compromise rather than seeking a novel option that is better for both parties. The equal outcomes rule tends to discredit options that provide unequal benefits even if such options are the only way to achieve high joint benefit (Marwell and Schmidt 1975).

Although norms often curtail conflict, they sometimes exacerbate it instead. This happens when they require one to challenge another person, for example to fight injustice or defend one's rights. This also happens when two or more parties disagree about which norms are applicable to their situation or how to interpret a norm that is clearly applicable. Norms often entail an emotional investment, especially when they involve fairness or provide guidance to one's rights. Hence, normatively based disagreements tend to be hard to resolve, a point that was made in Chapter 4.

Norms and negotiation

Norms are almost always important in negotiation (Zartman *et al.* 1990). They affect the positions taken, the arguments and concessions made, and the agreements reached. Fairness principles are particularly important, negotiators usually being more concerned about fairness to themselves than fairness to the other party (Thompson and Loewenstein 1992).

Fairness principles are important in people's thinking only if they can be applied. To apply the equality rule, it must be possible to compare one's own benefits with those of the other party. There must be some common scale of measurement. This may be hard to find if we are, for example, exchanging old clothes for food. To apply the equity rule, it must be possible to compare the ratio of benefits to contributions across the parties (Walster *et al.* 1978). To apply the needs rule, it must be possible to evaluate the relative strengths of the parties' needs. Such comparisons are not always possible.

Variations of the equality rule

Four types of equality rule have been observed in negotiation.

(1) *Equal outcomes.* Both parties benefit equally in the final agreement. For example, the standard solution to fee splitting in real estate sales in the USA is for the buyer's agent and the seller's agent each to get half of the commission. Komorita and Kravitz (1979) proposed an *equal excess* principle, a variation of the equal outcomes norm for cases where power differences exist owing to the parties having unequal alternatives to no agreement (BATNAs). Each side gets whatever it could get if no agreement was reached, and they split equally whatever benefit is left over beyond this distribution.

(2) *Equal concessions.* When outcomes cannot be compared, it is sometimes possible to identify equal concessions. For example, if a deadlock develops, with management advocating a 4 per cent raise and labor a 6 per cent raise, equal concessions would involve splitting the difference at 5 per cent. This is a very common solution in negotiation (Raiffa 1982). A variant on this solution is for the party that has conceded less in the last time period to make up the difference (Beriker and Druckman 1991; Druckman and Harris 1990). The equal concessions norm is one source of concession matching, which was discussed in Chapter 5.

(3) *Aspiration balance.* In splitting the difference between 4 per cent and 6 per cent, there is objective evidence about whether

concessions are equal. But such evidence is often not available, because the issues do not lie along an objective scale. In this case, a subjective scale must be used if the equality rule to be applied. Tietz and Weber (1978) have argued that negotiators sometimes equate concessions by comparing their levels of aspiration to those of the other party, a process they call "aspiration balancing."

These authors distinguish five levels of aspiration, ranging from most ambitious to least ambitious: first offer, optimistic goal, pessimistic goal, threatened breakoff point (the level below which one says one will not concede), and actual breakoff point (the limit below which one actually will not concede). Their evidence shows that at every point in negotiation, the two parties in their studies were at roughly the same aspiration level; for example, both proposing their pessimistic goal or both proposing their breakoff point. This implies that concession making often consisted of an effort to match or "balance" reductions in the other party's level of aspiration.

(4) *Outside precedent.* It is often possible to compare a negotiator's outcomes with those achieved by a similar party outside the negotiation. Fairness then becomes a matter of equating these two parties' outcomes. This is the basis for wage leadership in labor–management disputes, which was mentioned earlier. The first settlement that is achieved in an industry often sets the pattern for all the others.

Fairness principles and prominent solutions

There is evidence that agreement is more likely (Joseph and Willis 1963) and is reached more rapidly (Benton and Druckman 1973; Joseph and Willis 1963; Lamm and Rosch 1972) when a single fairness principle can be applied than when no principle can be applied. There is also more certainty about the outcome of the negotiation, because the fair solution is so likely to be adopted (Siegel and Fouraker 1960). There are two reasons for this. One is that both sides are likely to view fair outcomes as *correct*, and hence not quibble about them. The other is that both sides are likely to think that such outcomes are *inevitable*, because the other side cannot be expected to accept less than a fair outcome. An example of this phenomenon is that a team of workers that is paid as a whole will usually quickly divide the money in proportion to the amount of time each individual has worked (Messe 1971), an application of the equity rule.

Outcomes that satisfy a clear-cut fairness principle are *prominent solutions* – solutions that stand out as inevitable. Schelling (1960) argues that prominent solutions can also be produced by perceptual salience; for example, negotiators who are trying to decide the precise location of a boundary between two countries may fasten their attention on a river that lies between the countries. He suggests, in addition, that prominent solutions tend to structure the agreements reached in tacit coordination.

Even when there is a principle that clearly applies to the issues under consideration, agreement is not always reached. One reason for this is that the parties may disagree about how to interpret this principle or the nature of the evidence that pertains to it. For example, the principle of equal concessions is vulnerable to a *partisan bias* such that each party views the other's concessions as smaller than his or her own (Stillinger *et al.* 1991). After negotiation has gone on for a while, both parties may think that their own concessions have been larger than the other's, leading both of them to stop conceding.

Multiple principles

The situation is more complicated if *two or more* principles are applicable. Agreement should be especially easy to reach if all of the principles point to the same outcome. But there is a problem if they point to different outcomes, because each party is likely to show a partisan bias toward the principle(s) that favor(s) its own interests (Zartman *et al.* 1990). Such biases have been shown in settings where the following rules point in different directions: (a) the equity and equal outcome rules (Lamm and Kayser 1978), and (b) the equal outcome and equal concessions rules (Hamner and Baird 1978). It is harder to reach agreement in such cases than when all applicable principles point in the same direction (Hamner and Baird 1978).

Lamm and Kayser (1978) argue that it is better to have multiple principles pointing in different directions than no principles at all, because multiple principles tend to limit the range of options under consideration. The problem with this argument is that principles often have an emotional appeal – they seem righteous and moral, even when they are self-serving. Hence they tend to encourage rigidity with respect to one's demands, and hostility if the other party rejects these demands. This is likely to reduce the amount of problem solving and thus diminish the likelihood of agreement. Evidence that disputes involving opposing principles are especially hard to resolve can be seen in studies of both negotiation (Druckman *et al.* 1988) and mediation (Bercovitch 1989; Hiltrop 1985; Zubek *et al.* 1992). Such dynamics have led Kolb and Rubin (1991) to advise mediators to "be wary when matters of principle, not pragmatics are the central issues."

A critique of principled negotiation

The points just made lead to a mixed evaluation of the popular strategy of "principled negotiation" advocated by Fisher and Ury (1981). These authors urge bargainers to insist that agreements be based on fair standards and fair procedures and to seek objective information relevant to these standards whenever possible. They give as an example a tenant who is trying to persuade a landlord not to increase the rent by saying, "The Rent Control Examiner said it would take about $10,000 in improvements to justify an increase of $67 a month. How much money (did you spend) on improvements?" (Fisher and Ury 1981: 130).

Our analysis suggests that such a strategy will encourage agreement (which may well be in one's favor) *if* the other party accepts the principle proposed and the proposed interpretation of it, and *if* objective information is available allowing unambiguous application of the principle. But these are big ifs.

Clear-cut situations like the one described by Fisher and Ury are not all that common. A city administrator who can provide a precise formula for evaluating fairness is seldom on hand. If one embarks on principled negotiation, the other party may well reject the proposed principle and suggest another one that is equally plausible. The emotions accompanying such principles may then make it difficult for either side to concede, prolonging rather than solving the conflict. The parties would be better off haggling for terms than trying to solve the problem with principles. History is strewn with the wreckage of negotiations in which adherence to principles blocked the achievement of agreements that were otherwise mutually acceptable. For example, arms control negotiations have often failed because equal security or equal concession was sought in a realm where honest men could differ on how to interpret these concepts (Zartman *et al.* 1990).

Overcoming principle-based rigidity

This analysis suggests that in addition to negotiators being advised to seek jointly acceptable principles, they should be taught how to back off from these principles if the other side does not agree with them. They should also be taught how to overcome the other party's principle-based rigidity. Mediators may also benefit from this training. This training might include the following methods.

(1) Persuade the committed party that the principle is inapplicable to the case at hand; e.g. that the issue in arms control is not equal security but *adequate* security.

(2) Persuade the committed party that another equally or more valid principle contradicts the one that is being advocated. For example, an overseas student studying in the USA told a foreign student advisor that he was honor-bound by his religion to kill his roommate, who had failed to pay the rent. When the foreign student advisor urged him not to do so, he accepted her plea on the grounds that it would not be right to offend her (Pruitt 1981).

(3) Persuade the committed party that the principle, while applicable, can be satisfied in some other way, such as by requiring an offending party to apologize or make restitution rather than be punished (Peachey 1989).

(4) Find a win–win solution that satisfies both the committed party's principles and one's own priorities. For example, the United States has sometimes tried to persuade Israel to accept negotiation with PLO representatives by giving some other label to those representatives.

(5) Try to shift the discussion from principles to concrete issues (Lax and Sebenius 1986). For example, a woman accused a man she had lived with of "stealing" some of the household objects they had held in common. There was no way to reach agreement during mediation of this controversy, because she based her arguments on two principles: "stealing must be punished" and "thieves should not profit from their crimes." In an effort to overcome her rigidity, the mediator argued that the only way to retrieve any of her property was to work out a compromise.

Norm enforcement

Social norms, including those that govern and those that result from negotiation, are only effective if people comply with them. Compliance with norms is usually a *voluntary* matter. There are various reasons for voluntary compliance. Some norms are in our interest. Others are in the interest of people whose outcomes we value or whose criticism we fear. In other cases, we may abide by a norm because we view it as legitimate. Voluntary compliance is often predicated on trust – the assumption that other people will also follow the norm (see Chapter 9 for a discussion of trust).

Although voluntary compliance accounts for most conformity to norms, it is not a strong enough force to achieve universal conformity, particularly when there are strong incentives for deviation, as in many mixed-motive settings. Furthermore, there is danger to a group if even a few people begin to deviate from an important norm, because others may follow their lead, viewing the norm as discredited or fearing exploitation. Hence, groups adopt auxiliary strategies to encourage compliance.

One auxiliary strategy is the development of in-group *friendliness and solidarity*, which encourages concern about the welfare and opinions of other group members. This was shown in a study of five-person prisoner's dilemma by Bonacich (1972). Full communication was allowed, and a mutual cooperation norm developed in virtually all of the groups. There were two experimental conditions, which differed in the strength of incentives for individuals to deviate from this norm. In the high temptation condition group members gained much more money for noncooperation than in the low temptation condition. Bonacich found that the subjects rated their groups as more friendly in the high temptation condition than in the low temptation condition. He argues that group members were friendly to each other as a strategy to enhance compliance to the norm and thus counteract the temptation to defect.

Another auxiliary strategy is *social pressure* for norm following. Such pressure was apparent in the same study, where a larger temptation to defect produced stronger verbal support of the mutual cooperation norm. The group members in the high temptation condition talked more about defection and used stronger words to describe a potential defector (e.g. "fink" and "liar") than those in the low temptation condition. The potency of social pressure can also be seen in a finding that more people cooperate in the multi-person prisoner's dilemma (Bixenstine *et al.* 1966; Fox and Guyer 1978) and in resource dilemmas (Jorgenson and Papciak 1981) when their choices are known to the group than when they remain anonymous. When their choices are known, they have more to fear from their fellow group members.

A final strategy of norm enforcement is to develop a *sanction system* that systematically penalizes group members who fail to follow the norm. Yamagishi (1986) found that such a system encouraged cooperation in a four-person resource dilemma if the penalties were large enough. In larger groups, the administration of such a sanction system is often given to a corps of leaders who take responsibility for developing as well as enforcing the norms – in other words, to a governing body or bodies.

Another kind of strategy that can be adopted by a leadership corps in many resource dilemmas is to *administer directly* the collection or allocation of resources; for example, to require employers to deduct taxes from paychecks or to allocate water during a shortage. This makes it unnecessary to rely on individual compliance with norms. The dilemma is solved by taking decision making out of the hands of the individual.

Sanction systems and direct administration of resources are heavy medicine, usually effective but painful because of the loss of individual freedom they imply. Hence groups tend to adopt these procedures only when they expect that more voluntary methods will fail to produce cooperation, endangering the general welfare. Such expectations can be based on adverse experience – for example, a rapid depletion of resources (Messick *et al.* 1983; Samuelson *et al.* 1984; Sato 1987). Or they can be based on a general distrust in other people, which has been shown to encourage the adoption of a sanction system in resource dilemmas (Yamagishi 1986). Distrust is often decried because it tends to bring out the worst in those who are not trusted (Kruglanski 1970). But Yamagishi (1986) has shown that low trust is an asset in resource dilemmas that involve a strong temptation to defect, because it encourages the adoption of a sanction system that is powerful enough to achieve mutual cooperation. Voluntary compliance is a weak reed to lean on when there is a significant temptation to defect.

It seems reasonable to assume that these strategies of norm enforcement are relevant to negotiation – for example, that they are used during negotiation to encourage conformity to the equal concessions principle, and after negotiation to ensure adherence to the final agreement. However, there has been no research directly on this issue.

Summary and implications

Social norms clearly have an important impact on negotiation. They shape the positions negotiators take, the arguments they use, and the agreements they reach. Among the most important norms are the principles of fairness, which encourage, among other effects, efforts to achieve equal outcomes and concessions. Negotiation goes faster and agreement is more likely if the negotiators concur on what principles are applicable and how to interpret these principles. But negotiation goes slower and often founders when opposing principles are advocated on either side, because the emotions accompanying these principles tend to induce rigidity. Methods for overcoming such rigidity include seeking ways to satisfy both parties' principles and trying to shift the discussion from principles to concrete issues.

Although norms are of great importance in negotiation, they have not been much studied in this setting. This is probably because so many scholars have derived their ideas from the traditional theoretical paradigm (shown in Figure 1.1), which ignores the social context in which negotiation takes place. We turn now to another topic that is outside the framework of this paradigm: relationships among the negotiating parties.

Suggestions for further reading

Breslin, J. W. and Rubin, J. Z. (eds) (1991). *Negotiation theory and practice*. Cambridge, MA: Program on Negotiation at Harvard Law School.

Deutsch, M. (1985). *Distributive justice: A social-psychological perspective*. New Haven, CT: Yale University Press.

Komorita, S. S. and Kravitz, D. (1979). The effects of alternatives in bargaining. *Journal of Experimental Social Psychology*, 15, 147–57.

Schelling, T. C. (1960). *The strategy of conflict*. Cambridge, MA: Harvard University Press.

Yamagishi, T. and Sato, K. (1986). Motivational bases of the public goods problem. *Journal of Personality and Social Psychology*, 50, 67–73.

RELATIONSHIPS AMONG THE NEGOTIATING PARTIES

This chapter continues our exploration of the social context within which negotiation takes place. In Chapter 8, we looked at the impact of social norms. Here we look at pre-existing relationships between the negotiating parties. We are particularly interested in three aspects of these relationships: power, trust, and overall positivity versus negativity. The latter two topics are related, in that trust is an element of most positive relationships (and distrust an element of most negative relationships). But trust is a large enough topic for it to deserve its own section.

Power

Power may be thought of as the control of resources that, if used, will affect another party's future welfare. Two kinds of resources may be involved: the power to reward and the power to punish. There are two dimensions of power, when viewed as an element of the relationship between two parties: relative power and absolute power (Bacharach and Lawler 1981). Relative power is the extent to which one party is more powerful than the other; for example, most supervisors have more power than their subordinates. Absolute (also called "total") power is the extent to which the parties have power *over each other*. There will be a lot of absolute power in the relationship between two lawyers from the same firm who often work together, but little absolute power in the relationship between two lawyers from different firms who seldom deal with each other. This is because the former have more capacity to reward or punish each other than the latter.

Relative power

Relative power has been found to have a predictable effect on concession making in negotiation. In two studies involving unequal power to punish (i.e. to fine) the other negotiator, the party with higher power made fewer concessions than the one with lower power (Hornstein 1965; Michener et al. 1975). This accounts, at least in part, for the better outcome usually achieved by the party with higher power. In a related prisoner's dilemma study, the party with higher punishment power cooperated less (Lindskold and Bennett 1973).

One party's power is the other party's dependency (Bacharach and Lawler 1981); in other words, A has power over B when B is dependent on A. In a study of bargaining in romantic couples, Mullick and Lewis (1977) found that the party who was more in love achieved lower outcomes. This may have been because that party was the more emotionally dependent of the two. His or her partner had more power because of having less need for the relationship.

Another finding is that more powerful negotiators usually make more threats, a form of contentious behavior (Hornstein 1965; Michener et al. 1975). However, this generalization is not always valid when power differences are small. In a study by Hornstein (1965), *low* power negotiators made more threats than high power negotiators in a condition where there was a small discrepancy in power. There were also fewer agreements in this condition than in those involving equal power or large power discrepancies; and less money was made by either party.

Other aspects of the same data suggest that the mild discrepancy in power put the negotiators at cross purposes, producing what is sometimes called a "power struggle." The high power negotiators apparently expected to achieve more than their opponents, but the low power negotiators were unwilling to accept this lower status and fought for equal treatment. The high power negotiators put up a return fight, creating an escalation that often wrecked the negotiation. Such a struggle did not occur when there was a large discrepancy in power, presumably because the low power negotiators realized that struggle was hopeless.

A second study (Vitz and Kite 1970) showed similar results. Here power consisted of the capacity to contribute to a pool of resources that was useful to both parties. More disagreements were detected when there was a mild, as opposed to a large, discrepancy in power, indicating that contentious tactics and escalation were more common in this condition.

Absolute power

Several studies have looked at the impact of *absolute power* (Hornstein 1965; Bacharach and Lawler 1981). Fewer threats were made and more agreements were reached when the two parties had high punitive power rather than moderate or low power. Lawler *et al.* (1988) showed that high mutual threat capacity lowered the temptation to use coercion and the expectation that the other party would use coercion. It appears that each side's capacity to harm the other severely made the two sides very careful not to antagonize each other.

The findings about absolute power are interesting; but we must be careful not to overgeneralize them, because they are based on laboratory tasks that had an unusual feature. It was easy for the subjects to calibrate their relative power and thus tell whether one party was ahead of the other. In more realistic settings, this is often not the case, especially if the two parties differ in the type of power they hold. In such settings, it is common for each party to engage in wishful thinking, believing *itself* to be the stronger of the two parties and hence deserving of the larger outcome. This is an unstable situation that can easily lead to contending and escalation. A protracted struggle may be necessary in such a setting before each party's true strength is evident. The greater the absolute power, the more destructive will be this struggle.

An example of this would be the Vietnam War, which, it can be argued, was prolonged for years because of the different kinds of military strength on the two sides. The United States had a strong conventional army, while Vietnam had potent guerrilla forces. Hence, both sides thought they were going to win. Not until the Vietnamese Tet offensive did it become clear to the United States that military victory was unlikely, and only then was it possible to move toward an agreement.

Trust

Trust is the expectation that the other party will cooperate in the future. It is an individual cognition, and hence could have been discussed in Chapter 6. But it is also an aspect of the relationship between parties, in two ways: it deals with how the parties perceive each other, and it is often (but not always) similar on both sides – if A trusts (distrusts) B, B is likely to trust (distrust) A.

Trust is sometimes regarded as a *trait* – a general faith in humanity that is measured by a self-report inventory (Sato 1988, 1989; Yamagishi 1986; Yamagishi and Sato 1986). It can also be viewed as a *state* that is produced by *environmental conditions*, such as the following; the other has cooperated with oneself, especially if this happened recently (Kelley and Stahelski 1970), and has incurred costs in doing so (Komorita 1973). (Such costs presumably increase the likelihood that one will view the other's cooperation as genuine.) The other is known to have cooperated with other people in the past (Braver and Barnett 1976). The other is believed to be humble and self-effacing (Marlowe *et al.* 1966). The other is dependent on oneself (Solomon 1960). One has sent a message to the other requesting cooperation, or has received a message from the other indicating an intention to cooperate (Loomis 1959). The other is a member of one's own group (Kramer and Brewer 1984; Yamagishi and Sato 1986) or similar to oneself (Apfelbaum 1974). Third parties can be expected to punish the other for failing to cooperate (Yamagishi 1986).

The impact of trust in mixed-motive settings

In two studies of the effect of trust on negotiation, it was found that trust encouraged the exchange of information about values and priorities (Kimmel *et al.* 1980; Lindskold and Han 1988). Trust also made it easier to reach agreement in one of these studies (Lindskold and Han 1988). The latter effect should be even stronger in settings where agreements must be implemented, because trust should encourage a belief that the other party will uphold its end of the bargain.

Trust usually also encourages cooperation in prisoner's dilemmas and resource dilemmas. There are two related ways in which this can happen. One is by encouraging people to believe that their cooperation will be reciprocated. The other is by encouraging them to believe that their cooperation will not be exploited, that they will not be treated as suckers.

These interpretations help explain two findings about the effect of the personality variable of trust (Sato 1988). One was that trust predicted cooperation in three-person but not seven-person groups. The investigator explained this as indicating that, in larger groups, the individual's decision to cooperate has less proportional effect on the other group members and hence is less likely to be noticed. As a result, others will not be expected to reciprocate cooperative behavior, even if they are trusted as individuals. The second finding was that trust had progressively less impact on cooperation in the absence of feedback about how others were responding. This suggests that there is a limit to how far even the most trusting people will go in making themselves vulnerable to exploitation by others.

Level of trust appears to distinguish those who match from those who mismatch other people's selfish behavior during resource shortages. (Matching and mismatching were discussed in Chapter 5.) Trust was measured as a personality variable in two resource dilemma studies (Brann and Foddy 1988; Messick *et al.* 1983). People with high trust tended to mismatch their fellows, defending the common resource by restricting their withdrawals. People with low trust tended to match their fellows, withdrawing resources in response to withdrawals made by others, and thus further exacerbated the crisis.

There are two possible explanations for these results. One is that high trust encouraged a belief that the other subjects could be reformed by setting a good example. This seems unlikely since the high trusters continued to cooperate in the face of continuing greed on the part of their fellow group members. The second explanation is that high trusters were not worried about their reputation for toughness; in other words, were not afraid of looking like suckers. Perhaps trust makes people unconcerned about others taking advantage of them in later situations.

No studies have been made of the impact of trust on demands and concessions in negotiation. However, the results just cited suggest that more trusting negotiators may make more concessions and be more likely to fill the gap produced by the other party's failure to concede at a deadline.

Reducing reliance on trust

It is hard for people to cooperate in the absence of trust. But when there is a desire for cooperation and trust is low, it is sometimes possible to reduce reliance on trust. This can be done by making decisions *reversible*, so that they can be escaped if the other proves untrustworthy. Thus, Deutsch (1973) found high levels of cooperation in the prisoner's dilemma when both parties were free to reverse their decisions again and again until satisfactory results were obtained. In negotiation, reversibility is implicit in the rule sometimes adopted that no decisions are final until all issues have been agreed upon. This rule makes it possible to concede on some issues without full assurance that the adversary will concede on others. This rule was presented earlier as a way of maximizing the likelihood of finding tradeoffs among the issues. But it is also a way to move ahead despite distrust.

Another way to reduce reliance on trust involves *fractionation* of cooperation into many tiny moves, such that the risk entailed in any one of them is small (Fisher 1964). One can usually make a tiny cooperative move even if trust is low, and then wait to see if the other reciprocates before taking the next tiny move. Two negotiators sometimes move toward agreement in this way, each making tiny concessions that are reciprocated by the other until they arrive at a common position.

Positive and negative relationships

The rest of this chapter will concentrate on a broad characteristic of most relationships: how positive or negative they are. In positive relationships, the parties are concerned about each other's outcomes and usually avoid hostile actions toward each other. Furthermore, they have positive attitudes to and images of each other, and often feel warmly toward each other. Negative relationships have just the opposite features. Trust is an element of most positive relationships and distrust an element of most negative relationships.

The characteristics of positive and negative relationships just discussed are usually shared by both parties. Such sharing is extremely common. If A has a positive attitude toward B, B is likely to have a positive attitude toward A. If C trusts D, D is likely to trust C. We usually find two negotiators behaving in much the same way toward each other; for example, both engaging in problem solving or both employing threats (Bacharach and Lawler 1981; Hornstein 1965; Kimmel *et al.* 1980; Michener *et al.* 1975). There is also a very high correlation, in the prisoner's dilemma, between the level of cooperation exhibited by the two parties (Rapoport and Chammah 1965).

The impact of positive and negative relationships

The impact of positive relationships has usually been studied by bringing friends, lovers, or married couples into the laboratory. Sometimes behavior within these relationships is compared to behavior between strangers. At other times the quality of the relationship is measured with self-report instruments, and positive relationships are compared with negative relationships. In still other studies, relationships are produced in the laboratory by instructing people to work together.

As might be expected, there is more concession making and problem solving in negotiation between people with positive relationships than between those with negative relationships or no relationships (Fry *et al.* 1983; Schoeninger and Wood 1969; Syna 1984; Zubek *et al.* 1992). There is also less hostile and contentious behavior (Syna 1984; Zubek *et al.* 1992). Positive relationships also show more cooperation in the prisoner's dilemma (McClintock and McNeel 1967), and when the other transgresses, people in more positive relationships tend to retaliate less readily (Rusbult *et al.* 1991), though they will eventually respond if the other continues to annoy them (Gottman 1979).

We do not mean to imply that people with positive relationships always concede easily or bow quickly to each other's wishes. This sometimes happens in new romantic relationships, because the members are afraid of alienating each other and hence are "walking on eggs" with respect to one another's feelings. They tend to lower their aspirations to avoid conflict, resulting in simple compromise agreements that miss the integrative potential in the situation (Fry *et al.* 1983). But in more mature and secure relationships, people are likely to exhibit a combination of problem solving and concession making which commonly leads to high joint benefit. We call these "working relationships."

The characteristics of working relationships

Working relationships are often found between people with emotional ties, such as friends, relatives, or married couples. Working relationships are also common between people with instrumental ties, such as colleagues whose jobs require them to cooperate, and negotiators in counterpart relationships. An example of the latter would be a salesperson and a regular client.

Working relationships between negotiators might seem like a contradiction in terms, since negotiators are adversaries. But negotiation is a mixed-motive enterprise, and negotiators usually have a common interest in finding win–win solutions and reaching agreement. This means that they must collaborate as well as compete. Working relationships make collaboration possible.

Pruitt (1991) describes working relationships as involving three related norms for dealing with mixed-motive settings:

1 A norm of *problem solving*, which specifies that if both parties feel strongly about an issue, they should try to find a way for both of them to succeed.
2 A norm of *mutual responsiveness*, which specifies that if only one party feels strongly about an issue or if problem solving fails, the party who feels less strongly should concede to the other's wishes.
3 A norm of *truth in signaling*, which specifies that the parties should be honest about the strength of their feelings.

It can be argued that this set of norms is optimal for generating high joint benefit. Problem solving encourages high joint benefit on a single issue or a set of issues considered simultaneously, as discussed in Chapter 3. Mutual responsiveness encourages high joint benefit on a set of issues considered *sequentially* when these issues have logrolling potential as a group. This is because each party succeeds on the issues of greatest importance to itself. Truth in signaling is a necessary adjunct to the norm of mutual responsiveness, preventing people from exaggerating the strength of their needs. In the absence of this norm, neither party will trust the

Table 9.1 Joint benefit achieved under various combinations of concern and agenda

	Self-concern	Joint-concern
Simultaneous agenda	587	608
Sequential agenda	513	572

Source: Weingart et al. (1993)

other's statements about issue importance, and the norm of mutual responsiveness will collapse.

Evidence about working relationships

Weingart *et al.* (1993) have found evidence of the second and third norms in a study of multilateral four-party negotiation. The task was related to that shown in Tables 1.1 and 6.1A, in that the four negotiators had different priorities across the issues under discussion. Working relationships were produced in the laboratory by instructing some of the four-party groups to adopt a joint-concern, to "be concerned about how well the other parties are doing as well as how well you are doing." Other groups received self-concern instructions. Half of the groups in each condition employed a simultaneous agenda, in which all issues were discussed at the same time. The other half employed a sequential agenda in which the five issues were discussed one by one. The results are shown in Table 9.1. Groups that had received joint-concern instructions were able to achieve high joint benefit in both agendas; whereas those that had received self-concern instructions only achieved high joint benefit in the simultaneous agenda.

Verbalizations in the joint-concern, sequential agenda condition suggest that the subjects followed the norms of truth in signaling and mutual responsiveness, providing honest information about their priorities and letting others win on issues that were important to them. The result was logrolling across the five issues, with each person winning on his or her high priority issues, despite the fact that these issues were discussed at different times. This yielded a level of joint benefit that was almost as high as that produced by the ordinary problem solving that was possible in the simultaneous agenda conditions.

The results of this study suggest that the norms of mutual responsiveness and truth in signaling are readily available forms of behavior. We can speculate that these norms emerge under two conditions that were simultaneously manipulated (i.e. confounded) in the study: (a) the parties are motivated by a joint-concern, embracing both their own and the others' interests; and (b) the parties know that this is true, in other words they trust each other. Joint-concern is needed to make people willing to concede on issues of importance to others. Trust is needed to assure them that they will not be suckers if they make such concessions – that they will get something in return.

Sources of relationships

What are the sources of positive and negative relationships? The answer to this question comes in three parts. One part concerns conditions that affect the direction taken by relationships, whether positive or negative. A second part concerns mechanisms that cause people to share the same attitudes and behave in similar ways toward each other. The third part concerns the persistence of positive and negative relationships once established.

Conditions affecting the direction taken by relationships

Bonds

Positive relationships are encouraged by bonds of perceived similarity, kinship, and common group membership. People are better liked when they are seen as similar in attitudes and values (Byrne 1971), and there is also more readiness to cooperate with them in the prisoner's dilemma (Apfelbaum 1974; Dion 1973). Balance theory (Heider 1958) predicts that a positive relationship will also develop between people who see each other as part of the same group. Research (summarized by Brewer 1979) suggests that this effect is much enhanced if the parties can contrast their common (in-)group with an outgroup. For example, it has been found that attitudes toward the members of one's own group were more positive when there was a second group with a different name sitting at a nearby table than when the two groups were integrated at the same table and given a common name (Gaertner *et al.* 1990). A similar effect has also been demonstrated in a mixed-motive setting: Kramer and Brewer (1984) found that people turned to prudent harvesting in a resource dilemma when they were reminded that they were members of the same ingroup (residents of Berkeley, California) in contrast to an outgroup (residents of other communities).

If being part of the same group leads to positive attitudes and perceptions, one might expect that being part of different groups will lead to negative attitudes and perceptions. However, this effect, if it exists at all, appears to be small (Brewer 1979; Gaertner *et al.* 1990). Furthermore, Dion (1973) has shown that group solidarity, produced by perceived similarity to other group members, does not encourage negative views of outgroups.

Prior cooperation and competition
A large number of studies (summarized in Johnson *et al.* 1984) indicate that cooperation leads to improved interpersonal and intergroup relations. In the initial studies on this topic, Sherif (1967; see also Sherif and Sherif 1953) first produced animosity between two groups of boys in a summer camp by having them compete with and exploit each other. He was able to dispel this animosity in a second phase by having them cooperate on "superordinate goals," such as dismantling the camp's water tower and putting it on a truck for transportation to a repair shop. Other research has shown that the anticipation of cooperation also leads to improved interpersonal and intergroup relations (Brown and Abrams 1986; Ben-Yoav and Pruitt 1984a, b).

When actual cooperation is involved, the extent of success in this cooperation is an important variable. The impact of success depends on whether the decision to cooperate with the other party is voluntary or not (Turner *et al.* 1984). If cooperation is involuntary, the relationship improves if the joint venture is successful. But if cooperation is voluntary, *failure* leads to a more positive relationship than success. The latter effect is probably due to the subjects' efforts to reconcile the failure with the fact that they voluntarily decided to affiliate with the other party. The dissonance produced by this apparent contradiction is resolved by concluding that one likes the other party so much that it does not matter that they failed.

There are many possible explanations for the positive effect of cooperation on relationships. Cooperation may lead to reward at the hands of the other party. It may provide favorable information about the other party that would not otherwise be available. It may enhance perceived similarity and break down the conceptual boundary between groups (Gaertner *et al.* 1990). Helping the other may induce positive attitudes – another dissonance-resolving effect. Given the strength and reliability of the cooperation effect and the variety of conditions under which it is found, it seems likely that several of these explanations are valid.

If cooperation tends to improve relationships, what of competition – the pursuit of contradictory goals? In the first phase of his study, Sherif produced hostile relations by having his groups compete. Other research has found similar effects (Johnson *et al.* 1984). It seems likely, however, that competition that stays within normative boundaries is much less likely to produce negative relations than competition in which the other party appears to be trying to gain an unfair advantage.

Interdependence and role relationships

Interdependence is found when the parties can help or hurt each other in the future and hence must rely on one another's cooperation. The research on absolute power discussed earlier suggests that high interdependence encourages cooperation, provided, of course, that the parties perceive that they are interdependent.

In the prisoner's dilemma, the parties are interdependent; hence mutual cooperation is the most effective approach. However, this interdependence is more obvious in some cases than in others. In some versions of the prisoner's dilemma, each party seems to control the other's largest rewards; hence, it looks as if the parties must lean on each other. The result is a high level of mutual cooperation which should lead to a positive relationship. In other prisoner's dilemma situations, it appears that the parties are in control of their own largest rewards. This produces declining cooperation and a negative relationship, apparently because the parties do not feel interdependent even though they really are (Pruitt 1967, 1970).

Mutual cooperation is usually buttressed by *norms* in mixed-motive settings. These norms are followed in part because both parties know that the other party's cooperation is likely to be contingent on their own. Other norm enforcement mechanisms of the kind discussed in Chapter 8 may also be involved. Mutual cooperation norms often derive from the *roles* people play in groups and organizations. An example would be the norms associated with the complementary roles of office director (or assistant to the director) and purchasing agent. The norms governing the office director in this relationship include making firm decisions about the equipment and supplies that are needed for the office, and communicating these decisions to the purchasing agent in a clear and timely fashion. The norms governing the purchasing agent include locating suppliers, building inventories of the most commonly needed items, rationalizing and promulgating the procedures for placing orders, and moving rapidly on rush orders. Both parties are governed by norms requiring accessibility and cordiality.

Of course, role relationships sometimes impose an antagonistic, rather than a cooperative, relationship. An example would be the roles of soldiers in opposing armies.

Mechanisms that produce similar attitudes and behavior

Why do parties who are in a relationship so often share the same attitudes – positive or negative – toward each other and behave similarly when they interact? Part of the answer to this question concerns the nature of the phenomena explored in the previous section: bonds, prior cooperation and competition, interdependence, and role relationships. These tend to affect both parties similarly – if I am bonded to you, you are usually bonded to me; if I compete with you, you usually compete with me, etc. But this does not seem a sufficient explanation for the immense uniformity that is found between the members of most relationships.

Another part of the answer entails forces that encourage the *matching* of behavior; these were examined in Chapter 5. Noncooperation tends to be matched to avoid tangible loss and image loss (the perception that one is a sucker) and to pay the other back, in compliance with the norm of reciprocity. Such matching often leads to vicious circles in which A's negative behavior leads to B's negative behavior, which leads to more negative behavior from A, etc. The result is mutual noncooperation. Cooperation also tends to be matched, especially when there is future dependence on the other party (Pruitt and Kimmel 1977); and there are also benevolent circles, in which each party's cooperation strengthens the other's trust and sense of obligation, making it ever more likely that the other will respond cooperatively. In addition, there are strong forces that encourage matching the other's perceptions of and attitudes toward oneself.

The persistence of positive and negative relationships

Once established, positive and negative relationships tend to persist. People continue respecting and helping each other, or disliking and acting hostilely toward each other. Why is this?

Part of the explanation is a phenomenon called the "self-fulfilling prophecy," which causes perceptions of the other party to be self-reinforcing (Rosenthal and Jacobson 1968; Snyder *et al.* 1977). The mechanisms underlying this phenomenon are the vicious and benevolent circles just described. For example, suppose that A views B as unpleasant and lazy. A is likely to behave in a strained manner toward B and not to give B much responsibility. B's most likely reaction to this will be hostile and careless behavior, which will reinforce A's initial view and perpetuate the negative relationship between the parties. Similar circular processes can reinforce a flattering view of another party, perpetuating a positive relationship.

Perceptions and attitudes also perpetuate themselves by mechanisms of selective perception, selective memory, and attributional distortion (Cooper and Fazio 1979; Pruitt and Rubin 1986; also, see Chapter 6). Selective perception occurs whenever there is ambiguous evidence about the other party's behavior. People tend to notice negative behavior when they have hostile attitudes, and to notice positive behavior when their attitudes are friendly. For example, Hastorf and Cantril (1954) found that the events of a Dartmouth–Princeton football game were judged differently as a function of the viewer's allegiance. Princeton students thought that the Dartmouth team had committed twice as many infractions as the Princeton team, while Dartmouth students saw no difference in the number of violations. Selective memory is illustrated by a study (Zadney and Gerard 1974) in which subjects who had seen another person behave in a complex way tended to recall primarily those actions that confirmed their initial views of that person (see also Grzelak 1982). These are mechanisms of self-perpetuation because they tend to reinforce the perceptions and attitudes that give rise to them.

As mentioned in Chapter 6, attributions are the explanations one gives for another party's behavior. Attributions reinforce our pre-existing perceptions of another party in the following way (Holtzworth-Munroe and Jacobson 1985; Regan *et al.* 1974). When the other party behaves in accordance with our perceptions, we view this behavior as intentional and as reflecting the other's stable characteristics. This reinforces our perceptions of that party. But when the other behaves discrepantly from our perceptions, there is a tendency to attribute it to unstable causes in the immediate situation to which the other is reacting. Hence, this behavior is not seen as reflecting the other's basic characteristics, and there is no need to change our perceptions of those characteristics.

An illustration of attributional distortion can be seen in the way John Foster Dulles explained Soviet behavior over a period of several years (Holsti 1962). Dulles was the US Secretary of State at the height of the cold war. When Soviet behavior was hostile toward the West, Dulles explained it as a manifestation of their stable, aggressive characteristics. But when the Soviets were conciliatory, he attributed it to their military weakness, a transitory aspect of the situation. By these attributional manipulations, he was able to maintain his basically negative view of the Soviet Union, despite changes in their behavior toward the West.

Sometimes people actively seek information about others rather than receiving it passively, as in the case of the mechanisms reviewed so far. Attitudes and perceptions tend to be self-perpetuating even when this happens, because the search is often conducted differently depending on one's initial assumptions. Thus Snyder and Swann (1978) found that subjects who were trying to assess another person's social outlook asked different questions if they assumed he or she was an introvert as opposed to an extrovert. These questions tended to elicit answers that confirmed the initial assumptions.

The mechanisms described so far all involve the psychology of the individual. In addition, when groups (including organizations and nations) are involved, prevailing views of the other party tend to be reinforced by social pressure and the defense of vested interests (Pruitt and Rubin 1986). Examples of vested interests would be militant leaders and representatives of war industries, who sometimes encourage a continued view of another society as "the enemy" in order to preserve their dominant positions. Commercial ties between two societies can also produce vested interests that provoke social pressure in favor of a continued positive view of the other society.

The forces described in this section tend to perpetuate relationships in the mold they initially take. However, these forces are not totally overwhelming; relationships do change at times. In the next section, we will describe some of the conditions that encourage change in negative relationships.

Overcoming negative relationships

The motivation to overcome a negative relationship can come from two sources: disputants are often unhappy with such a relationship because it produces conflict and prevents needed collaboration; third parties who are close to the relationship may become concerned because they fear that conflict will spill over into their arena. What can either kind of party do to combat a bad relationship? There has been a flurry of theoretical work and some empirical research on this issue.

Stylistic guidelines
A number of stylistic guidelines have been proposed for improving a distressed relationship. Fisher and Brown (1988) suggest:

1 Be rational, even if they act emotional.
2 Try to understand them, even if they misunderstand you.
3 Consult them before deciding on matters that affect them, even if they are not listening.
4 Be honest and trustworthy even if they are trying to deceive you.
5 Avoid coercive tactics even if they are using them.
6 Be open to persuasion and try to persuade them.
7 Care about them and be open to learning from them even if they reject your concerns as unworthy of consideration.

Fisher and Ury (1981) add to this list:

8 Attack the problem not the people. This advice is supported by research which shows that attacks on the other party's competence produce derogation of the speaker and closed-mindedness about the speaker's position and arguments (Tjosvold *et al.* 1980).

Pruitt and Rubin (1986) emphasize the following further guidelines:

9 Maintain open communication channels.
10 Engage in active listening (see Chapter 3).
11 Openly express concern about the other's welfare.
12 Demonstrate a real interest in problem solving. Show willingness to change your proposals if a way can be found to bridge the two parties' interests.
13 Re-examine any elements of your supposed interests that are unacceptable to the other party to be sure they are essential to your own welfare.
14 Reward the other party for taking conciliatory initiatives.

Techniques developed by the Japanese in their constant quest for improved interpersonal relations can also be added to this list:

15 Do little favors: give presents, throw restaurant parties, attend weddings and funerals in the other party's family.
16 Try to locate any bonds between the parties, however remote.

All these suggestions make sense as ways to reverse an unpleasant relationship (and to build a positive relationship from scratch). However, it is not clear that they are powerful enough to break through the rough thickets of distrust that accompany a really bad relationship. The other party may simply discount such gestures by the methods of selective perception, selective memory, and attributional distortion described earlier. Social pressures and vested interests may also operate at the group level to block improved relations.

Unilateral conciliatory initiatives

When distrust is strong on the other side, it is sometimes possible to improve the relationship by taking a dramatic conciliatory initiative (See Lindskold 1986; Osgood 1962). An example is Egyptian President Anwar Sadat's trip to Jerusalem, which paved the way for peace between Egypt and Israel. Kelman (1985) has reported that most Israelis viewed this event as a genuine effort to improve relations. Another example is US President John F. Kennedy's 1963 announcement that he was stopping atmospheric tests of nuclear weapons, which was a step on the road to détente. A third example is Soviet Chairman Mikhail Gorbachev's withdrawal from Afghanistan, which was a major event in the dissolution of the cold war.

Several guidelines have been proposed for enacting unilateral initiatives (Osgood 1962). Two of these have received experimental verification: announce what you are doing ahead of time (Lindskold and Aronoff 1980), and carry out the initiatives as announced (Gahagan and Tedeschi 1968; Lindskold *et al.* 1976). In addition, it has been suggested that conciliatory initiatives should be irrevocable and noncontingent, so that they will be understood as efforts to resolve the conflict rather than to gain a quid pro quo (Mitchell 1991). They should be costly or risky to oneself, so that they cannot be construed as a cheap trick. They should be continued for a period of time so as to put pressure on the other party to reciprocate and to give the other party time to rethink its policy. Two other pieces of advice are added by the current authors. Unilateral initiatives should be noticeable and unexpected so that they will provoke thought. Their users should try to demonstrate a good and lasting reason for wanting to change the relationship; otherwise such initiatives may be viewed as a flash in the pan.

There is evidence that conciliatory initiatives are especially effective when the party taking them is of equal or greater strength than the party toward whom they are taken (Lindskold and Aronoff 1980). This makes sense from an attributional viewpoint. Concessions from strength are more likely to be viewed as genuine efforts at conciliation than concessions from weakness, a point that was made in Chapter 5.

Fisher and Brown (1988) have questioned the value of conciliatory initiatives, characterizing them as efforts to "buy a good relationship." This position seems arbitrary in light of the success of Sadat's mission, Kennedy's announcement, and Gorbachev's withdrawal, as well as the evidence from laboratory experiments just described.

There are two major problems that limit the effectiveness of conciliatory initiatives even when properly enacted. One is that the other party may not be interested in making peace. Conciliatory initiatives were worse than useless against Hitler, who viewed them as evidence that his adversaries were "little worms." The other is that neither party may be willing to take a conciliatory initiative. Such initiatives require high motivation to escape the conflict, a readiness to take risk, and a belief that the other party can be influenced. Such conditions are often absent in negative relationships. If neither party is willing to take an initiative, the relationship may not improve until a third party intervenes.

Contact and communication

Contact and communication are commonly employed in an effort to improve a negative relationship. They can have several beneficial effects. First, contact and communication allow the parties to explain actions and proposals that might otherwise elicit defensive reactions or retaliation. Second, they contribute to understanding the other party's motives and sensitivities; combating stereotypes and making it possible to act in ways that will not upset the other. Third, contact and communication permit problem-solving discussions in which substantive and procedural issues can be resolved. Finally, there is evidence that contact and communication contribute to the development of positive bonds (Ancona *et al.* 1991; Festinger *et al.* 1950; Friedman and Gal 1992; Zajonc 1968).

Contact and communication have, on the whole, been found to improve intergroup relations (Amir 1976). However, they should not be regarded as panaceas. They are most effective when the parties have a *moderately* negative relationship. If the parties are severely hostile toward each other, contact and communication tend to be useless or worse than useless (Rubin 1980). Under such conditions, people will often not employ available communication channels (Deutsch 1973). Or they may use them to threaten or trick the other side (Worchel 1979). Indeed communication between extreme adversaries can be exceedingly explosive, allowing angry, insulting interchanges. This was shown in Sherif's boys' camp study. When the warring cabins were brought together they only argued and called each other names, worsening the controversy. Furthermore, if there are fundamental differences in attitudes and values between the parties, communication may bring these out, making the parties even more dubious about each other (Druckman and Zechmeister 1973).

It is sometimes possible to tone down severely hostile relationships to the point where contact and communication can be effective. A third party may shuttle between the disputants for a while – encouraging ventilation, improving mutual images, and laying the groundwork for agreement – before allowing the parties to make direct contact with each other (Kelman and Cohen 1976; Walton 1969). While shuttling, the third party may have to coach the disputants to stay away from explosive topics that are not relevant to the issues at hand. A cooling-off period may also be useful if the parties become angry with each other once they get together (see Pilisuk *et al.* 1971). Third party tactics will be discussed in much greater detail in Chapter 11.

Contact that involves cooperation between the parties appears to be a good deal more effective at resolving differences than contact alone (Brown 1988b). The mechanisms by which cooperation works were discussed earlier in this chapter.

Wilder (1986) has pointed out that contact between groups or organizations inevitably involves a small number of individuals. Quite often the relations between these individuals improves while attitudes toward the larger groups remain the same. Hence, it is important to ask how improved relations between individuals can be generalized to the groups from which the individuals come. Wilder argues that this will only happen if the people with whom one has contact are seen as *typical* of the group from which they come. He did a study that manipulated two variables: the pleasantness versus unpleasantness of an interaction between students from two colleges, and whether or not the other person was viewed as typical of her college. There was only one condition in which attitudes improved toward the other college as a whole – when there had been a pleasant interaction with a person who was viewed as typical of her college.

Negotiating new relationships

Negotiation is often useful as a way to repair a distressed relationship. The parties confront some of the malfunctional features of their relationship and develop new norms that better suit their individual and collective purposes.

There is evidence, however, that simply devising an agreement about how to behave is not enough to repair really problematical relationships. Behavioral marital therapists experimented for a time with efforts to improve distressed marriages by developing contracts between spouses; but evaluation studies (Jacobson 1984) have not supported this approach. These studies suggest that "marital contracts" have a positive effect as long as there is contact with the therapist, but tend to deteriorate as soon as therapy is over. This result parallels a finding that the best contracts reached in community mediation were no better in the long run than the worst contracts (Pruitt et al. 1992b). There are two problems with contracts between people in distressed relationships, which may explain these results. One is that the disputants may not trust each other to uphold a contract, reducing their commitment to it. The other is that contracts tend to deal with the current issues in the relationship, and these often change over time.

Later versions of behavioral marital therapy have emphasized problem solving training, in which the parties are taught to discuss new issues in a productive way. Studies (Jacobson 1984; Johnson and Greenberg 1985) have shown the value of this approach, which is also supported by the finding that joint problem solving during community mediation sessions was predictive of later improved relations between the parties (Pruitt *et al.* 1992b). It makes sense that training and experience with problem solving should have a beneficial long-run effect, since problem solving facilitates the development of good agreements about *new issues* as they arise. In addition, it can be argued that such training and experience will tend to improve trust toward the other party, because one sees the other party actually trying to come up with solutions to common problems.

Summary and implications

Like the one before it, this chapter has dealt with an element of the social context within which negotiation takes place; in this case, the relationship between the parties. There are many ways to describe relationships, and we have only covered three of them: power, trust, and positivity versus negativity.

Having a power advantage in negotiation leads negotiators to concede less and make more use of contentious tactics than the other party. This ordinarily means that the advantaged party will achieve higher outcomes than the other. But if the disadvantaged party is only slightly less powerful, the result is likely to be a power struggle in which neither party does well. Such a struggle is also likely to ensue if the power relationship between the two parties is unclear because each party is likely to see itself as somewhat advantaged over the other. There is evidence that a high level of absolute power makes the parties fear escalation and hence exercise care not to antagonize each other.

Trust, the expectation that the other party will cooperate, encourages problem solving in negotiation and cooperation in the prisoner's dilemma. In resource dilemmas, trust also encourages making up for other people's depletion of resources, perhaps because trusting people do not fear looking like suckers. Cooperation is hard to achieve in the absence of trust, but it is not impossible if reversible decisions can be made or cooperation can be fractionated.

Parties in positive "working" relationships tend to engage in problem solving or to allow the party with the stronger feelings to win. The result is high joint benefit over a period of time. Positive relationships are produced by perceived similarity, kinship, common group membership, prior cooperation, perceived interdependence, and cooperative role obligations. There is also a strong tendency to match the positivity of the other's actions and apparent attitudes. This encourages parties to share orientations – positive or negative – toward each other. Once established, these orientations tend to be perpetuated by self-fulfilling prophecies and the mechanisms of selective perception, selective memory, and attributional distortion. These are cognitive processes that appear to have motivational components, and that are particularly relevant to relationships.

A variety of procedures are available for repairing negative relationships, including unilateral conciliatory initiatives, contact and communication, and problem solving training.

We turn now to a third chapter on the social context of negotiation, concerning negotiation by groups or organizations.

Suggestions for further reading

Bacharach, S. B. and Lawler, E. J. (1981). *Bargaining: Power, tactics, and outcomes.* Greenwich, CT: JAI Press.

Clark, M. S. and Reis, H. T. (1988). Interpersonal processes in close relationships. *Annual Review of Psychology,* 39, 609–72.

Fisher, R. and Brown, S. (1988). *Getting together: Building a relationship that gets to YES.* Boston: Houghton Mifflin.

Messick, D. M., Wilke, H., Brewer, M. B., Kramer, R. M., Zemke, P. E. and Lui, L. (1983). Individual adaptations and structural change as solutions to social dilemmas. *Journal of Personality and Social Psychology,* 44, 294–309.

Osgood, C. E. (1962). *An alternative to war or surrender.* Urbana: University of Illinois Press.

Sherif, M. and Sherif, C. W. (1953). *Groups in harmony and tension.* New York: Harper and Row.

10 / GROUP PROCESSES IN NEGOTIATION

Parties to negotiation are often groups; for example, families, committees, departments, companies, governments. When this is the case, negotiation usually takes place through representatives, individuals or small subgroups who are trying to protect the interests of the larger collective (Adams 1976; Walton and McKersie 1965). For example, the car dealer described in Chapter 1 represented the owner of the car franchise, and the labor lawyer mentioned in Chapter 6 represented the school board. Many international negotiations are conducted by diplomats who attempt to reach agreements that must then be sold to political leaders and other people back home. As mentioned in Chapter 4, the people whose interests are represented by a negotiator are called constituents.

Most negotiation theorists (e.g. Fisher and Ury 1981; Patchen 1989; Pruitt 1981) draw no clear distinction between interpersonal and intergroup negotiation. Events and outcomes are attributed to decisions made by unitary actors, the "negotiators" or negotiating "parties." And these decisions are assumed to result from psychological processes, especially motives and cognitions – as described in earlier chapters of this book. This outlook has some value, since collectives are made up of individuals, whose behavior is guided by psychological processes. But the outlook clearly has its limitations. For example, negotiations via group representatives increase the likelihood that messages between constituents will be distorted (Rubin and Sander 1988). Furthermore, groups are (often vast) collections of interests, which must be reconciled before or during negotiation (Pruitt 1990, 1992), adding an additional complication to intergroup negotiation. When groups and organizations face each other in negotiation, within-group dynamics can have important consequences for the between-group negotiation.

Winham (1979) has argued forcefully that the generalizations of negotiation theorists who view negotiations from an individual perspective "may bear little relevance to the behavior found in real negotiation because they fail to capture the complexity of the process" (p. 118). The complexities of within-group and between-group negotiation are apparent when the parties are large collectivities such as organizations or nations. The negotiation is typically handled by negotiation teams, subgroups that represent the larger collectives. In international negotiations, which usually involve many complicated issues, it is often expedient for top diplomats and their aides to negotiate an abstract formula or sketch of the overall agreement. Smaller, specialized committees, consisting of lower-ranking diplomats on both sides, then negotiate the finer details (Zartman 1977).

Even an ordinary negotiation over the price of a car typically involves people other than the salesperson and the customer. The salesperson has the owner of the dealership to consider, and the customer may have a spouse whose approval must be obtained before making an offer. Often there is considerable within-group negotiation before and during between-group negotiation (Walton and McKersie 1965). Consider the following example of a group whose members have differing interests and views regarding how a negotiation should turn out. You enter a car dealership with your spouse to negotiate the price of a new car. You approach the car dealer on the showroom floor ready to make an offer on your first choice, the grey family sedan. Then your spouse loudly proclaims that the two of you should buy the red sports coupé. You loudly proclaim that you thought the decision had already been made. The car dealer becomes curious about which one of you will handle the negotiation. This simple example of a within-group conflict points to a shortcoming of much negotiation theory: the failure to consider that negotiation is often not between unitary actors but between groups whose members are frequently in conflict.

In the sections below, we examine how theorists have tried to cope with the challenge of between-group and within-group negotiation. We focus on two aspects of group and intergroup negotiation: (a) the role of the representative *vis-à-vis* constituents, expanding our discussion of representatives in Chapter 4; and

(b) team negotiation, in which small groups on each side plan a negotiation strategy.

The role of the representative

Representation can pose problems for negotiators. Consider the dilemma faced by negotiators in a recent labor–management dispute described by Shapira (1990). Everyone on both sides expected the negotiation to be a major battle. When the negotiators from both sides met, however, the agreement came very quickly – it was reached in about an hour. Both sets of negotiators were happy with it. But the negotiators were reluctant to go back to their constituents so quickly. So they stayed in the hotel for two days, played cards, drank beer, let their beards grow (the ones who had beards), and then emerged with both sides telling their constituents that it was a major battle, and that the agreement was the result of a series of hard-won contests. Both sets of constituents – the rank-and-file union members and upper management – believed that the agreement was the best one possible since it had been so hard to achieve. Hence it was easy for them to accept the agreement.

Negotiation between representatives is inescapable when large collectives are involved. However, when groups are small, there is sometimes a choice between appointing a representative or having the group as a whole negotiate with the other side. Such a choice is also faced by individuals who are considering whether to employ an agent as their representative or to negotiate on their own behalf. Rubin and Sander (1988) argue that the use of representatives in negotiation ordinarily should be avoided, except in the following special circumstances:

1 When the representative has substantive knowledge in the domain under consideration; for example, hiring a tax attorney to handle your negotiation with an IRS auditor.
2 When the representative has process expertise, such as special skills as a negotiator.
3 When the representative has special influence, such as in the case of a Washington lobbyist.
4 When the negotiation is too emotionally charged for the principals to meet face to face. An example of this might be a bitter divorce, in which the parties are only willing to talk through their lawyers.

Greenhalgh (1987) is more sanguine about the use of representatives, arguing that they are often more rational than their constituents, having a better understanding of the other party's priorities and hence being more realistic about success.

Another argument for negotiation through representatives is that it provides an opportunity for the use of tactical stratagems, such as the "bad guy/good guy" routine (Rafaeli and Sutton 1991; Rubin and Sander 1988). In this routine, the representative adopts a cooperative stance, while one of his or her constituents shows a tough stance. For example, the representative might say, "I'd like to give you this really good price on the car; but I can only do so if my manager approves it, and he's pretty tough about these matters." Such a strategy has been shown to be effective in eliciting concessions (Hilty and Carnevale 1992). A related strategy, which involves a negotiator claiming "my hands are tied," invokes a constraint on one's ability to make a concession due to constituent pressures (Schelling 1960). It has been shown to be effective when it accompanies an offer within the bargaining range (see Chapter 4) (Friedland 1983).

Theorists who have examined the relationship between representatives and their constituents have taken one of three perspectives. Some theorists assume a one-way influence model: influence goes from constituents to negotiators, with constituents determining policy and negotiators following it (see Chapter 4). Other theorists assume a mutual-influence model, with negotiators and constituents influencing each other. And still other theorists assume a network model, which pictures representatives and constituents as parts of a larger communication network embracing both collectivities. We take up each of these perspectives in turn.

One-way influence model

The assumption that constituents determine policy and negotiators follow is seen most clearly in laboratory studies on concession making by social psychologists. Some of these studies have looked at the effect of being a representative *per se* (e.g. Enzle *et al.* 1992). Other studies have looked at the influence of the representative's accountability, status within the group, or surveillance by the constituent on concessions and contentious behavior. This literature was reviewed in some detail in Chapter 4.

Mutual-influence model

A few authors take the stance that representatives and constituents talk things over and often have considerable impact on each other (Adams 1976; Colosi 1983; Holmes *et al.* 1986; Pruitt 1964; Walton and McKersie 1965). In a book on labor negotiation, Walton and McKersie (1965) argued that representatives are often deeply involved in policy making about their negotiation. This is in part because of their closeness to the other party, which allows them to contribute a unique, realistic perspective on what can be achieved in the negotiation. Constituents tend to be overly optimistic about what can be achieved. Hence, representatives are often arguing for more concessions.

This stance can make representatives seem disloyal to their constituents, creating what is sometimes called "Adams's paradox," or the "cycle of distrust" (Adams 1976): representatives who are trusted and given autonomy by constituents will feel especially free to advocate concessions to the other side. The result of this behavior is likely to be suspicion of the representative's loyalty, leading to closer monitoring of the representative's behavior. This, in turn, may cause the representative to become rather tough with the other party, resulting in poor relations with that party, and a poor agreement. The poor agreement reinforces the constituent's monitoring and suspicion. According to Adams (1976: 1192), "The paradox is noteworthy, for it suggests that a rewarding organizational climate may be self-destructive and may lead eventually to less organizational effectiveness in boundary transactions than might be supposed."

In order to avoid Adams's paradox, representatives need to be attentive to their image with their constituents, advocating concessions to the other side within a context that makes their loyalty clear. One way of doing this is to make an initial, well publicized show of toughness in the negotiation. This establishes credentials of loyalty that can be drawn upon when one later presses for realism. An example of this is the two-day "battle" staged by the negotiators in the labor–management case described at the beginning of this chapter. Both sets of negotiators needed this event in order to sell their constituents on the compromises to which they had agreed.

Combining Walton and McKersie's insights with the results of experiments based on the one-way influence model, Holmes *et al.*

(1986) describe the representative's position as involving considerable *role conflict*. Representatives have to negotiate simultaneously with their constituents and the opposing group's representative (Frey and Adams 1972; Stephenson 1981). They must span the chasm between appearing completely loyal and urging realistic concessions derived from intimate knowledge of the other negotiator. Efforts to span this chasm can place them under a lot of stress (Friedman and Podolny 1992).

An implication of the mutual-influence model is that representatives often act as intermediaries, presenting each side's views to the other side. Drawing on his experience as a labor mediator, Colosi (1983: 231–2) writes: "The union spokesperson not only tries to get management to go along with labor's point of view but may also have to get the rest of the union team to accept management's view on the same points." Colosi also observes that chief negotiators often serve as "quasi-mediators" in their organization, trying to reconcile the differing views of constituents to develop a unified strategy. In a study of foreign policy making, Pruitt (1964) found that individuals in the US State Department, the "country desk officers," served the role of quasi-mediators during negotiation. These officers were either the main negotiators or in immediate contact with the main negotiators on their side.

Chains of intermediaries: A network model

Our network model of negotiation (Pruitt 1990, 1992) subsumes constituent–negotiator relations within a broader framework which is inspired by Colosi's analysis. The model applies to negotiation between any types of organizations, ranging from subdepartments in a small firm to the largest nations on earth. It postulates communication and influence chains involving organization members. These chains begin inside one organization, cut across the boundary between the two organizations, and continue inside the other organization.

To illustrate this model, we will rely on a modified version of the example of the teacher–school board negotiation that was presented in Chapter 6. A diagram of this example is shown in Figure 10.1.

Our two organizations are the teachers and their representatives (S1 to S3 and L1 to L3 in Figure 10.1), and the school board and

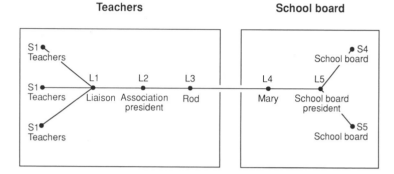

Figure 10.1   A negotiation chain involving two organizations

their representatives (S4, S5, and L4 and L5). At the ends of the chains lie "stake holders" (designated by "S"), whose needs and values are of concern to their organization ("L" stands for "link"). A single chain may have several stake holders at each end, as shown by S1 to S5, making it a "branching chain". Each point in the chain may represent an individual, or a team of individuals.

On the teachers' side, there are three groups of stake holders, each a distinct group of teachers: one from the high schools in the district (S1), one from the elementary schools (S2), and one from the special education schools (S3). For the school board, which is composed of officials elected by the broader community, the stake holders are two factions on the school board from rival political parties (S4 and S5). Note that we could extend this chain to include more remote stake holders: the political parties or the people in the community who elected the board members.

All other chain members are intermediaries, who are trying to reconcile the needs and values of the stake holders at the two ends of the chains. Intermediaries, or "links," are represented by L1 to L5 in Figure 10.1. L1 is a liaison within the teachers' association, who meets with the three groups of teachers (S1, S2 and S3) and also with the association's president (L2). Rod (L3), our tireless negotiator, reports to this president and deals with Mary (L4), the lawyer who represents the school board. Mary reports directly to the president of the school board (L5), who in turn has the two factions of school board members to worry about (S4 and S5).

Two adjacent chain members form an "arena." The members of an arena ordinarily take different positions, each presenting the viewpoints from the end of the chain to which he or she is closer. This means that intermediaries flip-flop allegiances as they shuttle from one arena to the other. For example, in Figure 10.1, Rod (L3) will present the viewpoints of the teacher groups (S1, S2, and S3) in discussions with Mary (L4) and the viewpoints of the school board members (S4 and S5) in discussions with the teachers' association president (L2). In other words, two adjacent chain members can be seen as boundary spanners, or "linking pins," facing different directions (see Kahn 1991; Likert 1961).

The most important activities in an arena are *information transmission*, *persuasion*, and *problem solving*. Exchange of information about the views of the stake holders is the minimum function of an arena. Accurate information about the positions, interests, priorities, and assumptions of the stake holders must flow through subsidiary arenas. Most arenas are also the site of some sort of negotiation. Contentious tactics aimed at winning are often seen in these arenas, as is problem solving. Potential agreements must be presented to powerful stake holders. If key stake holders are not persuaded, they are likely to block agreement. In some cases, it is useful to assume a "value-added" perspective, viewing intermediaries as adding their own needs and values to the network, as they pass messages and the agreements reached in negotiation along the chain.

People with the formal title of "negotiator" (Rod and Mary, L3 and L4) are usually intermediaries, as is also true of the constituents to whom they immediately report (L2 and L5). Hence the model draws no firm distinction between negotiators and constituents, viewing both roles as part of a broader communication network.

The sharpest conflicts in a network of this kind are not necessarily between the two formal negotiators (Rod and Mary in our example). The negotiators may only be exchanging information (Colosi 1983); or they may be sufficiently attuned to one another that they are mainly involved in problem solving. In such cases, the sharpest differences, and the heaviest contentious behavior, are likely to be found within one of the organizations. For example, the sharpest disagreements might well be between the teacher liaison and the president of the teachers' association. Likewise, in an international negotiation, the US State and Defense Departments may well be engaged in a fiercer battle than the American and Spanish negotiators.

Similarly, the most effective problem solving may well take place in an arena other than that involving the formal negotiators (Rod and Mary); for example, in conversations between Mary (L4) and the president of the school board (L5). These two might be best equipped to come up with a proposal that will be acceptable to the teachers. In general, it can be argued that the most effective problem solving will take place in those arenas whose occupants are best informed, best able to communicate with each other, and most trustful of each other.

How are agreements reached in such networks? Messages go back and forth along the chain, and efforts are made at various points in the chain to persuade, sharpen the issues, and develop new ideas. Larger groups are sometimes assembled involving several points along the chain. Agreement is reached when winning coalitions in both organizations embrace the same idea (Colosi, personal communication).

At present, little is known about the conditions under which conflict is most likely to be resolved in such networks, though we can speculate that it has to do with the level of information the two networks have about each other and the degree of trust and communication that exists in the arenas along the chain. We suspect that there will be optimal problem solving when there are good relations throughout the chain, and people at all points feel responsibility for the success of those on either side of them. This idea has its roots in the dual concern model described in Chapter 7.

Negotiation teams

The concept of negotiation teams adds a further degree of complexity to the network picture of negotiation shown in Figure 10.1. We noted earlier that each of the points in the figure could represent an individual, or it could represent a negotiation team, a group of individuals who make collective decisions on how to negotiate with the individuals or teams that are adjacent to them in the chain. Although Walton and McKersie (1965) drew attention to the importance of within-group negotiation more than 25 years ago, little is known about these effects. What happens within such a team may have important consequences for the between-team negotiation.

Members of negotiation teams may disagree on matters of substance (what offers to make) and on matters of style (how to negotiate, when to make an offer, whether a threat should be issued, etc.). Ancona *et al.* (1991) identify group processes that may pose problems for team negotiation. For example, it is often difficult to coordinate team members, especially in adopting new procedures for conducting the negotiation. The lead negotiator might fear that members of the team will "give away" key information in the between-group negotiation. Moreover, the lead negotiator may suppress participation out of fear of losing power and influence.

In the sections below, we examine three related issues regarding negotiation teams: (a) the differences between negotiation teams and individuals; (b) the role of perceived group boundaries; and (c) the reciprocal influence of within-group and between-group processes in negotiations.

Teams and individuals in negotiation

Several studies suggest that negotiation teams are likely to adopt a more competitive approach to negotiation than are individuals. Evidence from prisoner's dilemma research indicates that intergroup interactions are more competitive than interactions between individuals (Komorita and Lapworth 1982; Lindskold *et al.* 1977). In a related study, Peirce *et al.* (1991) obtained marginally significant evidence that groups are more likely than individuals to opt for struggle tactics when given a choice of procedures for dealing with conflict.

Evidence that between-group interactions are more competitive than between-individual interactions has been obtained in a series of prisoner's dilemma experiments by Insko and colleagues (e.g. Insko *et al.* 1990). These authors interpret their findings in terms of individual's beliefs and expectations that "intergroup relations are competitive, unfriendly, and aggressive . . . in contrast to beliefs regarding intragroup cooperativeness, loyalty, and friendliness" (Schopler *et al.* 1991: 613). In addition, there is reason to believe that as a negotiation team grows larger in size, it is more likely to adopt a competitive approach in between-group negotiations (Kramer 1991b).

There are two reasons to believe that groups may be better at problem solving and discovering win–win agreements than individuals. Keenan and Carnevale (1992) reported that three-person negotiation teams, although more likely than individuals to adopt contentious tactics in negotiation, were also more likely to discover tradeoffs among the issues. This is probably because there are a greater number of thinkers in a group, an "$N + 1$ heads are better than 1" effect (Hill 1982). Rubin and Sander (1988: 398) note that representatives who participate in their group's decision making can be useful for problem solving in negotiation: "they can help articulate interests, options, and alternatives.... Four heads are clearly better than two."

Second, Friedman and Podolny (1992) show that negotiation teams can lessen the role conflict associated with boundary spanning. Role conflict can be avoided when several different individuals on the team take on different functions of boundary spanning, such as communicating *out from* versus communicating *into* the boundary spanning team. This role differentiation helps individuals avoid problems of carrying information in opposing directions, and presumably improves the quality of that information.

The salience of group boundaries

When there are two or more groups in a setting, people are ordinarily more attracted to and cooperative with members of their own group than members of other groups (Tajfel *et al.* 1971; Tajfel and Turner 1986). Several studies support this generalization in negotiation (Brewer and Kramer 1986; Kramer 1991a). For example, Rothbart and Hallmark (1988) found that conciliation is seen as a more effective strategy for dealing with ingroup members, whereas coercion is seen as more effective for dealing with outgroup members. Keenan and Carnevale (1992) found that subjects who negotiated with a member of their own group made more concessions and were more likely to adopt a problem solving strategy than those who negotiated with a member of another group. Negotiations within-group were characterized by greater trust, and greater concern that both parties should attain a good outcome. Friedman and Gal (1992) and Pruitt and Rubin (1986) argue that bypassing formal roles and creating relationships that cut across group boundaries is an important element of problem solving in between-group negotiation (see Chapter 9).

Within-group and between-group processes

Several studies suggest that within-group processes can have important reciprocal effects on between-group negotiation (Bornstein *et al.* 1989; Dion 1979; Fisher 1989; Rabbie 1982). Keenan and Carnevale (1989), for example, found that groups whose members engaged in a cooperative or competitive negotiation within their group adopted the same approach to a subsequent negotiation with an outgroup. Within-group cooperation made between-group cooperation more likely, and within-group conflict diminished the likelihood of between-group cooperation. Similarly, Friedman and Gal (1992) reported that solidary labor and management negotiation teams were more likely to come together to form a solidary, joint negotiating team in the between-group negotiation.

Another source of evidence on the important influence of within-group processes in between-group negotiation is research on the effects of mediation. Lim and Carnevale (1990) found that mediator suggestions that were made when there were internal disagreements within a negotiation team decreased the likelihood of agreement in the between-group negotiation. Like throwing gasoline on glowing coals, the mediator's suggestion apparently inflamed an already smoldering situation.

Summary and implications

This chapter continued our discussion of the social context of negotiation and our effort to expand the framework of the traditional paradigm described in Chapter 1. Most theorists who examine the role of representative *vis-à-vis* constituents assume a one-way influence model: influence goes from constituents to negotiators, with constituents determining policy and negotiators following it (see Chapter 4). Other theorists assume a mutual-influence model, with negotiators and constituents influencing each other (Walton and McKersie 1965). The most comprehensive framework is the network model, which pictures representatives and constituents as parts of a larger communication network that embraces both collectivities (Figure 10.1).

Sometimes negotiations are conducted by a team or committee of individuals, which poses unique problems and opportunities. Negotiation teams may be more hostile than individuals in between-group negotiation (Schopler *et al.* 1991), but they may also have positive effects on information exchange and problem solving (Friedman and Podolny 1992).

Our understanding of the behavior of negotiators in group contexts is highly limited. We can rely on only a few studies to develop conclusions about these effects. Basic questions have gone unanswered. For example, we know practically nothing about the effects of team decision rules, such as majority vote versus unanimity, on negotiations between groups. We also know little about different forms of representation. Is there a difference in negotiation behavior between representatives who were elected or appointed by a group, and representatives who were hired by a single person to represent his or her interests? As of yet, no study offers an answer.

We now turn to the mediation of disputes, a topic that has generated much research in recent years. In mediation, a new link is introduced to the model shown in Figure 10.1, in between the two negotiators L3 and L4. To follow our example from Chapter 6, which was continued in this chapter, a mediator, Chuck, enters the scene to help Rod and Mary reach an agreement.

Suggestions for further reading

Argote, L. and McGrath, J. E. (1993). Group processes in organizations: continuity and change. In C. Cooper and I. T. Robertson (eds), *International review of industrial and organizational psychology*. Chichester: John Wiley & Sons.

Brown, R. (1988). *Group processes: Dynamics within and between groups.* Oxford: Basil Blackwell.

Colosi, T. (1983). Negotiation in the public and private sectors: a core model. *American Behavioral Scientist*, 27, 229–53.

Levine, J. M. and Moreland, R. L. (1990). Progress in small group research. *Annual Review of Psychology*, 41, 585–634.

Messick, D. M. and Mackie, D. (1989). Intergroup relations. *Annual Review of Psychology*, 40, 45–81.

Turner, J. C. and Giles, H. (eds) (1981). *Intergroup behavior*. Chicago: University of Chicago Press.

11 / MEDIATION

Another stalemate! For Chuck, it was not the first, nor would it be the last. Chuck is a professional mediator working for the state mediation board, and his job is to help negotiators reach agreement when they cannot do so on their own. In this stalemate, facing each other across the table, were Rod and Mary, our tireless labor negotiators from Chapter 6. The meeting was convened by Chuck, who sat at the head of the table.

In *mediation*, the negotiation continues but is helped along by the third party. Mediation can be distinguished from *arbitration*, where the third party makes a binding decision about the issues. Mediation preserves the voluntary, joint-decision features of negotiation – the disputants retain the right to accept or reject any suggestion made by the mediator. Hence mediation is a special case of negotiation. This chapter presents an overview of psychological research on mediation.

Mediation has wide scope. It has long been an important part of labor relations and international negotiation. Pick up any newspaper on any day and you will almost always find a report of a mediator attempting to help disputing parties reach agreement in one or both of these areas. In the USA, mediation has been introduced into realms as diverse as neighborhood feuds, civil and criminal litigation, police interventions, family disputes and divorce, environmental planning and surveying, and informal decision making in organizations (Kressel and Pruitt 1989; Rubin 1981, 1985; Susskind and Ozawa 1985; Wall and Lynn 1992). It is by no means a new phenomenon. One of the earliest recorded mediations occurred more than four thousand years ago in Mesopotamia. A

Sumerian ruler helped to avert a war between neighboring groups and to develop an agreement in a dispute over land (Kramer 1963).

Mediation can take on a variety of shapes and forms. Like negotiation, a mediator's decisions and inferences are often made in the context of complex social, organizational, and cultural systems that have legal constraints and historical underpinnings (Karambayya and Brett 1989). Such is the case for Chuck, our labor mediator in the teacher–school board negotiation. Like all mediators, Chuck had to make decisions about two main issues: whether to enter the dispute, and what behaviors – *strategies* and *tactics* – to employ if he did. These decisions will be examined in this chapter. There will also be a discussion of disputant reactions to mediation, which is important for understanding the effectiveness of mediation.

Contractual versus emergent mediation

When the discussion between the disputing parties breaks down, sometimes one or both parties may contact a third party to intervene. In other cases, a third party may volunteer his or her services. When is a potential mediator likely to intervene in a dispute? This depends in part on the mediator's own perspective and in part on that of the disputants, who must often decide whether to invite or accept mediation. The context in which mediation occurs, whether *contractual* or *emergent*, is important in understanding what leads people to mediate or to accept mediation (Kolb 1989; Kressel and Pruitt 1989; Smith 1985; Touval 1985).

Contractual mediation

Contractual mediation occurs within a set of rules and guidelines that have been previously established by the community. It is usually done by a professional who has received formal training, and is available for more than one case. Labor mediation is usually of a contractual nature. In the teacher–school board dispute, Chuck was a representative of the state's Public Employment Relations Board. In this dispute, much like other disputes involving public sector employees in many states in the USA, mediation occurred because it was required. By law, the parties had to accept mediation if they failed to reach agreement on their own. In contractual mediation, the mediator meets the parties for a relatively short period of time, and usually does not have a continuing relationship with the parties.

Another example of contractual mediation is "community mediation." Community mediation is now common in the USA, especially as an alternative to court (McGillis 1981). More than 300 community conflict resolution centers now exist in the USA, many affiliated with the court system, others relying on self-referral or referral by social agencies (Duffy *et al.* 1991). The disputes usually involve people who have some sort of ongoing relationship: e.g. family members, neighbors, landlords and tenants, consumers and merchants. Typical disputes involve noise, damage to property, theft, assault and battery, harassment, and so on.

Emergent mediation

In contrast to contractual mediation, emergent mediation has no formally defined mediation role (Kolb 1989; Murnighan 1986). The mediator typically has an ongoing relationship with the disputants, and is an interested party who emerges from the organization or system in which the dispute has occurred. For example, in a dispute among two coworkers in a business, another coworker may step in as a mediator. In a dispute between two nations over the location of a common border, a third nation may offer to mediate.

Emergent mediation occurs either because the mediator has an interest in the outcome of the dispute, or because the mediator seeks to make a good impression on one or both parties (Touval and Zartman 1985, 1989). An example of the former is a nation that mediates a border dispute between two of its neighbors because it fears that the conflict will spill over its own borders.

Mediators are often genuinely interested in seeing the negotiators reach an agreement; but they occasionally use mediation as a tactic for furthering or preserving their own interests. Sometimes, mediators see their best interests as being served by the negotiators continuing to fight, and needing to rely on the mediator (Zartman and Touval 1985). This is particularly likely in emergent mediation. This suggests that mediator goals are important, not only in entering disputes, but in their decisions regarding what to do in mediation. According to Touval and Zartman (1989: 118), "A third party may hope to win the gratitude of one or both parties in a conflict, either by getting them out of the conflict or by helping one achieve better terms. . . . Mediators can also increase their influence by becoming guarantors of whatever agreement is reached." Van de Vliert (1992) adds to this:

> Maybe the most striking example of self-serving intervention is the mediator who, in fact, conquers everybody by operating as a *tertius gaudens*, as the one who is sitting pretty. In some fashion or another the third party in the middle draws advantage from the conflict because the principal parties hold each other in check, so that the mediator can make a gain which one of the parties would otherwise deny him or her.

The problem of bias

In both contractual and emergent mediation, mediators usually need to steer a precise course between the disputants lest they alienate one side and lose their credibility and acceptability. There is always a danger that one or both parties will come to believe that the mediator is hostile or biased against them. Such beliefs have been shown to reduce disputant receptivity to mediators (Welton and Pruitt 1987).

While all of this is true, the traditional view that mediator bias is totally incompatible with success (Young 1972) has been challenged by several authors (Brookmire and Sistrunk 1980; Kressel 1972; Smith 1985; Touval 1975; Touval and Zartman 1985, 1989). These authors argue that a biased mediator is sometimes the only one available to mediate the conflict and is often the person with the greatest influence over the party that most needs to change. There are two kinds of mediator bias: (a) the mediator's general alignment with one side before the start of mediation and (b) the mediator's support for one side's position during the mediation. Carnevale and Conlon (1990) showed that negotiators were more concerned about the latter than the former kind of bias during a dispute. Indeed, the negotiators were very receptive to a mediator who was unfavorably aligned provided that the mediator was even-handed during the negotiation.

Strategies and tactics of mediation

Negotiators find it difficult to reach agreement for a variety of reasons: their aspirations may be too high, they may have too much hostility toward each other, they have no good ideas for an agreement, so a mediator may come in to help. A typical mediator will try to figure out what the problem is, and then try to solve it. Mediators will almost always do certain things, such as get information, and try to build rapport with the parties. Other activities are tied to the nature of the problem.

Much of the recent literature on mediation focuses on what mediators do in their effort to assist disputants; in other words, the *tactics* of mediation. More than one hundred different mediator tactics have been identified (Wall 1981; Wall and Lynn 1992), including controlling communication processes, thinking up and suggesting new ideas for possible agreements, arguing for or against certain options, and even trying to mold the disputants' relationship, such as balancing their power relationship.

The mediation literature offers many typologies and distinguishing factors of mediator interventions (Fisher and Keashly 1988; Prein 1987). The best known is perhaps that by Kressel (1972), which was updated by Kressel and Pruitt (1989) and has received some empirical support (Lim and Carnevale 1990; McLaughlin et al. 1991).

Mediators often use tactics to get negotiators to accept mediation, to trust in the mediator, and to have confidence in the mediation process. Kressel (1972) and Kressel and Pruitt (1989) call these behaviors "reflexive tactics." For example, in a private conversation with Mary, Chuck, the mediator, told an amusing story about one of his recent fishing trips. This personal anecdote helped establish rapport with Mary, which Chuck hoped would help Mary trust him. Several studies have shown that rapport with and trust in the mediator are important predictors of agreement (Carnevale and Pegnetter 1985; Pruitt et al. 1989).

Mediators also attempt to control communication. Perhaps the most widely used technique for controlling communication in mediation is the caucus, where the mediator separates the parties and meets privately with each side. The caucus is used for getting information about one party's values and priorities without the other party hearing. Caucuses are usually called when the parties are showing high levels of hostility toward one another and little joint problem solving (Pruitt et al. 1989). They remedy these difficulties by providing an alternative location for problem solving, involving discussions between the mediator and each of the disputants (Pruitt *et al.* 1989). However, there is one danger in caucusing: disputants may make derogatory statements about the other party – who is not present to refute them – and these statements may be misleading to the mediator (Pruitt *et al.* 1989; Welton *et al.* 1988).

Dealing with the issues is central to mediation. It includes identifying the issues, uncovering the negotiators' underlying interests and concerns, setting an agenda, packaging, sequencing and prioritizing the issues, interpreting and shaping proposals. One task facing Chuck in his mediation was what to do with the nineteen different issues on the table. Which issues should be considered first? Which issues were more or less important for each side? Which issues could be traded off with one another?

In dealing with the issues, mediators often seek out the interests and aspirations underlying the parties' positions and use this information to reconceptualize the issues under discussion. They are aided in this effort by the parties, who will share secrets with them that they refuse to reveal to the other side. Being in close touch with both parties' perspectives makes it possible for mediators to discover new, creative options that they can propose and that might actually solve the conflict (Kolb and Rubin 1991; Lax and Sebenius 1986; Raiffa 1983).

Some mediator behaviors are designed to reduce a party's resistance to making concessions or reaching agreements; for example, helping them to save face when making concessions (Johnson and Tullar 1972; Pruitt and Johnson 1970; Stevens 1963), helping them to deal with recalcitrant constituents (Wall 1981), or helping them to resolve internal disagreements, as mentioned in Chapter 10 (Lim and Carnevale 1990).

Chuck realized right away that the teacher negotiation team had internal disagreements. Rod, the chief negotiator, was having great difficulty dealing with a militant faction of teachers who had no interest at all in reaching agreement. To deal with this problem, Chuck met privately with Rod and the negotiation team and argued vehemently – including some fist pounding on the table – that such a militant approach was unacceptable. Chuck's persuasive appeals helped to fortify Rod's position as leader of the teacher negotiation team and bolstered Rod's cooperative approach to the negotiation.

Mediators sometimes also influence the parties' motivation to reach agreement by applying negative sanctions, threats, and arguments, or by adding positive incentives for agreement or concession making (Bercovitch 1984, 1989; Carnevale 1986; Lovell 1952; Touval and Zartman 1985).

Sometimes mediators actively attempt to remedy power imbalances. They can do this, for example, by encouraging the more passive party to speak up or by criticizing and challenging the more aggressive party. Interestingly, in a study by Ippolito and Pruitt (1990) the mediators were not perceived as biased, even though they were attempting to remedy power imbalances. Perhaps the balancing was seen as justified, or perhaps the disputants did not detect it. An important question is, "How far can a mediator go in 'tipping the scales' and still not be perceived as biased?" As mentioned earlier, this may be more of a problem in the context of emergent than contractual mediation.

Mediator behavior often unfolds over time in consistent patterns (Donohue 1991). Pruitt et al. (1989) have developed a three-stage descriptive model of mediation. Stage 1 is "setting the stage," which includes clarifying the ground rules and gathering information about the dispute. Stage 2 is "problem solving," which includes posing issues and generating alternatives. Stage 3 is "achieving a workable agreement," which includes pressing the parties to reach agreement. A similar stage model was reported by Shaw et al. (1973) and Landsberger (1955b).

Determinants of mediator behavior

Many factors can influence the mediator's decision about what strategies and tactics to use. Researchers agree that much mediator behavior is contingent on characteristics of the context, on mediator goals, and on mediator perceptions (Kressel and Pruitt 1989). Mediator behavior is often adaptive, in the sense that mediators often vary their tactics to suit the nature of the dispute and the events of the mediation session (Shapiro et al. 1985). Sheppard et al. (1989) have shown that mediators tend to emphasize fact finding and clarification of the issues when the disputants are interdependent and the issues are complex. But they tend to emphasize solution identification when they are concerned about efficiency or are in a position of authority over the disputants.

Basic strategies

Much of the work on typologies of mediator behavior provides descriptions of mediator behaviors but offers little in the way of explanation of why mediators do different things in different situations. To help explain why mediators make the choices that they do, Carnevale (1986) developed a simple classification of mediator behavior that connects some of the various tactics, using four basic strategies:

1 *Problem solving*, also referred to as integration, which involves efforts to discover a win–win solution that satisfies both parties' limits or major aspirations.
2 *Compensation*, which involves efforts to entice the parties into concessions or agreement by promising them rewards or benefits.
3 *Pressure*, which involves efforts to force the parties into concessions or agreements by punishment or the threat of punishment.
4 *Inaction*, which involves a conscious effort to let the parties handle the conflict on their own.

The focus of our next section is the important question of why mediators make the choices that they do – and the circumstances and conditions that influence mediator choice of strategy and tactics.

Concern-likelihood model

Carnevale (1986) has developed a strategic choice model to predict contingent mediator behavior. The model first classifies mediator behavior into the four basic strategies mentioned above: problem solving, compensation, pressure, and inaction. It postulates two antecedent variables that interact to predict mediator behavior: (a) the mediator's likelihood estimate of a win–win agreement ("perceived common ground"); and (b) the mediator's level of concern that the parties achieve their aspirations. The model is shown in Figure 11.1.

Mediators are predicted to emphasize an integrative (i.e. a problem-solving) strategy aimed at discovering win–win solutions when they have high concern for the parties' aspirations and perceive that the likelihood of a win–win agreement is high. They are predicted to use compensation to entice the parties into concessions

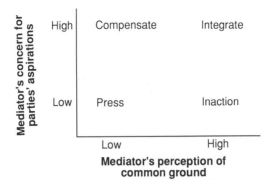

Figure 11.1 The concern-likelihood model of mediator behavior

and agreements when they have high concern for the parties' aspirations and perceive that the likelihood of a win–win agreement is low. They are predicted to employ pressure to force the parties to reduce their aspirations and make concessions when they have little concern for the parties' aspirations and perceive that the likelihood of a win–win agreement is low. Finally, they are predicted to be inactive – letting the parties handle the dispute on their own – when they have low concern for the parties' aspirations and perceive that the likelihood of a win–win agreement is high.

These predictions of the model incorporate effects noted in the literature. For example, several studies indicate that mediators become more active and forceful as the level of conflict increases (Donohue 1989; Landsberger 1955a, b). Imagine what Chuck would do if Rod lost his temper and began slamming his shoe on the table. Chuck might well raise his voice and shout that such behavior will not be tolerated, and any continuation of it will terminate the mediation. Chuck might add that he will give the news media a detailed account of Rod's disruptive behavior if it continues.

Research has supported and extended parts of the concern-likelihood model (Carnevale and Conlon 1988; Chaudhry and Ross 1989; Harris and Carnevale 1990). For example, Carnevale and Conlon (1988) found that mediators were less directive at first but shifted in the direction of pressure tactics and compensation tactics as time progressed and as time pressure increased. This was explained by a corresponding decrease in the mediator's perception of common ground. Wall and Rude (1991) found a similar effect for assertiveness in judicial mediation.

Of course, there are many other determinants of mediator behavior that the concern-likelihood model does not address. These include features of the context and mediator goals.

The context

The context, whether emergent or contractual, can play an important role in encouraging certain mediator behaviors and precluding others. A labor mediator, for example, can put pressure on the parties to make concessions, but can rarely give compensation to the negotiators. In contractual mediation, mediator training can be an important factor in predisposing mediators to a certain style of behavior. In emergent mediation, the range of possible mediator behaviors appears to be greater. Mediators is these contexts show a full range of social influence tactics (Touval 1985). Also in these contexts, mediator interests and biases often have a large impact on their behavior.

Mediator goals

It may be that some outcomes in mediation can only be achieved at the expense of others. If a mediator wants a quick settlement, having a goal of a win–win agreement may go by the wayside (Lissak and Sheppard 1983; Sheppard 1984; Thomas 1982). According to Lissak and Sheppard (1983: 63) in their discussion of various mediator goals, "It would be relatively difficult for any one procedure to satisfy all of these criteria. . . . The apparent incompatibility of some of these criteria suggests that different procedures may be necessary depending upon what criteria are particularly important in a given situation."

Effectiveness of mediation

We begin our review of the effectiveness of mediation by focusing on the overall impact of this procedure. Does mediation make a difference? We follow this with a discussion of the effectiveness of specific mediation tactics.

An important issue in the evaluation of mediation, and mediator behavior, is the definition of effectiveness. Lissak and Sheppard (1983) offer four criteria to evaluate intervention strategies: (a) fairness (concerns for equity, disputant control, protection of individual rights); (b) participant satisfaction (concern for the attainment of disputants' objectives, minimization of injury, participation, commitment); (c) general effectiveness (quality, permanence, implementability); and (d) efficiency (time and cost considerations as well as potential disruptions of other activities). With a few exceptions, researchers see agreement as the *sine qua non* of effectiveness.

General evaluation of mediation

Most of the research suggests that mediation is effective in general – agreements are usually reached, participants are ordinarily satisfied, and compliance is high (see Kressel and Pruitt 1989). However, this general question of the overall effectiveness of mediation is clearly too broad. More interesting research questions are "Under what circumstances is mediation effective?" and "Which mediation tactics are effective under various circumstances?"

Conditions in which mediation is effective

As is also true of negotiation, mediation is more effective when conflict is moderate rather than intense (Glasl 1982; Pruitt *et al.* 1992b), and when the parties are highly motivated to reach settlement, as they are in a "hurting stalemate" (Touval and Zartman 1985). As mentioned in Chapter 1, a dispute is a hurting stalemate when it reaches an intolerable impasse – so painful or costly that inaction is unthinkable – and the parties search for a way out, possibly through the help of a mediator.

Mediation is also more effective when the parties are committed to mediation (Hiltrop 1989), when there is not a severe resource shortage (Kochan and Jick 1978), when the issues do not involve general principles (Bercovitch 1989; Pruitt *et al.* 1989), and when the parties are relatively equal in power (Bercovitch 1989; but see Ippolito and Pruitt 1990 for a failure to find this effect).

Mediation has also been shown to be more effective when arbitration is threatened as a next step. In a field experiment at a community mediation center, McGillicuddy *et al.* (1987) compared mediation to two forms of mediation–arbitration: (a) med–arb(same), where the mediator becomes an arbitrator and issues a binding decision if agreement is not reached during mediation; and (b) med–arb(diff), where a fourth party, not present during mediation, becomes an arbitrator. The results indicated that the med–arb(same) condition produced the highest levels of problem solving and the lowest levels of hostility, although there were no differences in the likelihood of agreement.

Effectiveness of mediator behavior

Noncontingent effectiveness

Some kinds of mediator behavior appear to be effective regardless of the dispute situation. For example, in a study of labor mediation, Hiltrop (1985, 1989) found that mediators can control the communication between the parties and help the parties to understand one another's positions, and such efforts are positively related to settlement. Lim and Carnevale (1990) and Zubek *et al.* (1992) have found that mediator efforts to structure an agenda increase the chances of success in mediation. In our example, Chuck approached the task of agenda building by putting several simpler issues early in the discussion. This made it possible for the parties to reach agreement at an early stage in the mediation. Such an agenda produces "momentum," a belief that agreement is possible, which often contributes to achieving agreement on later, more difficult issues (Huber *et al.* 1986). Ross *et al.* (1990) reported that a friendly style of mediation was effective regardless of the time pressure on the disputants.

Mediators can help to overcome the problem of reactive devaluation (see Chapter 6), advancing as their own proposal a position that is acceptable to the other party but would be rejected if the other party put it forward (Stillinger *et al.* 1991). Conceding to the mediator instead of the other party also helps disputants to save face because it is less likely to be seen as a sign of weakness (Peters 1952). In addition, mediators can reduce negotiator optimism about the likelihood that the other party will make large concessions (Kochan and Jick 1978). As this kind of optimism declines, the parties are more likely to make concessions of their own, moving the controversy toward agreement.

There is evidence that, as mediators become more active or use more mediation tactics, they perceive that their efforts are more effective (Wall and Rude 1991).

Contingent effectiveness

The effectiveness of other kinds of mediator tactics seems to be contingent on the dispute circumstances (Shapiro *et al.* 1985). A broad generalization can be derived from all of the findings on this topic: direct, forceful mediator intervention is effective when the conflict between the disputants is so intense that they are unable to engage in joint problem solving. But such intervention is counter-productive when the disputants are capable of talking things over themselves.

The most direct evidence for this generalization comes from a study of divorce mediation by Donohue (1989), which showed that agreement was most likely to be reached if the mediator interrupted the disputants when their discussion was becoming more hostile and refrained from doing so when their discussion was becoming more friendly. Similar results were obtained for British labor mediation by Hiltrop (1985, 1989). Forceful, substantive mediator tactics were positively associated with reaching agreement when hostility was high, but negatively associated with reaching agreement when hostility was low. Hiltrop (1989) also found that efforts to improve communication and understanding between the parties were especially effective when hostility was high and positional differences were large.

Related to this are findings from a study of community mediation (Zubek *et al.* 1992). When there was high hostility and little joint problem solving by the disputants, agreement was more likely to be reached if the mediator stimulated thought by posing problems to be solved – challenging the parties to come up with new ideas, suggesting new ideas, and requesting reactions to new ideas. Lim and Carnevale (1990) reported similar results from a survey of US labor and community mediators. They also showed that pressure tactics (e.g. telling the parties that their positions are unrealistic) were positively associated with reaching agreement when conflict intensity was high, and negatively associated with reaching agreement when conflict intensity was low.

Timing of mediator behavior

Earlier we mentioned that mediators are advised to wait to enter the dispute until the parties are in a "hurting stalemate" in order to maximize their receptivity. However, Donohue (1991) argues that mediators need to intervene immediately if one disputant verbally attacks the other disputant in the presence of the mediator. If the mediator waits, an attack–defense spiral may develop, causing the conflict to escalate out of control. In addition, Bercovitch (1989) has found that, in international mediation, the more fatalities that have occurred as a result of the conflict, the less is achieved in mediation. This favors a pattern of early intervention when overt hostilities are imminent.

Long-term success

Most research in this field deals with the antecedents of short-term mediation success: reaching agreement, serving disputant goals, and producing immediate disputant satisfaction. One exception to this trend is a study by Pruitt et al. (1992b) that focused on the determinants of long-term success in community mediation: compliance with the terms of the agreement, improvement in the relationship between the parties, and the absence of new problems. Surprisingly, no relationship was found between short-term and long-term success: agreements that achieved the disputants' goals were no more effective in the long run than those that did not. The best predictors of long-term success were joint problem solving during the discussion and procedural justice, the disputants' perceptions that fair procedures were used in the mediation hearing and that they were given a chance to voice their concerns. We will return to this and related issues in Chapter 12.

Current areas of research

Several topics are currently the focus of research interest in mediation. These include mediator cognition and decision processes, mediator power, and negotiator behavior toward the mediator.

Mediator cognition and decision processes

Researchers have been interested in integrating recent work on information processing (see Chapter 6) into the study of mediation. Kolb and Rubin (1991) note that "it is possible from their third-party vantage point, they may assist disputants to become more rational and systematic in their negotiations."

Several studies suggest, however, that mediators are as susceptible to the same cognitive shortcomings as disputants, of the sort described in Chapter 6. Thompson (1991b) reported that neutral observers (e.g. mediators) were no more likely to understand the tradeoffs that were available in a negotiation task (i.e. logrolling potential) than were the negotiators. Consistent with the latter finding, Carnevale and Conlon (1988) reported that mediators in a laboratory study were poor judges of integrative potential. Mediators only recommended win–win agreements when the negotiators were already offering such agreements. In a field study, Carnevale and Pegnetter (1985) found that professional labor mediators were overconfident about the likelihood that they could resolve a dispute. This might be explained on the grounds that mediators tend to underestimate the negotiators' aspirations (Thompson 1991b).

Research derived from decision theory (e.g. Kahneman and Tversky 1979) suggests that mediators work harder to avoid a loss for themselves than to achieve a gain. Carnevale and Mead (1990) gave mediators either a positive decision frame (i.e. the mediators would gain money if the bargainers reached agreement) or a negative frame (i.e. they would lose money if the bargainers did not reach agreement). Mediators who had something to lose adopted more forceful tactics than those who had something to gain, even though the money they could earn in each case was identical.

Mediator power

Mediator power sometimes stems from reputation and authority and sometimes from the capacity to reward or punish the disputants (Carnevale 1986; Kressel and Pruitt 1989; Touval and Zartman 1985). Power has been found to encourage mediators to use more forceful tactics. For example, community mediators who had the capacity to arbitrate were especially likely to use threats and heavy advocacy (McGillicuddy et al. 1987). This is consistent with the finding that judges who mediate often use strong-arm tactics (Wall and Rude 1989). It is also consistent with a recent finding by Conlon *et al.* (1993). In a laboratory study, mediators who could impose an outcome were more likely than other mediators to use forceful, pressure tactics, and were also more confident and saw themselves as more influential. Powerful mediators imposed outcomes in 66 per cent of the cases, doing so more often when they viewed the disputants as uncooperative than as cooperative. Only 44 per cent of the imposed outcomes reflected the disputants' underlying interests, but this was greater when the powerful mediator had high compared to low concern for the disputants' aspirations.

Mediator power also affects disputant behavior. Harris and Carnevale (1990) found that when mediators made suggestions, mediators with punitive power were more effective in eliciting concessions than mediators without punitive power and mediators who only had reward power. Sometimes disputants have power over the mediator, as when a labor negotiator can influence the mediator's reputation with other labor negotiators. Welton and Pruitt (1987) found that disputants who had high power over a mediator were more accepting of the mediator and behaved less contentiously, but they were also less influenced by the mediator.

Negotiator behavior toward the mediator

Several studies indicate that negotiators use concession making in an effort to influence the mediator's choice of strategy. Negotiators sometimes make concessions in order to avoid the intervention of a potentially coercive mediator (Hiltrop and Rubin 1982; Harris and Carnevale 1990). By contrast, they tend to reduce their concession making when faced with a mediator who can provide rewards in the future (Harris and Carnevale 1990; Idaszak and Carnevale 1989), perhaps with the thought of later trading their concessions for rewards. Rubin (1981) and Touval and Zartman (1985) cite instances of this in international mediation.

A happy ending

We end this chapter on a happy note. Rod and Mary, as representatives of the teachers' association and school board, were successful in their negotiation, with Chuck's help. Their words were music to Chuck's ears: "We want to give this conflict up, Chuck – we have a solution that we can live with." Not only did Rod and Mary discover a win–win agreement but they learned enough about problem solving that they were confident that they could handle any future disputes on their own, without the help of a third party. And that may be the ultimate test of the effectiveness of a mediator: the parties are able to resolve future conflicts on their own.

Summary and implications

Mediation is an extension of negotiation, where a third party helps the negotiators reach their own agreement. Sometimes mediation is *contractual*, where the mediator has a short-term relationship with the parties and is primarily concerned about settlement. At other times, mediation is *emergent*: the mediator is a member of the social system with the disputants, expects to interact with them in the future, and has interests in the outcome of the negotiation. In the latter case, the issue of *mediator bias* takes on a different meaning (Touval and Zartman 1985, 1989). It is often tolerated by the negotiators.

Researchers have identified many specific mediator tactics that can have a positive impact on negotiation. And recent theorizing has had some success in predicting the occurrence of these behaviors. Many mediator behaviors are used in a contingent manner, and their effectiveness depends on features of the dispute context.

Research on mediation is in its infancy. There are many important questions that have incomplete answers. Many mediation tactics have been identified, and studies that assess their effectiveness usually focus on the effects of a single tactic or set of tactics that reflect the same underlying theme, e.g. pressure tactics. Few studies have examined the impact of combinations of mediator tactics on negotiation, either simultaneous or in sequence. But it is likely that mediator behavior has multiple effects. It is often a two-way street, affecting both the disputants and the mediator. For example, listening carefully to a disputant's views on an issue will very likely lead the mediator to understand better the issues and the disputant's interests (see Johnson 1971). But it may also convey an impression of sincerity and competence, which may increase the chances that the disputant will be more responsive to the mediator's suggestions at a later point in the mediation. In addition, the use of mediator tactics is not mutually exclusive. Several can occur at the same time. For example, conducting a caucus may simultaneously allow the mediator to develop rapport with one party and enhance that party's understanding of the other's position, and give the mediator an opportunity to offer that party an incentive for concession making.

Mediation often occurs in the context of a broad set of choices of dispute handling procedures. In our next chapter, we look at disputant preferences among various procedures for addressing conflict – including negotiation, mediation, arbitration, and struggle. We also look at the organization of dispute resolution systems that encourage an optimal mixture of these procedures.

Suggestions for further reading

Bercovitch, J. (1984). *Social conflicts and third parties: Strategies of conflict resolution*. Boulder, CO: Westview Press.

Donohue, W. A. (1991). *Communication, marital dispute and divorce mediation*. Hillsdale, NJ: Lawrence Erlbaum.

Duffy, K. G., Grosch, J. W. and Olczak, P. W. (eds) (1991). *Community mediation: A handbook for practitioners and researchers*. New York: Guilford.

Kressel, K. and Pruitt, D. G. (eds) (1989). *Mediation research*. San Francisco: Jossey-Bass.

Touval, S. and Zartman, I. W. (1985). *International mediation in theory and practice*. Boulder, CO: Westview Press.

Touzard, H. (1977). *La mediation et la resolution des conflicts* (Mediation and the resolution of conflicts). Paris: PUF.

12 / CHOICES AMONG PROCEDURES IN SOCIAL CONFLICT

This chapter focuses on the choices people make among the procedures that are available for dealing with conflict. Procedures are shared activities, entered into by the disputants with the aim of coping with perceived divergences of interest. Negotiation and mediation are among the available procedures; hence, this chapter will in part examine the origins of negotiation and mediation.

In Chapter 1, we mentioned three main classes of procedures: joint decision making, third party decision making, and separate action. The procedures that have received attention within these classes are:

Joint decision making
- Negotiation
- Mediation

Third party decision making
- Adjudication
- Arbitration
- Autocratic decision making

Separate action
- Retreat
- Struggle
- Tacit coordination

The following is an example of a case involving choices among all but one of these alternatives. Two neighbors are in a dispute because one claims that the other is playing the radio too loud and the other claims that the first is using his or her lawn as a junk yard. Negotiation would involve talking these issues over, and mediation would involve doing so with the help of a third party.

Adjudication would involve going to court, while arbitration would involve a hearing and decision by an official of lesser rank than a judge. (Both mediators and arbitrators are available in many communities.) It would be autocratic decision making if the third party gathered the information rather than inviting testimony in a hearing. However, this procedure is not available in any community we know, though it is used in many organizations. If one of the neighbors simply gave in and turned down the radio or cleaned up the yard, it would be yielding. It would be struggle if one or both of them employed harassing moves, such as making anonymous late night phone calls, or tried to get other members of the community to bring additional pressure. Finally, it would be tacit coordination if the two parties tried to work out an exchange of concessions without talking – for example, if one turned down the radio somewhat and the other reciprocated with some cleaning of the lawn.

At any given point in negotiation, disputants may differ in their preferences among these procedures. But with the single exception of retreat, they almost always end up using the same procedure. This is because joint decision making, third party decision making, and tacit coordination require that both parties participate. Struggle is the default procedure if the parties cannot agree on any of the others; and one party's decision to engage in struggle almost always brings out struggle in the other for reasons of self-defense.

Theory and research about choices among procedures has focused on one or another subset of those just listed. There are two traditions: one *normative*, providing advice about what procedures should be employed, the other *descriptive*, providing information about the circumstances that determine what procedures will be employed.

Designing dispute resolution systems

A strong normative tradition has emerged in the area of procedural choice, involving advice to third parties about how to design dispute resolution systems. Its proponents (Ury *et al.* 1988) argue that the joint decision making procedures (they call them the "interest oriented approach") are usually the best ones to use because they allow disputants to reconcile their separate interests. This encourages the development of win–win solutions that are satisfying and lasting, and that contribute to a positive future relationship. The authors contrast these procedures with third party decision making (the "rights-oriented approach"), which can damage the relationship between the parties, and struggle (the "power-oriented approach"), which can be very costly and often produces escalatory spirals.

Another argument in favor of joint decision making is that the other two approaches often create additional problems. Evidence of this comes from a study by Lewin (1987), which showed that filing a grievance in an organization (seeking a third party decision) led to negative outcomes (e.g. less likelihood of promotion) for both the employee who filed the grievance and the supervisor who was the target of the grievance, regardless of who won the grievance. Carnevale et al. (1992) replicated this effect in a laboratory simulation of an organizational grievance system and further showed the importance of informality in such systems. Students played the role of a manager and received a grievance from a subordinate (actually a confederate). When the grievance was handled in a formal manner (it was delivered via a written document), negative outcomes were more likely than when the *same* grievance was handled informally (in a private discussion).

Occasionally, according to Ury et al. (1988), joint decision making is infeasible because of special circumstances, such as the following: (a) joint decision making is impossible because one or both parties will not participate; (b) joint decision making is unlikely to produce an agreement because principles are very strong, power ambiguity is great, or there is no middle ground; (c) an authoritative decision is needed in a matter of public policy. In these cases, one of the other procedures is needed.

These authors describe a third party role that goes beyond the traditional roles of mediator and arbitrator: the designer of social systems that will get disputants into productive joint problem solving. Disputants can also design such systems for themselves. An example of such a system was one these authors set up at a coal mine for dealing with persistent grievances that had previously produced a number of antagonistic work stoppages. According to these authors, such systems should have the following characteristics:

1 Provide for an early discussion of differences.
2 Include several negotiation partners on each side, in the hope that at least one channel will become operational during a crisis.

3 Provide for a multi-step negotiation in which "a dispute that is not resolved at one level of the organizational hierarchy moves to progressively higher levels, with different negotiators involved at each step" (Ury *et al.* 1988: 45).

4 Give potential negotiators enough authority that people on the other side will find it worthwhile dealing with them.

5 Provide easy access to intermediaries (e.g. ombudsmen, mediators) who can encourage negotiation or coordinate the development of a consensus.

6 Teach the disputants problem solving skills – how to listen, probe for interests, explore creative options.

7 Build in "loop-backs" to negotiation, which move disputants from a rights or a power orientation to an interest orientation. Among the loop-back mechanisms they recommend are:

   (a) Cooling-off periods, in which hostilities are temporarily suspended at a point where, "the parties are on the verge of a costly power contest or are in the midst of one" (Ury *et al.* 1988: 54). During cooling-off periods, disputants get a chance to think more clearly about the relative advantages of negotiation in contrast to the struggle to which they seem committed.

   (b) Active mediation, in which potential third parties search for emerging disputes and quickly offer their services.

   (c) Advisory arbitration, a hybrid procedure in which disputants satisfy their rights orientation by getting an arbitrator's opinion about the issues, but are then encouraged to negotiate their differences.

   (d) Med–arb, another hybrid procedure in which disputants who seek arbitration are encouraged to allow the third party to try mediation first.

8 Start with low cost procedures and move to high cost procedures only if they do not work.

Critique

The notion of designing dispute resolution systems has the virtue of changing our focus of attention. Most of the normative literature (reviewed in many sections of this book) provides advice to negotiators and mediators about *how to behave* in the conflict at hand. The systems design approach seeks to advise third parties and disputants about *how to set up conditions that will encourage proper behavior* at a later time when conflict arises.

The guidelines just listed seem effective for encouraging negotiation and mediation rather than arbitration, adjudication, and struggle. Hence, it makes sense to install such systems in circumstances where struggle is potentially injurious to the two parties or the broader community, or where a third party's decision may destroy a useful relationship. However, injurious outcomes are not inevitable; and arbitration, adjudication, and struggle sometimes make sense even when negotiation and mediation are feasible. While most people would object to brothers going to court against each other or management thugs beating up strikers, it is harder to argue that a court suit should not be launched against a vendor who has taken money without providing services, or that unions should never strike to achieve wages that are equal to those achieved by other comparable workers.

In short, dispute resolution systems are important innovations. But they are not a universal elixir.

Preferences among procedures

A series of empirical studies has been done to assess the determinants of people's feelings about the procedures that are available in conflict and their preferences among them.

Procedural justice

A persistent finding in this research is that arbitration is preferred over autocratic decision making (Houlden *et al.* 1978; LaTour *et al.* 1976; Lind *et al.* 1980; Thibaut *et al.* 1974). Thibaut and Walker (1975) have interpreted these findings as showing that people place a value on *process control*, the capacity to regulate the events in a conflict resolution procedure. In their view, the most critical element of process control is *voice*, the right to present one's viewpoint to a third party. They argue that process control is valued because it produces a sense of *procedural justice*; in other words, a sense that fair procedures have been used.

These conclusions have held up well in subsequent research

on decisions made by authorities such as policemen, judges, and superiors in organizations (Lind and Tyler 1988). It has been shown that the sense of procedural justice is equal to, and in some studies more important than, gain to the self as a determinant of satisfaction with these decisions. A sense of procedural justice is also antecedent to satisfaction with the system of which these authorities are a part (Alexander and Ruderman 1987; Tyler 1984). Tyler (1987a) has presented evidence that voice is most effective in producing a sense of procedural justice if it is believed that the authority has considered one's viewpoint in making his or her decision. Other research has shown that voice and perceived procedural justice encourage compliance and long-term satisfaction with agreements reached in mediation (McGillicuddy *et al.* 1992).

Other findings on procedural preferences

Another finding in the early research was that subjects preferred arbitration to negotiation and advisory arbitration. Houlden *et al.* (1978) interpreted these preferences as suggesting that people generally like to give third parties *decision control*, the capacity to make the final decision in a controversy. However, these findings have not always been replicated; nor is arbitration consistently chosen over mediation, as would be expected if there were a general preference for third party decision control (Arnold and Carnevale 1992; Heuer and Penrod 1986; Leung 1987; Peirce *et al.* 1991; Valley 1990). Furthermore, naturalistic studies have shown that people who have experienced mediation generally prefer this procedure over court, a form of arbitration (Brett and Goldberg 1983; Roehl and Cook 1989). Hence, it appears that there are *no general preferences* among arbitration, mediation and negotiation. Instead, preferences among these procedures seem to depend on the situation.

Evidence about the impact of the situation comes from studies of both disputant and third party preferences. One consistent finding is that time pressure increases attraction to arbitration (LaTour *et al.* 1976; Lewicki and Sheppard 1985; Sheppard *et al.* 1989). Peirce (1990) also found that time pressure encouraged third parties to have a preference for autocratic decision over arbitration. It appears that people – probably realistically – view autocratic decision making as the most time-efficient procedure, followed by arbitration, and then negotiation and mediation. Sheppard *et al.* (1989) also found that third parties tended to favor arbitration over negotiation and mediation when the dispute was complex and important.

Another common finding is that mediation is preferred over arbitration and struggle when it is necessary for the disputants to cooperate in the future. This has been shown in organizational settings in the USA (Lewicki and Sheppard 1985; Sheppard *et al.* 1989) and is echoed in the anthropological literature. For example, Collier (1973) and Witty (1980), studying two distinct societies, found that disputants preferred mediation over court hearings for claims against members of their own village but not members of other villages. In a study of three nonindustrial societies, Merry (1989) found that mediation was preferred to violence (a form of struggle) when the disputants were members of the same family or were residents of the same village. These were societies in which violence is ordinarily employed to settle a wide range of disputes, including those over debts, breach of contract, adultery, trespass, and murder. But mediation was preferred in close relationships, presumably because it helps to preserve the disputants' capacity to live together amicably in the future. Struggle and arbitration, being adversarial, are more likely than mediation to destroy a relationship.

Given the danger to relationships posed by other procedures, it is not surprising that joint decision making is considered the most normative approach to dealing with everyday controversies in our society. This conclusion is based, in part, on a laboratory study in which the subjects played the roles of a student and a professor in a controversy about what would be covered on the final examination (Peirce *et al.* 1991). Subjects rated negotiation and mediation as the most "proper approach to take, that is, the way one ought to or should behave." Arbitration was viewed as the next most proper procedure, followed by inaction (doing nothing) and struggle, in that order. The actual preferences among these procedures were consistent with these normative judgments: joint decision procedures were preferred over arbitration, which was preferred over inaction and struggle. In another set of ratings, subjects overwhelmingly endorsed struggle (e.g. threats) as advantageous to their self-interest. Nevertheless, they placed struggle *last* in their preference ordering, probably because it seemed so counter-normative.

Another finding in this study was that respondents (the targets of a complaint, in this case the professors) were more favorable to inaction than were complainants (those bringing a complaint, in this case the students). This appeared to be a matter of self-interest. In the setting studied, as is often the case, the status quo favored the respondents, making inaction a way to win. In addition, there was some evidence that the complainants had a stronger preference for third party procedures as a whole than did the respondents, who were more partial to negotiation. This may have been due to the fact that the respondents (the professors) had authority over the complainants (the students). Similarly, Valley (1990) has found that disputants with greater authority in a firm are less likely to endorse third party intervention in a controversy and more likely to endorse negotiation. Arnold and Carnevale (1992) found that a lower status individual in a conflict judged the higher status individual as less likely to prefer third party intervention. This is presumably because third parties tend to treat disputants as equals in our society, which may disrupt authority relationships that exist between the disputants.

Sequences of preferences

The study just described and interviews with real-life disputants (Arnold and Carnevale 1992; Pruitt *et al.* 1992a; Sarat 1976) show that people in conflict often go through a sequence of procedures, turning to a new procedure if the old one is ineffective. Such sequences ordinarily begin with negotiation – in the sense of talking with the other party. If this fails, third parties may be approached to intervene with the other party. Only if these two procedures fail do disputants seek binding arbitration (e.g. go to court) or turn to struggle tactics. This progression of procedures seems to move from low risk to high risk. Arbitration is more risky than negotiation in two ways: the process and outcome of arbitration are more likely to disrupt the relationship between the disputants; and decision control is lost in arbitration, making it possible that this decision will totally favor the other party. Struggle is more risky than negotiation because of the danger to relationships and the potential for escalation.

Summary and implications

The systems design perspective assumes that negotiation and mediation, the main topics of this book, are of great significance. Third party decision making may be a way to find out who is right, and struggle may be a way to find out who is more powerful. But these procedures run some risks, and only joint decision procedures are fully capable of locating hidden alternatives that provide benefit to both sides. The value of joint decision making can clearly be overstated. Sometimes third parties need to step in to clarify rights or provide speedy action, and sometimes there is more to be gained from struggle than can possibly be achieved by discussion. But negotiation and mediation are clearly powerful medicine. It is hoped that the contents of this book will make this medicine more useful and more generally available than heretofore.

Perhaps the best way to summarize the findings on procedural preference is to ask what they imply about the design of dispute resolution systems. Some of these findings suggest that voice and a sense of procedural justice are important for the success of all dispute resolution procedures. This has been shown repeatedly for various kinds of third party decision making, and a recent study has found the same dynamics in mediation (Pruitt *et al.* 1992b). Other research suggests that third parties (e.g. managers, officials) are tempted to take over decision making when there is high time pressure and when they perceive that the dispute is complex and important (Sheppard *et al.* 1989). Such takeovers run the risk that the disputants will feel they have little voice, which will often alienate them from the process and the decision. Hence, designers of dispute resolution systems need to develop plans for counteracting these tendencies.

We have reviewed a number of findings suggesting that people in close relationships prefer joint decision making procedures over third party decision and struggle. This seems rational, since the latter procedures run a greater risk of alienating the disputants from each other. This suggests that it is particularly important to develop systems that encourage negotiation and mediation for people who are in close relationships, especially if they must rely on each other in the future.

We turn now to our final chapter, a review of some of our most important conclusions. In it, we point to some deficiencies in existing theory and research, as well as some opportunities for further development of knowledge in this area.

Suggestions for further reading

Lewin, D. and Peterson, R. B. (1988). *The modern grievance procedure in the United States: A theoretical and empirical analysis*. Westport, CT: Quorum.

Lind, E. A. and Tyler, T. R. (1988). *The Social Psychology of Procedural Justice*. New York: Plenum.

Sheppard, B. H., Blumenfeld-Jones, K. and Roth, J. (1989). Informal thirdpartyship: studies of everyday conflict intervention. In K. Kressel and D. G. Pruitt (eds), *Mediation Research*. San Francisco: Jossey-Bass, pp. 166–89.

Thibaut, J. and Walker, L. (1975). *Procedural Justice: A Psychological Analysis*. Hillsdale, NJ: Erlbaum.

Ury, W. L., Brett, J. M. and Goldberg, S. B. (1988). *Getting disputes resolved: Designing systems to cut the costs of conflict*. San Francisco: Jossey-Bass.

$\Big/13\Big/$ CONCLUSIONS

In this book we have described and attempted to integrate the behavioral literature on negotiation. Our aim was to present a behavioral analysis of this topic, detailing the conditions that determine the ways that negotiators behave and the effects of this behavior. In this chapter, we step back to take an overview of this product, assess its strengths and weaknesses, and examine the prospects for future research and theory on negotiation.

Here, we briefly review the dominant theoretical paradigm in negotiation, its limitations, and our efforts to expand it. Next, we point out some further gaps we have detected in current research and theory on negotiation, and some prospects for future research to fill those gaps. We also review in some detail Morley's critique of the dominant theoretical paradigm (Morley 1986, 1992; Morley et al. 1988). Morley's critique provides a fundamental challenge to this paradigm in rejecting the view (implied in Figure 1.1) that negotiation is a sequence of tactics that moves the parties toward an agreement. This is a much more fundamental critique than ours and could possibly lead to a complete reconceptualization of negotiation.

Overview of current theory and research

In Chapter 1, we presented the dominant theoretical paradigm that underlies much of the behavioral research and theory on negotiation. While recognizing that this paradigm paints a simplistic picture (see the diagram in Figure 1.1), we used it as a model of thought to organize the first half of this book. In Chapter 2, we examined the issues under discussion in negotiation, the possible outcomes of negotiation, and other settings that involve a divergence of interest ("games of moves").

Working within the dominant paradigm, some researchers and theorists have focused their attention on *tactics* and their effect on negotiation *outcomes* (path D in Figure 1.1). These tactics include holding firm, conceding, and the various forms that contending and problem solving can take. The work of these investigators was summarized in Chapter 3.

Other investigators have looked at various conditions that have an impact on the choice of tactics and the outcome of negotiation. Two kinds of psychological processes are assumed to be affected by these conditions. Many investigators stress human *motivation* – emphasizing constructs such as goals and limits, hostility toward the other party, and fear of being a sucker (Chapters 4 and 5). Other investigators emphasize *cognitive* processes, such as availability, framing, and the fixed-pie perception (Chapter 6).

Limitations of the dominant paradigm

In the course of writing this book, we have mentioned limitations of the dominant theoretical paradigm just described and have tried to expand the paradigm. All of the limitations can be traced to a historical accident, the fact that this paradigm had its origin in mathematical models aimed at providing advice to negotiators about how to maximize their self-interest. One main limitation of the dominant paradigm is its reliance on a self-interest assumption, and we have drawn attention to the importance of other-interest in negotiation (Chapter 7). Other limitations that we have addressed pertain to the social context of negotiation, including social norms (Chapter 8), relationships (Chapter 9), group processes (Chapter 10), mediators (Chapter 11), and the broad set of conflict-handling choices within which negotiation is but one (Chapter 12). Here, we say a few more words about our efforts to expand the paradigm in each of these directions.

Other-interest in negotiation

A main limitation of the dominant paradigm is the premise that negotiators are only motivated by *self-interest*. This premise may be valid for negotiations between parties who have little in common and no other relationship. But many negotiations are not of this kind; they involve parties who have some degree of genuine or strategic concern about the other party's welfare ("other-interest" or "other-concern"). Furthermore, it turns out that other-interest affects the way that many of the variables function in negotiation. Limit level, time pressure, accountability, negative framing, and various negotiator strategies such as sequential versus simultaneous consideration of the issues have a different impact on negotiators who are solely self-interested and those who have some other-interest as well. The dual-concern model (Chapter 7), which takes the degree of other-interest into account, moves us beyond this limitation of the dominant paradigm.

Other limitations of the dominant paradigm deal with the social context of negotiation. These include the absence of focused research interest on norms, relationships, group processes and networks, third parties such as mediators, and procedural choice.

Norms

The traditional theoretical model (shown in Figure 1.1) ignores the social context in which negotiation takes place, and ignores norms. Social norms have a huge impact on negotiation, shaping offers and arguments, and the outcomes of negotiation. We have worked on this limitation in Chapter 8 by focusing on: (a) principles of fairness that encourage, among other effects, efforts to achieve equal outcomes and concessions; (b) the facilitating effects on negotiation when negotiators concur on what principles are applicable and how to interpret these principles; (c) the inhibiting effects on negotiation when opposing principles are advocated on either side; and (d) methods to satisfy both parties' principles and to shift negotiations from discussion of principles to concrete issues.

Relationships

A third limitation of the dominant paradigm is its view of negotiation as a stand-alone process, divorced from the ongoing relationship between the parties. We have worked on this limitation in Chapter 9 by focusing on: (a) the way positive and negative relationships between the parties affect cognitions as well as choices among tactics in negotiation; and (b) the nature and origins of such relationships.

Group processes and networks

A fourth limitation of the dominant paradigm is that it often fails to distinguish between individuals and groups (the term includes organizations) as parties to the negotiation. This distinction is an important one to make, because groups and organizations make decisions in different ways from individuals, and because they usually deal with each other through representatives. We have tried to relieve this limitation in Chapter 10, on group processes in negotiation. This chapter introduced our greatest departure from the dominant paradigm: a systems model of negotiation between organizations, which views negotiation as the product of conversations in various arenas that are linked by a broad communication network embracing the organizations.

Mediation

Communications networks often include mediators (Chapter 11). Aside from the influence of negotiation theory, the study of mediation has been mainly descriptive. Most writers have confined their efforts to the development of isolated theoretical propositions that fit one data set, or at the most two. An exception to this trend is the concern-likelihood model of mediator choice presented in Chapter 11, which implies a number of hypotheses and has been successfully tested in several studies.

Since mediation is assisted negotiation, it seems worthwhile to try to develop an integrated theory that embraces both negotiation and mediation. A possible basis for such a theory might be the systems model of negotiation between organizations presented in Chapter 10. This model focuses on multiple discussion arenas linked in a communication network. The entry of a mediator produces two new arenas, between the mediator and each of the two negotiators. By this analysis, the likelihood that the mediator can be of any assistance depends on the strength of these new arenas, which rests on the extent to which the mediator gains information about both sides' perspectives, speaks both parties' language, and is trusted by both parties.

Negotiation as a choice among procedures

Another limitation of the dominant paradigm is its failure to examine alternatives to negotiation and how the parties choose among them. We have dealt with this limitation in Chapters 1 and 12 in a discussion of procedural preference. Three broad classes of procedures were distinguished: joint decision making (negotiation and mediation), separate action (struggle, tacit coordination, retreat), and third party decision making (decision by judges, arbitrators, higher executives).

Prospects for future research

The goal of this section is to spark interest in areas of research that we believe will help fill gaps in current knowledge of negotiation. In pointing to these areas of research, we do not intend to map out a research agenda that dictates what research should be done, because such an effort could easily suppress creative, new efforts. But we do want to point to some areas that seem quite underdeveloped and that offer exciting opportunities for future study.

Cultural similarities and differences

We have not said much about the cultural context of negotiation and mediation in this book. There is evidence for cross-cultural similarities and differences in negotiation behavior (Cohen 1991; Gulliver 1979, 1988; Roth *et al.* 1991) and in preferences among dispute resolution procedures (Leung 1987). Mediation is a prominent feature of many non-western societies (Cohen 1966), and there is evidence that it can change from one cultural context to another (Wall and Blum 1991). Hence, it seems important to develop a theory of negotiation and mediation that allows for cultural variation. A mature theory should also help us to understand what happens in negotiation between representatives of different cultures and how to overcome the problems in such negotiation (Dupont and Faure 1991). Preliminary efforts in this direction have mainly involved efforts to characterize the negotiation styles found in various cultures (e.g. Weiss and Stripp 1985). There are a few broader overviews of the impact of cultural variables (Cohen 1991; Janosik 1987), but this field of study is still in its infancy.

One perspective on cultural differences in negotiation derives from the theory of collectivism and individualism (Triandis 1989). Chan *et al.* (1992) had subjects in Hong Kong and the USA negotiate with a friend or a stranger in the integrative bargaining task shown in Table 1.1. Consistent with the theory, the results indicated that negotiators in the collectivist culture (Hong Kong) were more sensitive to ingroup/outgroup differences than negotiators in the individualist culture (United States). Negotiators in Hong Kong were more cooperative in dealing with a friend and more competitive in dealing with a stranger, compared to negotiators in Champaign, Illinois.

Individual differences

We have not said much about individual differences in negotiation and mediation. The study of personality and other individual differences in negotiation has had a mixed history. Earlier efforts to relate broad personality variables to negotiation behavior yielded a confusing and inconsistent pattern (Pruitt 1981; Rubin and Brown 1975). However, there are indications in research on the prisoner's dilemma (e.g. Kuhlman and Marshello 1975) and on the dual concern model (see Chapter 7) that direct measures of the strength of self-concern, other-concern, and joint-concern will be related to negotiation behavior. We discussed the literature on individual differences in conflict style in Chapter 7. We also discussed literature on trust as a personality variable in Chapter 9. Negotiation studies should begin to incorporate these measures (see Rahim 1986; van de Vliert and Prein 1989; Yamagishi and Sato 1986).

The results on gender differences are also inconsistent. Some studies show that men are more likely than women to adopt a forceful style in both negotiation and mediation (Kimmel *et al.* 1980; Lim and Carnevale 1990), and that negotiation is likely to produce better outcomes for men than for women (Gerhart and

Rynes 1991). Other studies show no differences between men and women in negotiation behavior and outcome (Pruitt *et al.* 1986). The theoretical variables underlying gender differences are unclear; but the absence of clear-cut findings suggests that gender interacts with personality and situational variables. An example of such an interaction is the finding that women who held traditional sex-role attitudes did more poorly in negotiation with their romantic partners when they had low aspirations but not when their aspirations were high (Williams and Lewis 1976).

Multilateral negotiation

Multilateral negotiation, involving more than two parties, is a common phenomenon that is becoming increasingly important as international organizations grow in prominence and more and more actors become involved in domestic issues (Touval 1989). However, there is very little research on this topic, probably because the dominant theoretical paradigm assumed two parties.

There are only a few laboratory experiments on multilateral negotiation, with occasional extensions of the bilateral theory to three-person (Mannix *et al.* 1989) and five-person (Weingart *et al.* 1993) negotiation (see Esser *et al.* 1990). Druckman (1991) has done a statistical study of a multilateral arms control conference involving two coalitions of nations. One of his findings was that as members of one coalition became firmer in their statements, members of the other coalition became less diverse in the positions they advocated. Both Winham (1991) and Morley (1982) observe that multilateral negotiation creates cognitive problems well beyond those encountered in bilateral negotiation. Kramer (1991b) presents a very useful analysis of the general characteristics and problems of multi-party negotiation, including the number of parties involved, complexity of decision making (e.g. agreement by simple majority versus consensus), and heterogeneity, which refers to the number of distinct social categories represented in the negotiation (e.g. men versus women, old versus young). Certainly one important feature of multilateral negotiation is the opportunity for coalitions to form (Komorita 1984).

In recent years mediated multilateral negotiation has become prominent in the United States (Susskind and Ozawa 1985). Disputes about the siting of dams, oil wells and the like are often settled that way because of the large number of interests involved. The same is true of some disputes about the allocation of public resources. Gray (1989) has published a book on the dynamics of such procedures. Among the tasks mediators must often perform in such settings are finding all the parties ("stake holders") who have an interest in the issues under consideration, seeking agreement on a body of ground rules, and advising the representatives about how to deal with their constituents.

Negotiation support systems (NSS)

The use of computers in the conduct of negotiation and mediation is an interesting new development in the field. A number of computerized expert systems have been developed which accept data relevant to a particular negotiation and provide it to negotiators on demand. Kolodner and Simpson (1989), for example, developed a program called MEDIATOR, which uses case-based reasoning for different tasks in problem solving, where previous solutions to problems are remembered and adapted to fit new cases.

Other efforts by Poole *et al.* (1991) and Nyhart and Samarasan (1989) on support systems for negotiation extend concepts from group decision making to negotiation. Hollingshead and McGrath (1992) and McGrath and Hollingshead (1993) provide reviews and theoretical synthesis of the literature on computer support systems for group decision making. Nyhart and Samarasan (1989) report some success in assisting negotiators by using computers in complex multilateral negotiations. Although it is far from conclusive, there is evidence that computer structuring can have both positive and negative effects on negotiation. Arunachalam (1991) reported that computer-mediated negotiations took longer to complete, were more hostile, and led to poorer outcomes than face-to-face negotiation, although negotiators with a computer-based structure showed marked improvement in outcomes over repeated negotiations. Clearly more work is needed in this area.

Pre- and post-negotiation phases

There are almost always preliminary activities before negotiation starts. The individual parties must decide to seek negotiation

(Zartman and Berman 1982). Then they must decide what issues are to be discussed and where they stand on them. Pre-negotiation meetings between the parties are often held to continue this process. Writing about international negotiations, Druckman (1986; see also Druckman and Mahoney 1977) describes such meetings as involving efforts to reach agreement on rules of conduct, the issues to be discussed later, and the order in which these issues are to be discussed. He also argues that such meetings provide an opportunity for the parties to obtain information about one another's intentions. Sjostedt (1991) suggests that pre-negotiation preparations are more important and take longer the greater the complexity of the issues. Of all the realms in which negotiation can take place, the international probably involves the most complex issues. Hence, it is not surprising to learn that preparation for international negotiation often takes months or even years.

There has been very little research on pre-negotiation activities. This is probably because the dominant theoretical paradigm in negotiation research assumes that the issues have already been determined and focuses on negotiator efforts to reach substantive agreements about these issues. Decrying this gap in theory, Saunders (1985), a retired foreign service officer, writes

> This article is written from the perspective of someone who spent much of two decades dealing with the Arab-Israeli-Palestinian conflict, where most of the parties refuse to talk or even to recognize each other. In my opinion, negotiating theory that concentrates only on what happens around the negotiating table does not provide the President and Secretary of State as useful a theory of negotiation as they need to conduct the nation's foreign policy. (Saunders 1985: 249)

A theory of the pre-negotiation phases might build, in part, on the analysis of procedural preference presented in Chapters 1 and 12 of this book.

Saunders (1985: 261) also points out that we are woefully ignorant about the post-negotiation period and the events during negotiation that shape it. In his words, "The implementation of any agreement is an important part of the negotiating process." Negotiated agreements can be considered as new norms. Hence, the ideas on norm enforcement presented at the end of Chapter 8 may be a useful building block in the construction of a theory in this area.

Morley's critique: Room for a new view

In this our last section, we point to a current criticism of negotiation theory that may ultimately lead to a fundamental shift in
how negotiation is construed and investigated. Morley (1986, 1992;
Morley *et al.* 1988) has developed a much more fundamental
critique of the dominant theoretical paradigm than is embodied in
the criticisms mentioned above. An important element of his critique
is rejection of the view (implied in Figure 1.1) that negotiation
can be adequately understood as a sequence of tactics employed
by the two parties on the road to an agreement. Rather, he sees
negotiation as an event in an ongoing relationship in which the
parties decide whether, and in what direction, to change their
relationship. The critical dynamic in this process is not a progression of tactical choices but an effort to make sense of the situation
and to develop "a collective rationale, linking what is happening
now to what has happened in the past and what needs to happen
in the future" (Morley 1992: 206). Development of such a rationale
involves both cognitive and political events. The cognitive events
involve individual efforts to understand what is happening. The
political events occur because the parties are usually organizations
in which "different people have different views" but consensus
must be built. As a result of the need to build consensus within
organizations, "bilateral negotiations sometimes turn into multilateral negotiations."

In rejecting the view of negotiation as a sequence of negotiator
tactics moving toward agreement, Morley strikes at the heart of
much of the thinking presented in this book. Nevertheless, we take
Morley's criticism seriously, regard his ideas as intriguing, and
accept the possibility that they may eventually eclipse the field.
Abrupt paradigmatic changes are the essence of real scientific
progress (Kuhn 1962). Unfortunately, there is little more to Morley's
current position than a critique of current trends, a sketch of what
he regards as the right direction for theory, and some illustrative
case materials. What is needed is for Morley, or someone influenced
by him, to develop a theory about the processes by which negotiating parties make sense of their situation and develop a collective rationale about how their relationship should change (see
Friedman 1989). This theory must imply a set of variables and a
set of hypotheses that can be subjected to empirical test. Unless and
until Morley's (or some other novel) sketch is so elaborated, the

expanded view of negotiation presented in this book is likely to persist as the dominant thinking in this field.

Summary and implications

Most behavioral studies of negotiation that fall in the traditional, dominant paradigm treat negotiators as unitary decision makers, self-interested, and without any past history or future involvement. These are real limitations of the paradigm. In the course of writing this book, particularly in the last six chapters, we have attempted to expand the paradigm. We have drawn attention to the importance of other-interest in negotiation, the social context of negotiation including social norms, relationships, group processes, mediators, and the broad set of conflict-handling choices within which negotiation is but one. But the literature on these topics is quite thin. Hence there is room for much more work on these and other topics in negotiation.

We regard research on negotiation as an exciting, vigorous tradition that has generated many useful ideas. Nevertheless, this field is still immature. There is much further work to be done, and current concepts are likely to be substantially altered as we move ahead.

Suggestions for further reading

Cohen, R. (1991). *Negotiating across cultures*. Washington, DC: United States Institute of Peace.

Friedman, R. A. (1989). Interaction norms as carriers of organizational culture: a study of labor negotiations at International Harvester. *Journal of Contemporary Ethnography*, 18, 3–29.

McGrath, J. E. and Hollingshead, A. B. (1993). *Technology and groups*. Newberry Park, CA: Sage.

Morley, I. E. (1992). Intra-organizational bargaining. In J. F. Hartley and G. M. Stephenson (eds), *Employment relations*. Cambridge, MA: Blackwell.

Pruitt, D. G. (1986). Trends in the scientific study of negotiation and mediation. *Negotiation Journal*, 2, 237–44.

Smith, W. P. (1987). Conflict and negotiation: trends and emerging issues. *Journal of Applied Social Psychology*, 17, 641–77.

BIBLIOGRAPHY

Abelson, R. P. (1981). The psychological status of the script concept. *American Psychologist*, 36, 715–29.

Abric, J. C. (1982). Cognitive processes underlying cooperation: The theory of social representation. In V. J. Derlega and J. Grzelak (eds), *Cooperation and helping behavior: Theories and research*, pp. 73–94. New York: Academic Press.

Adams, J. S. (1976). The structure and dynamics of behavior in organization boundary roles. In M. D. Dunnette (ed.), *Handbook of industrial and organizational psychology*. Chicago: Rand McNally.

Adelberg, S. and Batson, C. D. (1978). Accountability and helping: When needs exceed resources. *Journal of Personality and Social Psychology*, 36, 342–50.

Alexander, S. and Ruderman, M. (1987). The role of procedural and distributive justice in organizational behavior. *Social Justice Research*, 1, 117–98.

Amir, Y. (1976). The role of intergroup contact in change of prejudice and ethnic relations. In P. A. Katz (ed.), *Toward the elimination of racism*. Elmsford, New York: Pergamon Press.

Ancona, D. G., Friedman, R. A. and Kolb, D. M. (1991). The group and what happens on the way to "Yes". *Negotiation Journal*, 2, 155–73.

Apfelbaum, E. (1974). On conflicts and bargaining. In L. Berkowitz (ed.), *Advances in experimental social psychology*, Vol. 7. New York: Academic Press.

Arnold, J. A. and Carnevale, P. J. (1992). *Preference for dispute resolution procedures: The role of intentionality, expected future interaction, and consequences*. Presented at the Fifth Annual Meeting of the International Association of Conflict Management, Minneapolis.

Arunachalam, V. (1991). Decision aiding in multi-party transfer negotiation: The effects of computer-mediated communication and structured interaction. PhD thesis, University of Illinois, Urbana.

Asch, S. E. (1956). Studies on independence and conformity: a minority of one against an unanimous majority. *Psychological Monographs*, 70, 416.

Axelrod, R. (1984). *The evolution of cooperation*. New York: Basic Books.

Bacharach, S. B. and Lawler, E. J. (1981). *Bargaining: Power, tactics, and outcomes*. Greenwich, CT: JAI Press.

Bar-Tal, D. and Geva, N. (1986). A cognitive basis of international conflicts. In S. Worchel and W. G. Austin (eds), *Psychology of intergroup relations*, pp. 118–33. Chicago: Nelson-Hall.

Bar-Tal, D., Kruglanski, A. W. and Klar, Y. (1989). Conflict termination: An epistemological analysis of international cases. *Political Psychology*, 10, 233–55.

Baron, R. A. (1984). Reducing organizational conflict: An incompatible response approach. *Journal of Applied Psychology*, 69, 272–9.

Baron, R. A. (1985). Reducing organizational conflict: The role of attributions. *Journal of Applied Psychology*, 70, 434–41.

Baron, R. A. (1988a). Attributions and organizational conflict: The mediating role of apparent sincerity. *Organizational Behavior and Human Decision Processes*, 41, 111–27.

Baron, R. A. (1988b). Negative effects of destructive criticism: Impact on conflict, self-efficacy, and task performance. *Journal of Applied Psychology*, 73, 199–207.

Baron, R. A. (1990). Environmentally induced positive affect: Its impact on self-efficacy, task performance, negotiation, and conflict. *Journal of Applied Social Psychology*, 20, 368–84.

Baron, R. A. and Ball, R. L. (1974). The aggression-inhibiting influence of non-hostile humor. *Journal of Experimental Social Psychology*, 10, 23–33.

Baron, R. A., Fortin, S. P., Frei, R. L., Hauver, L. A. and Shack, M. L. (1990). Reducing organizational conflict: The role of socially-induced positive affect. *International Journal of Conflict Management*, 1, 133–52.

Bartos, O. J. (1974). *Process and outcome in negotiation*. New York: Columbia University Press.

Bartunek, J., Benton, A. and Keys, C. (1975). Third party intervention and the behavior of group representatives. *Journal of Conflict Resolution*, 19, 532–57.

Bazerman, M. H. and Carroll, J. S. (1987). Negotiator cognition. In B. M. Staw and L. L. Cummings (eds), *Research in organizational behavior*, Vol 9, pp. 247–88. Greenwich, CT: JAI Press.

Bazerman, M. H., Magliozzi, T. and Neale, M. A. (1985). Integrative bargaining in a competitive market. *Organizational Behavior and Human Decision Processes*, 35, 294–313.

Bendor, J., Kramer, R. M. and Stout, S. (1991). When in doubt...: Cooperation in a noisy prisoner's dilemma. *Journal of Conflict Resolution*, 35, 691–719.

Benton, A. A. (1972). Accountability and negotiations between group representatives. *Proceedings of the Eightieth Annual Conference of the American Psychological Association*, pp. 227–8.

Benton, A. A. (1975). Bargaining visibility and the attitudes and negotiation behavior of male and female group representatives. *Journal of Personality*, 43, 661–75.

Benton, A. A. and Druckman, D. (1973). Salient solutions and the bargaining behavior of representatives and nonrepresentatives. *International Journal of Group Tensions*, 3, 28–39.

Benton, A. A. and Druckman, D. (1974). Constituent's bargaining orientation and intergroup negotiations. *Journal of Applied Social Psychology*, 4, 141–50.

Benton, A. A., Kelley, H. H. and Liebling, B. (1972). Effects of extremity of offers and concession rate on the outcomes of bargaining. *Journal of Personality and Social Psychology*, 24, 73–83.

Ben-Yoav, O. and Pruitt, D. G. (1984a). Accountability to constituents: A two-edged sword. *Organizational Behavior and Human Performance*, 34, 283–95.

Ben-Yoav, O. and Pruitt, D. G. (1984b). Resistance to yielding and the expectation of cooperative future interaction in negotiation. *Journal of Experimental Social Psychology*, 34, 323–35.

Bercovitch, J. (1984). *Social conflicts and third parties: Strategies of conflict resolution*. Boulder, CO: Westview.

Bercovitch, J. (1989). Mediation in international disputes. In K. Kressel and D. G. Pruitt (eds), *Mediation research*, pp. 284–99. San Francisco: Jossey-Bass.

Beriker, N. and Druckman, D. (1991). Models of responsiveness: The Lausanne Peace Negotiations (1922–1923). *Journal of Social Psychology*, 131, 297–300.

Bixenstine, V. E. and Gaebelein, J. W. (1971). Strategies of "real" opponents in eliciting cooperative choice in a prisoner's dilemma game. *Journal of Conflict Resolution*, 15, 157–66.

Bixenstine, V. E., Levitt, C. A. and Wilson, K. R. (1966). Collaboration among six persons in a prisoner's dilemma game. *Journal of Conflict Resolution*, 10, 488–96.

Bixenstine, V. E. and Wilson, K. R. (1963). Effects of level of cooperative choice by the other player on choices in a prisoner's dilemma game. Part II. *Journal of Abnormal Social Psychology*, 67, 139–47.

Blake, R. R. and Mouton, J. S. (1964). *The managerial grid*. Houston: Gulf.

Bonacich, P. (1972). Norms and cohesion as adaptive responses to potential conflict: An experimental study. *Sociometry*, 35, 357–75.

Bornstein, G., Rapoport, A., Kerpel, L. and Katz, T. (1989). Within and between group communication in intergroup competition for public goods. *Journal of Experimental Social Psychology*, 25, 422–36.

Bottom, W. P. and Studt, A. (1993). The nature of risk and risk preference in bargaining. *Organizational Behavior and Human Decision Processes* (in the press).

Brann, P. and Foddy, M. (1988). Trust and the consumption of a deteriorating common resource. *Journal of Conflict Resolution*, 31, 615–30.

Braver, S. L. and Barnett, B. (1976). Effects of modeling on cooperation in a prisoner's dilemma game. *Journal of Personality and Social Psychology*, 33, 161–9.

Breaugh, J. A. and Klimoski, R. J. (1977). Choice of group spokesman in bargaining: member or nonmember. *Organizational Behavior and Human Performance*, 19, 325–36.

Brett, J. M. and Goldberg, S. B. (1983). Mediator-advisors: A new third-party role. In M. H. Bazerman and R. J. Lewicki (eds), *Negotiating in organizations*, pp. 165–76. Newbury Park, CA: Sage.

Brewer, M. B. (1979). In-group bias in the minimal intergroup situation: A cognitive-motivational analysis. *Psychological Bulletin*, 86, 307–24.

Brewer, M. B. and Kramer, R. M. (1986). Choice behavior in social dilemmas: Effects of social identity, group size, and decision framing. *Journal of Personality and Social Psychology*, 50, 543–9.

Brodt, S. E. (1990). Inside information and negotiator decision behavior. Presented at the Third Annual Meeting of the International Association Conflict Management, Vancouver, British Columbia.

Brodt, S. E. (1991). Negotiating with friends in a competitive context: Affect and outcomes. Presented at the Fourth Annual Meeting of the International Association Conflict Management, Ernst Sillem Hoeve, Den Dolder, The Netherlands.

Brookmire, D. and Sistrunk, F. (1980). The effects of perceived ability and impartiality of mediators and time pressure on negotiation. *Journal of Conflict Resolution*, 24, 311–27.

Brown, B. R. (1968). The effects of need to maintain face on interpersonal bargaining. *Journal of Experimental Social Psychology*, 4, 107–22.

Brown, R. (1988a). *Group processes: Dynamics within and between groups*. Oxford: Basil Blackwell.

Brown, R. (1988b). Intergroup relations. In M. Hewstone, W. Stroebe, J. P. Codel and G. M. Stephenson (eds), *Introduction to social psychology*. Oxford: Basil Blackwell.

Brown, R. and Abrams, D. (1986). The effects of intergroup similarity and goal interdependence on intergroup attitudes and tasks performance. *Journal of Experimental Social Psychology*, 22, 78–92.

Burton, J. W. (1984). *Global conflict*. College Park, MD: Center for International Development, University of Maryland.

Byrne, D. (1971). *The attraction paradigm*. New York: Academic Press.

Campbell, J. C. (1976). *Successful negotiation: Trieste (1954)*. Princeton, NJ: Princeton University Press.

Carnevale, P. J. (1986). Strategic choice in mediation. *Negotiation Journal*, 2, 41–56.

Carnevale, P. J. (1991). Cognition and affect in cooperation and conflict. Presented at the Fourth Annual Meeting of the International Association Conflict Management, Ernst Sillem Hoeve, Den Dolder, The Netherlands.

Carnevale, P. J. and Conlon, D. E. (1988). Time pressure and strategic choice in mediation. *Organizational Behavior and Human Decision Processes*, 42, 111–33.

Carnevale, P. J. and Conlon, D. E. (1990). Effects of two forms of bias in the mediation of disputes. Presented at the Third Annual Meeting of International Association Conflict Management, Vancouver, British Columbia.

Carnevale, P. J. and Isen, A. M. (1986). The influence of positive affect and visual access on the discovery of integrative solutions in bilateral negotiation. *Organizational Behavior and Human Decision Processes*, 37, 1–13.

Carnevale, P. J. and Keenan, P. A. (1990). Frame and motive in integrative bargaining: The likelihood and the quality of agreement. Presented at the Third Annual Meeting of the International Association for Conflict Management, Vancouver, British Columbia.

Carnevale, P. J. and Lawler, E. J. (1986). Time pressure and the development of integrative agreements in bilateral negotiation. *Journal of Conflict Resolution*, 30, 636–59.

Carnevale, P. J. and Mead, A. (1990). Decision frame in the mediation of disputes. Presented at the Annual Meeting of the Judgment and Decision Making Society, New Orleans.

Carnevale, P. J., Olson, J. B. and O'Connor, K. M. (1992). Reciprocity and informality in a laboratory grievance system. Presented at the Fifth Annual Meeting of the International Association of Conflict Management, Minneapolis.

Carnevale, P. J. and Pegnetter, R. (1985). The selection of mediation tactics in public-sector disputes: A contingency analysis. *Journal of Social Issues*, 41, 65–81.

Carnevale, P. J. and Pruitt, D. G. (1992). Negotiation and mediation. *Annual Review of Psychology*, 43, 531–82.

Carnevale, P. J., Pruitt, D. G. and Britton, S. D. (1979). Looking tough: The negotiator under constituent surveillance. *Personality and Social Psychology Bulletin*, 5, 118–21.

Carnevale, P. J., Pruitt, D. G. and Seilheimer, S. (1981). Looking and competing: Accountability and visual access in integrative bargaining. *Journal of Personality and Social Psychology*, 40, 111–20.

Carroll, J. S., Bazerman, M. H. and Maury, R. (1988). Negotiator cognitions: A descriptive approach to negotiators' understanding of their opponents. *Organizational Behavior and Human Decision Processes*, 41, 352–70.

Carroll, J. S. and Payne, J. (1991). An information processing approach to two-party negotiations. In M. H. Bazerman, R. J. Lewicki and B. H. Sheppard (eds), *Research on negotiation in organizations, Vol. 3.* Greenwich, CT: JAI.

Chan, D. K-S., Triandis, H., Carnevale, P. J. and Tam, A. (1992). A cross-cultural comparison of negotiation: Effects of collectivism, relationship between negotiators, and concession pattern on negotiation. Manuscript submitted for publication.

Chaudhry, S. S. and Ross, W. R. (1989). Relevance trees and mediation. *Negotiation Journal*, 5, 63–73.

Chertkoff, J. and Baird, S. L. (1971). Applicability of the big-lie technique and the last clear choice doctrine to bargaining. *Journal of Personality and Social Psychology*, 20, 298–303.

Church, R. M. (1969). Response suppression. In B. A. Campbell and R. M. Church (eds), *Punishment and aversive behavior*. New York: Appleton-Century-Crofts.

Clark, M. S. and Mills, J. (1979). Interpersonal attraction in exchange and communal relationships. *Journal of Personality and Social Psychology*, 37, 12–24.

Cohen, D. (1966). Chinese mediation on the eve of modernization. *California Law Review*, 54, 1201–26.

Cohen, R. (1991). *Negotiating across cultures*. Washington, DC: United States Institute of Peace.

Colosi, T. (1983). Negotiation in the public and private sectors: A core model. *American Behavioral Scientist*, 27, 229–53.

Collier, J. (1973). *Law and social change among the Zinacantan*. Palo Alto, CA: Stanford University Press.

Conlon, D. E., Carnevale, P. J. and Murnighan, J. K. (1993). Intravention: Third-party intervention with clout. *Organizational Behavior and Human Decision Processes* (in the press).

Cooper, J. and Fazio, R. H. (1979). The formation and persistence of attitudes that support intergroup conflict. In W. G. Austin and S. Worchel (eds), *The social psychology of intergroup relations*, pp. 149–59. Monterey, CA: Brooks/Cole.

Dawes, R. M. (1989). Statistical criteria for establishing a truly false consensus effect. *Journal of Experimental Social Psychology*, 25, 1–17.

De Dreu, C. K. W. and Carnevale, P. J. (1992). Communicated frame and orientation in bilateral negotiation: Effects on negotiator cognition and behavior. Unpublished manuscript, Department of Social and Organizational Psychology, University of Groningen, Groningen, The Netherlands.

De Dreu, C. K. W., Emans, B. J. M. and Van de Vliert, E. (1992). Frames of reference and cooperative social decision making. *European Journal of Social Psychology* (in the press).

Deutsch, M. (1969). Conflicts: Productive and destructive. *Journal of Social Issues*, 25, 7–41.

Deutsch, M. (1973). *The resolution of conflict.* New Haven, CT: Yale University Press.

Deutsch, M. (1975). Equity, equality, and need: What determines which value will be used as the basis of distributive justice? *Journal of Social Issues*, 31, 137–50.

Deutsch, M. (1982). Interdependence and psychological orientation. In V. J. Derlega and J. Grzelak (eds), *Cooperation and helping behavior: Theories and research*, pp. 15–42. New York: Academic Press.

Deutsch, M. (1985). *Distributive justice: A social-psychological perspective.* New Haven, CT: Yale University Press.

Deutsch, M. and Krauss, R. M. (1962). Studies of interpersonal bargaining. *Journal of Conflict Resolution*, 6, 52–76.

Dion, K. L. (1973). Cohesiveness as a determinant of ingroup–outgroup bias. *Journal of Personality and Social Psychology*, 28, 163–71.

Dion, K. L. (1979). Intergroup conflict and intragroup cohesiveness. In W. G. Austin and S. Worchel (eds), *The social psychology of intergroup relations*. Monterey, CA: Brooks/Cole Publishers.

Donohue, W. A. (1981). Analyzing negotiation tactics: Development of a negotiation interact system. *Human Communication Research*, 7, 273–87.

Donohue, W. A. (1989). Communicative competence in mediators. In K. Kressel and D. G. Pruitt (eds), *Mediation research*, pp. 322–43. San Francisco: Jossey-Bass.

Donohue, W. A. (1991). *Communication, marital dispute and divorce mediation.* Hillsdale, NJ: Lawrence Erlbaum.

Douglas, A. (1962). *Industrial peacemaking.* New York: Columbia University Press.

Druckman, D. (ed.) (1977). *Negotiations: social psychological perspectives.* Beverly Hills, CA: Sage.

Druckman, D. (1986). Stages, turning points, and crisis: Negotiating military base rights, Spain and the United States. *Journal of Conflict Resolution*, 30, 327–60.

Druckman, D. (1991). Content analysis. In V. A. Kremenyuk (ed.), *International negotiation: Analysis, approaches, issues*, pp. 409–23. San Francisco: Jossey-Bass.

Druckman, D., Broome, B. J. and Korper, S. H. (1988). Values differences and conflict resolution. *Journal of Conflict Resolution*, 32, 489–510.

Druckman, D. and Harris, R. (1990). Alternative models of responsiveness in international negotiation. *Journal of Conflict Resolution*, 34, 234–52.

Druckman, D. and Mahoney, R. (1977). Process and consequences of international negotiations. *Journal of Social Issues*, 33, 60–87.

Druckman, D., Solomon, D. and Zechmeister, K. (1972). Effects of representative role obligations on the process of children's distribution of resources. *Sociometry*, 35, 489–501.

Druckman, D. and Zechmeister, K. (1973). Conflict of interest and value dissensus: Propositions in the sociology of conflict. *Human Relations*, 26, 449–66.

Duffy, K. G., Grosch, J. W. and Olczak, P. W. (eds) (1991). *Community mediation: A handbook for practitioners and researchers*. New York: Guilford.

Dupont, C. (1982). *La negociation: Conduite, theorie, applications*. Paris: Dalloz.

Dupont, C. and Faure, G. (1991). The negotiation process. In V. A. Kremenyuk (ed.), *International negotiation: Analysis, approaches, issues*, pp. 40–57. San Francisco: Jossey-Bass.

Edney, J. J. and Harper, C. S. (1978). The commons dilemma: A review of contributions from psychology. *Environmental Management*, 2, 491–507.

Enzle, M. E., Harvey, M. D. and Wright, E. F. (1992). Implicit role obligations versus social responsibility in constituency representation. *Journal of Personality and Social Psychology*, 62, 238–45.

Esser, J., Calvillo, M. J., Scheel, M. R. and Walker, J. L. (1990). Oligopoly bargaining: Effects of agreement pressure and opponent strategies. *Journal of Applied Social Psychology*, 20, 1256–71.

Esser, J. and Komorita, S. S. (1975). Reciprocity and concession making in bargaining. *Journal of Personality and Social Psychology*, 31, 864–72.

Faley, T. E. and Tedeschi, J. T. (1971). Status and reactions to threats. *Journal of Personality and Social Psychology*, 17, 192–9.

Festinger, L., Schachter, S. and Back, K. (1950). *Social pressures in informal groups: A study of human factors in housing*. New York: Harper and Row.

Filley, A. C. (1975). *Interpersonal conflict resolution*. Glenville, IL: Scott, Foresman.

Fisher, R. (1964). Fractionating conflict. In Roger Fisher (ed.), *International conflict and behavioral science: The Craigville papers*. New York: Basic Books.

Fisher, R. (1989). Negotiating inside out: What are the best ways to relate internal negotiations with external ones. *Negotiation Journal*, 5, 33–41.

Fisher, R. and Brown, S. (1988). *Getting together: Building a relationship that gets to YES*. Boston: Houghton Mifflin.

Fisher, R. and Ury, W. (1981). *Getting to YES: Negotiating agreement without giving in*. Boston: Houghton Mifflin.

Fisher, R. J. and Keashly, L. (1988). Third party interventions in intergroup conflict: Consultation is *not* mediation. *Negotiation Journal*, 4, 381–93.

Fiske, S. T. and Taylor, S. E. (1991). *Social cognition*, 2nd edn. New York: McGraw-Hill.

Fobian, C. S. and Christensen-Szalanski, J. J. J. (1992). Ambiguity and liability negotiations: The effects of the negotiators' role and the sensitivity zone. *Organizational Behavior and Human Decision Processes* (in the press).

Follett, M. P. (1940). Constructive conflict. In H. C. Metcalf, L. Urwick (eds), *Dynamic administration: The collected papers of Mary Parker Follett*, pp. 30–49. New York: Harper and Row.

Fox, J. and Guyer, M. (1977). Group size and others' strategy in an n-person game. *Journal of Conflict Resolution*, 21, 323–38.

Fox, J. and Guyer, M. (1978). "Public" choice and cooperation in N-person prisoner's dilemma. *Journal of Conflict Resolution*, 22, 468–81.

Freedman, S. C. (1981). Threats, promises, and coalitions: A study of compliance and retaliation in a simulated organizational setting. *Journal of Applied Social Psychology*, 11, 114–36.

Frey, R. L. and Adams, J. S. (1972). The negotiator's dilemma: Simultaneous in-group and out-group conflict. *Journal of Experimental Social Psychology*, 8, 331–46.

Friedland, N. (1983). Weakness as strength: The use and misuse of a "My hands are tied" ploy in bargaining. *Journal of Applied Social Psychology*, 13, 422–6.

Friedman, R. A. (1989). Interaction norms as carriers of organizational culture: A study of labor negotiations at International Harvester. *Journal of Contemporary Ethnography*, 18, 3–29.

Friedman, R. A. and Gal, S. (1992). Managing around roles: Building groups in labor negotiations. *Journal of Applied Behavioral Science* (in the press).

Friedman, R. A. and Podolny, J. (1992). Differentiation of boundary spanning roles: Labor negotiations and implications for role conflict. *Administrative Science Quarterly* (in the press).

Fry, W. R., Firestone, I. J. and Williams, D. L. (1983). Negotiation process and outcome of stranger dyads and dating couples: Do lovers lose? *Basic and Applied Social Psychology*, 4, 1–16.

Gaertner, S. L., Mann, J. A., Dovidio, J. F., Murrell, A. J. and Pomare,

M. (1990). How does cooperation reduce intergroup bias? *Journal of Personality and Social Psychology*, 59, 692–704.

Gahagan, J. P. and Tedeschi, J. T. (1968). Strategy and the credibility of promises in the prisoner's dilemma game. *Journal of Conflict Resolution*, 12, 224–34.

Gaski, J. F. (1986). Interrelations among a channel entity's power sources: Impact of the exercise of reward and coercion on expert, referent, and legitimate power sources. *Journal of Marketing Research*, 23, 62–77.

Gerhart, B. and Rynes, S. (1991). Determinants and consequences of salary negotiations by male and female MBA graduates. *Journal of Applied Psychology*, 76, 256–62.

Gilovich, T. (1981). Seeing the past in the present: The effect of associations to familiar events on judgments and decisions. *Journal of Personality and Social Psychology*, 40, 797–808.

Glasl, F. (1982). The process of conflict escalation and roles of third parties. In G. B. J. Bomers and R. B. Peterson (eds) (1982), *Conflict management and industrial relations*, pp. 119–40. Boston: Kluwer Nijhoff.

Gottman, J. M. (1979). *Marital interaction: Experimental investigations.* New York: Academic Press.

Gray, B. (1989). *Collaborating: Finding common ground for multiparty problems.* San Francisco, CA: Jossey-Bass.

Greenhalgh, L. (1987). Relationships in negotiations. *Negotiation Journal*, 3, 235–43.

Gruder, C. L. (1971). Relationship with opponent and partner in mixed-motive bargaining. *Journal of Conflict Resolution*, 15, 403–16.

Gruder, C. L. and Rosen, N. (1971). Effects of intergroup relations on intergroup bargaining. *International Journal of Group Tensions*, 1, 301–17.

Grzelak, J. L. (1982). Preferences and cognitive processes in interdependence situations: A theoretical analysis of cooperation. In V. J. Derlega and J. Grzelak (eds), *Cooperation and helping behavior: Theories and research*, pp. 95–122. New York: Academic Press.

Grzelak, J. (1988). Conflict and cooperation. In M. Hewstone, W. Stroebe, J. Codol and G. M. Stephenson (eds), *Introduction to social psychology*. Oxford: Basil Blackwell.

Gulliver, P. H. (1979). *Disputes and negotiations: A cross-cultural perspective.* New York: Academic Press.

Gulliver, P. H. (1988). Anthropological contributions to the study of negotiations. *Negotiation Journal*, 4, 247–55.

Haccoun, R. and Klimoski, R. J. (1975). Negotiator status and accountability source: A study of negotiator behavior. *Organizational Behavior and Human Performance*, 14, 342–59.

Hammond, K. R. and Grassia, J. (1985). The cognitive side of conflict:

From theory to resolution of policy disputes. In S. Oskamp (ed.), *Applied social psychology annual*, Vol. 6, pp. 233–54. Beverly Hills: Sage.

Hamner, W. C. (1974). Effects of bargaining strategy and pressure to reach agreement in a stalemated negotiation. *Journal of Personality and Social Psychology*, 30, 458–67.

Hamner, W. C. and Baird, L. S. (1978). The effect of strategy, pressure to reach agreement and relative power on bargaining behavior. In H. Sauermann (ed.), *Bargaining behavior*. Tübingen: Mohr.

Hamner, W. C. and Harnett, D. L. (1975). The effects of information and aspiration level on bargaining behavior. *Journal of Experimental Social Psychology*, 11, 329–42.

Hardin, G. (1968). The tragedy of the commons. *Science*, 162, 1243–8.

Harford, T. and Solomon, L. (1967). "Reformed sinner" and "lapsed saint" strategies in the prisoner's dilemma game. *Journal of Conflict Resolution*, 11, 104–9.

Harris, K. L. and Carnevale, P. J. (1990). Chilling and hastening: The influence of third-party power and interests on negotiation. *Organizational Behavior and Human Decision Processes*, 47, 138–60.

Hastie, R. (1981). Schematic principles in human memory. In E. T. Higgins, C. P. Heiman and M. P. Zanna (eds), *Social cognition: The Ontario symposium*, pp. 39–88. Hillsdale, NJ: Erlbaum.

Hastie, R. (1991). A review from a high place: The field of judgment and decision making as revealed in its current textbooks. *Psychological Science*, 2, 135–8.

Hastorf, A. H. and Cantril, C. (1954). They saw a game: A case study. *Journal of Abnormal and Social Psychology*, 49, 129–34.

Heider, F. (1958). *The psychology of interpersonal relations*. New York: Wiley.

Hermann, M. G. and Kogan, N. (1968). Negotiation in leader and delegate groups. *Journal of Conflict Resolution*, 12, 332–44.

Heuer, L. B. and Penrod, S. (1986). Procedural preference as a function of conflict intensity. *Journal of Personality and Social Psychology*, 51, 700–10.

Hewstone, M. (1988). Attributional bases of intergroup conflict. In W. Stroebe, A. W. Kruglanski, D. Bar-Tal and M. Hewstone (eds), *The social psychology of intergroup conflict: Theory, research, and applications*, pp. 47–72. New York: Springer-Verlag.

Hill, G. (1982). Group versus individual performance: Are $N + 1$ heads better than one? *Psychological Bulletin*, 91, 517–39.

Hiltrop, J. M. (1985). Mediator behavior and the settlement of collective bargaining disputes in Britain. *Journal of Social Issues*, 41, 83–99.

Hiltrop, J. M. (1989). Factors associated with successful labor mediation. In K. Kressel and D. G. Pruitt (eds), *Mediation research*, pp. 241–62. San Francisco: Jossey-Bass.

Hiltrop, J. M. and Rubin, J. Z. (1982). Effects of intervention conflict of interest on dispute resolution. *Journal of Personality and Social Psychology*, 42, 665–72.

Hilty, J. and Carnevale, P. J. (1992). Bad-guy/Good-guy strategy in bilateral negotiation. *Organizational Behavior and Human Decision Processes* (in the press).

Hollander, E. P. (1958). Conformity, status, and idiosyncrasy credit. *Psychological Review*, 65, 117–27.

Hollingshead, A. B. and Carnevale, P. J. (1990). Positive affect and decision frame in integrative bargaining: A reversal of the frame effect. Best Papers Proceedings of the Fiftieth Annual Conference of the Academy of Management, pp. 385–9.

Hollingshead, A. B. and McGrath, J. E. (1992). The whole is less than the sum of its parts: A critical review of research on computer assisted groups. In R. A. Guzzo and E. Salas (eds), *Team decision and team performance in organizations*. San Francisco: Jossey-Bass.

Holmes, J. G., Ellard, J. H. and Lamm, H. (1986). Boundary roles and intergroup conflict. In S. Worchel and W. G. Austin (eds), *The social psychology of intergroup relations*, 2nd edn. Chicago: Nelson Hall.

Holmes, J. G., Throop, W. F. and Strickland, L. H. (1971). The effects of prenegotiation expectations on the distributive bargaining process. *Journal of Experimental Social Psychology*, 7, 582–99.

Holsti, K. (1983). *International politics: A framework of analysis*, 4th edn. Englewood Cliffs, NJ: Prentice-Hall.

Holsti, O. R. (1962). The belief system and national images: A case study. *Journal of Conflict Resolution*, 6, 244–52.

Holtzworth-Munroe, A. and Jacobson, N. S. (1985). An attributional approach to marital dysfunction and therapy. In J. E. Maddux, C. D. Stoltenberg and R. Rosenwein (eds), *Social processes in clinical and counseling psychology*, pp. 153–69. New York: Springer-Verlag.

Hopmann, P. T. and Smith, T. C. (1977). An application of a Richardson process model: Soviet–American interactions in the Test Ban Negotiations, 1962–3. *Journal of Conflict Resolution*, 21, 701–26.

Horai, J. and Tedeschi, J. (1969). Effects of credibility and magnitude of punishment on compliance to threats. *Journal of Personality and Social Psychology*, 12, 164–9.

Hornstein, H. A. (1965). Effects of different magnitudes of threat upon interpersonal bargaining. *Journal of Experimental Social Psychology*, 1, 282–93.

Hornstein, H. A. (1976). *Cruelty and kindness: A new look at aggression and altruism*. Englewood Cliffs, NJ: Prentice-Hall.

Houlden, P., LaTour, S., Walker, L. and Thibaut, J. (1978). Preference for modes of dispute resolution as a function of process and decision control. *Journal of Experimental Social Psychology*, 14, 13–30.

Huber, E. L., Pruitt, D. G. and Welton, G. L. (1986). The effect of prior negotiation experience on the process and outcome of later negotiation. Poster presented at the annual meeting of the Eastern Psychological Association, New York.

Hulse, S. E., Egeth, H. and Deese, J. (1980). *The psychology of learning.* New York: McGraw-Hill.

Idaszak, J. R. and Carnevale, P. J. (1989). Third party power: Some negative effects of positive incentives. *Journal of Applied Social Psychology,* 19, 499–516.

Ikle, F. (1964). *How nations negotiate.* New York: Harper.

Insko, C. A., Schopler, J., Hoyle, R. H., Dardis, G. J. and Graetz, K. A. (1990). Individual-group discontinuity as a function of fear and greed. *Journal of Personality and Social Psychology,* 58, 68–79.

Ippolito, C. A. and Pruitt, D. G. (1990). Power balancing in mediation: Outcomes and implications of mediator intervention. *International Journal of Conflict Management,* 1, 341–56.

Isen, A. M. (1970). Success, failure, attention, and reaction to others. The warm glow of success. *Journal of Personality and Social Psychology,* 15, 294–301.

Isen, A. M. and Levin, P. A. (1972). Effect of feeling good on helping: Cookies and kindness. *Journal of Personality and Social Psychology,* 21, 384–8.

Isen, A. M., Johnson, M. M. S., Mertz, E. and Robinson, G. (1985). The influence of positive affect on the unusualness of word associations. *Journal of Personality and Social Psychology,* 48, 1413–26.

Jacobson, N. S. (1984). The modification of cognitive processes in behavioral marital therapy: Integrating cognitive and behavioral intervention strategies. In K. Hahlweg and N. S. Jacobson (eds), *Marital interaction: Analysis and modification,* pp. 285–308. New York: Guilford Press.

Janosik, R. J. (1987). Rethinking the culture-negotiation link. *Negotiation Journal,* 3, 85–95.

Jervis, R. (1976). *Perception and misperception in international politics.* Princeton, NJ: Princeton University Press.

Johnson, D. F. and Tullar, W. L. (1972). Style of third party intervention, face saving, and bargaining behavior. *Journal of Experimental Social Psychology,* 6, 319–30.

Johnson, D. W. (1967). The use of role reversal in intergroup competition. *Journal of Personality and Social Psychology,* 7, 135–41.

Johnson, D. W. (1971). The effects of warmth of interaction, accuracy of understanding, and the proposal of compromises on the listener's behavior. *Journal of Counseling Psychology,* 18, 207–16.

Johnson, D. W., Johnson, R. and Maruyama, G. (1984). Goal interdependence and interpersonal attraction in heterogenous classrooms: A metanalysis. In N. Miller and M. B. Brewer (eds), *Groups in contact:*

The psychology of desegregation, pp. 187–212. New York: Academic Press.

Johnson, D. W., Maruyama, G., Johnson, R. T., Nelson, D. and Skon, S. (1981). Effects of cooperative, competitive, and individualistic goal structures on achievement: A metaanalysis. *Psychological Bulletin*, 89, 47–62.

Johnson, S. M. and Greenberg, L. C. (1985). Differential effects of experiential and problem-solving interventions in resolving marital conflict. *Journal of Consulting and Clinical Psychology*, 53, 175–84.

Jorgenson, D. O. and Papciak, A. S. (1981). The effects of communication, resource feedback, and identifiability on behavior in a simulated commons. *Journal of Experimental Social Psychology*, 17, 373–85.

Joseph, M. L. and Willis, R. H. (1963). An experiment analog to two party bargaining. *Behavioral Science*, 8, 117–27.

Judd, C. M. (1978). Cognitive effects of attitude conflict resolution. *Journal of Conflict Resolution*, 22, 483–98.

Kabanoff, B. and van de Vliert, E. (1990). *Behavioral congruence in conflicting dyads*. Kensington: The University of New South Wales, Australian Graduate School of Management.

Kahan, J. P. (1968). Effects of level of aspiration in an experimental bargaining situation. *Journal of Personality and Social Psychology*, 8, 154–9.

Kahn, R. L. (1991). Organization theory. In V. A. Kremenyuk (ed.), *International negotiation: Analysis, approaches, issues*, pp. 40–57. San Francisco: Jossey-Bass.

Kahneman, D. (1992). Reference points, anchors, norms and mixed feelings. *Organizational Behaviour and Human Decision Processes*, 51, 296–312.

Kahneman, D. and Tversky, A. (1979). Prospect theory: An analysis of decision under risk. *Econometrica*, 47, 263–91.

Karambayya, R. and Brett, J. M. (1989). Managers handling disputes: Third party roles and perceptions of fairness. *Academy of Management Journal*, 32, 687–704.

Katz, N. H. and Lawyer, J. W. (1985). *Communication and conflict resolution skills*. Dubuque, IA: Kendall/Hunt.

Kazdin, A. E. (1975). *Behavior modification in applied settings*. Homewood, IL: Dorsey.

Keenan, P. A. and Carnevale, P. J. (1989). Positive effects of within-group cooperation on between-group negotiation. *Journal of Applied Social Psychology*, 19, 977–92.

Keenan, P. A. and Carnevale, P. J. (1992). Negotiation teams: Within-group and between-group negotiation. Unpublished manuscript, Department of Psychology, University of Illinois, Champaign.

Kelley, H. H. (1966). A classroom study of the dilemmas in interpersonal negotiations. In K. Archibald (ed.), *Strategic interaction and conflict:*

Original papers and discussion. Berkeley, CA: Institute of International Studies.

Kelley, H. H., Beckman, L. L. and Fischer, C. S. (1967). Negotiating the division of reward under incomplete information. *Journal of Experimental Social Psychology*, 3, 361–98.

Kelley, H. H. and Grzelak, J. (1972). Conflict between individual and common interest in an N-person relationship. *Journal of Personality and Social Psychology*, 21, 190–7.

Kelley, H. H. and Schenitzki, D. P. (1972). Bargaining. In C. G. McClintock (ed.), *Experimental social psychology*, pp. 298–337. New York: Holt.

Kelley, H. H. and Stahelski, A. J. (1970). Social interaction basis of cooperators' and competitors' beliefs about others. *Journal of Personality and Social Psychology*, 16, 190–7.

Kelley, H. H. and Thibaut, J. W. (1978). *Interpersonal relations: A theory of interdependence.* New York: Wiley.

Kelman, H. C. (1985). Overcoming the psychological barrier: An analysis of the Egyptian–Israeli peace process. *Negotiation Journal*, 1, 213–35.

Kelman, H. C. and Cohen, S. P. (1976). The problem-solving workshop: A social-psychological contribution to the resolution of international conflicts. *Journal of Peace Research*, 13, 79–90.

Kerr, N. L. (1983). Motivation losses in groups: A social dilemma analysis. *Journal of Personality and Social Psychology*, 45, 819–28.

Kerr, N. L. (1986). Motivational choices in task groups: A paradigm for social dilemma research. In H. A. M. Wilke, D. M. Messick and C. G. Rutte (eds), *Experimental social dilemmas*, pp. 1–27. New York: Lang.

Kimmel, M., Pruitt, D. G., Magenau, J., Konar-Goldband, E. and Carnevale, P. J. (1980). The effects of trust, aspiration, and gender on negotiation tactics. *Journal of Personality and Social Psychology*, 38, 9–23.

Klimoski, R. J. (1972). The effect of intragroup forces on intergroup conflict resolution. *Organizational Behavior and Human Performance*, 8, 363–83.

Klimoski, R. J. and Ash, R. A. (1974). Accountability and negotiation behavior. *Organizational Behavior and Human Performance*, 11, 409–25.

Knapp, A. (1989). *The effects of the behavioral and verbal aspects of self-presentational tactics on an opponent's performance in a resource dilemma task.* Mainz: Psychological Institute of Johannes Gutenberg University.

Kochan, T. A. and Jick, T. A. (1978). The public sector mediation process: A theory and empirical examination. *Journal of Conflict Resolution*, 22, 209–40.

Kogan, N., Lamm, H. and Trommsdorff, G. (1972). Negotiation constraints in the risk-taking domain: Effects of being observed by partners of higher or lower status. *Journal of Personality and Social Psychology*, 23, 143–56.

Kolb, D. (1989). Labor mediators, managers, and ombudsmen: Roles mediators play in different contexts. In K. Kressel and D. G. Pruitt (eds), *Mediation research*, pp. 91–114. San Francisco: Jossey-Bass.

Kolb, D. and Rubin, J. Z. (1991). Mediation from a disciplinary perspective. In M. H. Bazerman, R. J. Lewicki and B. H. Sheppard (eds), *Research on negotiation in organizations, Vol. 3*. Greenwich, CT: JAI.

Kolodner, J. L. and Simpson, R. L. (1989). The MEDIATOR: Analysis of an early case-based problem solver. *Cognitive Science*, 13, 507–49.

Komorita, S. S. (1973). Concession making and conflict resolution. *Journal of Conflict Resolution*, 17, 745–62.

Komorita, S. S. (1984). Coalition bargaining. In L. Berkowitz (ed.), *Advances in experimental social psychology, Vol. 18*. New York: Academic Press.

Komorita, S. S. and Barnes, M. (1969). Effects of pressures to reach agreement in bargaining. *Journal of Personality and Social Psychology*, 13, 245–52.

Komorita, S. S. and Esser, J. K. (1975). Frequency of reciprocated concessions in bargaining. *Journal of Personality and Social Psychology*, 32, 699–705.

Komorita, S. S. and Kravitz, D. (1979). The effects of alternatives in bargaining. *Journal of Experimental Social Psychology*, 15, 147–57.

Komorita, S. S. and Lapworth, C. W. (1982). Cooperative choice among individuals versus groups in an *n*-person dilemma situation. *Journal of Personality and Social Psychology*, 42, 487–96.

Komorita, S. S. and Mechling, J. (1967). Betrayal and reconciliation in a two-person game. *Journal of Personality and Social Psychology*, 6, 349–53.

Komorita, S. S., Parks, C. D. and Hulbert, L. G. (1992). Reciprocity and the induction of cooperation in social dilemmas. *Journal of Personality and Social Psychology*, 62, 607–17.

Komorita, S. S., Sheposh, J. P. and Braver, S. L. (1968). Power, the use of power, and cooperative choice in a two-person game. *Journal of Personality and Social Psychology*, 8, 134–42.

Kramer, R. M. (1989). Windows of vulnerability or cognitive illusions: Cognitive processes and the nuclear arms race. *Journal of Experimental Social Psychology*, 25, 79–100.

Kramer, R. M. (1991a). Intergroup relations and organizational dilemmas: The role of categorization processes. In L. L. Cummings and B. M. Staw (eds), *Research in organizational behavior, Vol. 13*, pp. 191–228. Greenwich, CT: JAI Press.

Kramer, R. M. (1991b). The more the merrier? Social psychological aspects of multiparty negotiations in organizations. *Research on Negotiation in Organizations*, 3, 307–32.

Kramer, R. M. and Brewer, M. B. (1984). Effects of group identity on resource use in a simulated commons dilemma. *Journal of Personality and Social Psychology*, 46, 1044–57.

Kramer, R. M., Newton, E. and Pommerenke, P. (1990). Self-enhancement biases in negotiations: Antecedents and consequences. Unpublished manuscript, Department of Organizational Behavior, Stanford University, Stanford, California.

Kramer, S. (1963). *The Summarians: Their history, culture, and character.* Chicago: University of Chicago Press.

Kremenyuk, V. (ed.) (1991). *International negotiation: Analysis, approaches, issues.* San Francisco: Jossey-Bass.

Kressel, K. (1972). *Labor mediation: An exploratory survey.* Albany, NY: Association of Labor Mediation Agencies.

Kressel, K. and Pruitt, D. G. (1985). Themes in the mediation of social conflict. *Journal of Social Issues*, 41, 179–98.

Kressel, K. and Pruitt, D. G. (eds) (1989). *Mediation research.* San Francisco: Jossey-Bass.

Kruglanski, A. W. (1970). Attributing trustworthiness in supervisor–worker relations. *Journal of Experimental Social Psychology*, 6, 214–32.

Kuhlman, D. M. and Marshello, A. (1975). Individual differences in game motivation as moderators of preprogrammed strategic effects in prisoner's dilemma. *Journal of Personality and Social Psychology*, 32, 922–31.

Kuhn, T. S. (1962). *The structure of scientific revolutions.* Chicago: University of Chicago Press.

Lamm, H. and Kayser, E. (1978). An analysis of negotiation concerning the allocation of jointly produced profit or loss: The role of justice norms, politeness, profit maximization, and tactics. *International Journal of Group Tensions*, 8, 64–80.

Lamm, H. and Rosch, E. (1972). Information and competitiveness of incentive structure as factors in two-person negotiation. *European Journal of Social Psychology*, 2, 459–62.

Landsberger, H. A. (1955a). Interaction process analysis of professional behavior: A study of labor mediators in twelve labor–management disputes. *American Sociological Review*, 20, 566–75.

Landsberger, H. A. (1955b). Interaction process analysis of the mediation of labor–management disputes. *Journal of Abnormal and Social Psychology*, 51, 552–9.

LaTour, S., Houlden, P., Walker, L. and Thibaut, J. (1976). Some determinants of preference for modes of conflict resolution. *Journal of Conflict Resolution*, 20, 319–56.

Lawler, E. J., Ford, R. S. and Blegen, M. A. (1988). Coercive capability in conflict: A test of bilateral deterrence versus conflict spiral theory. *Social Psychology Quarterly*, 51, 93–107.

Lax, D. A. and Sebenius, J. K. (1986). *The manager as negotiator.* New York: Free Press.

Leung, K. (1987). Some determinants of reactions to procedural models for conflict resolution: A cross national study. *Journal of Personality and Social Psychology*, 53, 898–908.

Leventhal, G. S. (1976). *Fairness in social relationships.* Morristown, NJ: General Learning Press.

Lewicki, R. J. and Sheppard, B. H. (1985). Choosing how to intervene: Factors affecting the use of process and outcome control in third party dispute resolution. *Journal of Occupational Behavior*, 6, 49–64.

Lewin, D. (1987). Dispute resolution in the nonunion firm: A theoretical and empirical analysis. *Journal of Conflict Resolution*, 31, 465–502.

Lewis, S. A. and Fry, W. R. (1977). Effects of visual access and orientation on the discovery of integrative bargaining alternatives. *Organizational Behavior and Human Performance*, 20, 75–92.

Liebert, R. M., Smith, W. P., Hill, J. H. and Keiffer, M. (1968). The effects of information and magnitude of initial offer on interpersonal negotiation. *Journal of Experimental Social Psychology*, 4, 431–41.

Likert, R. (1961). *New patterns of management.* New York: McGraw-Hill.

Lim, R. and Carnevale, P. J. (1990). Contingencies in the mediation of disputes. *Journal of Personality and Social Psychology*, 58, 259–72.

Lind, E. A., Kurtz, S., Musante, L., Walker, L. and Thibaut, J. W. (1980). Procedure and outcome on reactions to adjudicated resolution of conflicts of interest. *Journal of Personality and Social Psychology*, 39, 643–53.

Lind, E. A. and Tyler, T. R. (1988). *The social psychology of procedural justice.* New York: Plenum.

Lindskold, S. (1986). GRIT: Reducing distrust through carefully introduced conciliation. In S. Worchel and W. G. Austin (eds), *Psychology of intergroup relations.* Chicago: Nelson-Hall.

Lindskold, S. and Aronoff, J. (1980). Conciliatory strategies and relative power. *Journal of Experimental Social Psychology*, 16, 187–96.

Lindskold, S. and Bennett, R. (1973). Attributing trust and conciliatory intent from coercive power capability. *Journal of Personality and Social Psychology*, 28, 180–6.

Lindskold, S., Bennent, R. and Wayner, M. (1976). Retaliation level as a foundation for subsequent conciliation. *Behavioral Science*, 21, 13–18.

Lindskold, S. and Han, G. (1988). GRIT as a foundation for integrative bargaining. *Personality and Social Psychology Bulletin*, 14, 335–45.

Lindskold, S., McElwain, D. C. and Wayner, M. (1977). Cooperation and the use of coercion by groups and by individuals. *Journal of Conflict Resolution*, 21, 531–50.

Lissak, R. I. and Sheppard, B. H. (1983). Beyond fairness: The criterion problem in research on dispute intervention. *Journal of Applied Social Psychology*, 13, 45–65.

Logan, F. A. (1960). *Incentive*. New Haven, CT: Yale University Press.

Loomis, J. (1959). Communication: The development of trust and co-operative behavior. *Human Relations*, 12, 305–15.

Lovell, H. (1952). The pressure lever in mediation. *Industrial and Labor Relations Review*, 6, 20–33.

Luce, R. D. and Raiffa, H. (1957). *Games and decisions: Introduction and critical survey*. New York: Wiley.

McClintock, C. G. and McNeel, S. P. (1967). Prior dyadic experience and monetary reward as determinants of cooperative and competitive game behavior. *Journal of Personality and Social Psychology*, 5, 282–94.

McGillicuddy, N. B., Pruitt, D. G. and Syna, H. (1984). Perceptions of firmness and strength in negotiation. *Personality and Social Psychology Bulletin*, 10, 402–9.

McGillicuddy, N. B., Welton, G. L. and Pruitt, D. G. (1987). Third party intervention: A field experiment comparing three different models. *Journal of Personality and Social Psychology*, 53, 104–12.

McGillis, D. (1981). Conflict resolution outside the courts. In L. Bickman (ed.), *Applied social psychology annual*. Beverly Hills, CA: Sage.

McGrath, J. E. (1984). *Groups: Interaction and performance*. Englewood Cliffs, New Jersey: Prentice-Hall.

McGrath, J. E. and Hollingshead, A. B. (1993). *Technology and groups*. Newberry Park: Sage.

Mackintosh, N. J. (1974). *The psychology of animal learning*. New York: Academic.

McLaughlin, M., Carnevale, P. J. and Lim, R. (1991). Professional mediators' judgments of mediation tactics: MDS and cluster analyses. *Journal of Applied Psychology*, 76, 465–72.

Mannix, E. A., Thompson, L. L. and Bazerman, M. H. (1989). Negotiation in small groups. *Journal of Applied Psychology*, 74, 508–17.

Markus, H. and Zajonc, R. B. (1985). The cognitive perspective in social psychology. In G. Lindzey and E. Aronson (eds), *The handbook of social psychology*, Vol. 1, 3rd edn, pp. 137–230. New York: Random House.

Marlowe, D., Gergen, K. T. and Doob, A. N. (1966). Opponents' personality, expectation of social interaction, and interpersonal bargaining. *Journal of Personality and Social Psychology*, 3, 206–13.

Marwell, G. and Schmidt, D. R. (1975). *Cooperation: An experimental analysis*. New York: Academic Press.

Mather, L. and Yngvesson, B. (1981). Language, audience, and the transformation of disputes. *Law and Society Review*, 15, 755.

Merry, S. E. (1989). Mediation in nonindustrial societies. In K. Kressel and D. G. Pruitt (eds), *Mediation research*, pp. 68–90. San Francisco: Jossey-Bass.

Messe, L. A. (1971). Equity in bilateral bargaining. *Journal of Personality and Social Psychology*, 17, 287–91.

Messick, D. M. and Brewer, M. B. (1983). Solving social dilemmas: A review. In L. Wheeler and P. Shaver (eds), *Review of personality and social psychology*, Vol. 4, pp. 11–44. Beverly Hills: Sage.

Messick, D. M., Wilke, H., Brewer, M. B., Kramer, R. M., Zemke, P. E. and Lui, L. (1983). Individual adaptations and structural change as solutions to social dilemmas. *Journal of Personality and Social Psychology*, 44, 294–309.

Michener, H. A., Vaske, J. J., Schleiffer, S. L., Plazewski, J. G. and Chapman, L. J. (1975). Factors affecting concession rate and threat usage in bilateral conflict. *Sociometry*, 38, 62–80.

Mitchell, C. R. (1991). A willingness to talk: Conciliatory gestures and de-escalation. *Negotiation Journal*, 7, 405–30.

Mogy, R. B. and Pruitt, D. G. (1974). Effects of a threatener's enforcement costs on threat credibility and compliance. *Journal of Personality and Social Psychology*, 29, 173–80.

Mook, D. G. (1983). In defense of external invalidity. *American Psychologist*, 38, 379–87.

Moore, C. W. (1986). *The mediation process: Practical strategies for resolving conflict*. San Francisco: Jossey-Bass.

Morley, I. E. (1982). Preparation for negotiation: Conflict, commitment, and choice. In H. Brandstatter, J. H. Davis and G. Stocker-Kreichgauer (eds), *Group decision making*. New York: Academic Press.

Morley, I. E. (1986). Negotiating and bargaining. In O. Hargie (ed.), *A handbook of communication skills*, pp. 303–24. London: Croom Helm.

Morley, I. E. (1992). Intra-organizational bargaining. In J. F. Hartley and G. M. Stephenson (eds), *Employment relations*. Cambridge, MA: Blackwell.

Morley, I. E. and Stephenson, G. M. (1977). *The social psychology of bargaining*. London: Allen and Unwin.

Morley, I. E., Webb, J. and Stephenson, G. M. (1988). In W. Stroebe, A. W. Kruglanski, D. Bar-Tal and M. Hewstone (eds), *The social psychology of intergroup conflict: Theory, research, and applications*, pp. 117–34. New York: Springer-Verlag.

Mullick, B. and Lewis, S. A. (1977). Sex roles, loving and liking: A look at dating couple's bargaining. Paper presented at the 85th annual convention of the American Psychological Association.

Murnighan, J. K. (1986). The structure of mediation and intravention: Comments on Carnevale's strategic choice model. *Negotiation Journal*, 2, 351–6.

Neale, M. A. (1984). The effect of negotiation and arbitration cost salience on bargainer behavior: The role of arbitrator and constituency in negotiator judgment. *Organizational Behavior and Human Performance*, 34, 97–111.

Neale, M. A. and Bazerman, M. H. (1983). The role of perspective-taking ability in negotiating under different forms of arbitration. *Industrial and Labor Relations*, 36, 378–88.

Neale, M. A. and Bazerman, M. H. (1985). The effects of framing and negotiator overconfidence on bargaining behaviors and outcomes. *Academy of Management Journal*, 28, 34–9.

Neale, M. A. and Bazerman, M. H. (1991). *Negotiator cognition and rationality*. Free Press: New York.

Neale, M. A., Huber, V. L. and Northcraft, G. B. (1987). The framing of negotiations: Contextual versus task frames. *Organizational Behavior and Human Decision Processes*, 39, 228–41.

Neale, M. A. and Northcraft, G. B. (1986). Experts, amateurs, and refrigerators: Comparing expert and amateur decision making on a novel task. *Organizational Behavior and Human Decision Processes*, 38, 305–17.

Northcraft, G. B. and Neale, M. A. (1987). Experts, amateurs, and real estate: An anchoring and adjustment perspective on property pricing decisions. *Organizational Behavior and Human Performance*, 39, 84–97.

Nyhart, J. D. and Samarasan, D. K. (1989). The elements of negotiation management: Using computers to help resolve conflict. *Negotiation Journal*, 5, 43–62.

O'Connor, K. M. and Carnevale, P. J. (1992). Strategic misrepresentation in bilateral negotiation. Presented at the Fifth Annual Meeting of the International Association of Conflict Management, Minneapolis.

O'Quin, K. and Aronoff, J. (1981). Humor as a technique of social influence. *Social Psychology Quarterly*, 44, 349–57.

Organ, D. W. (1971). Some variables affecting boundary role behavior. *Sociometry*, 34, 524–37.

Osgood, C. E. (1962). *An alternative to war or surrender*. Urbana: University of Illinois Press.

Oskamp, S. (1971). Effects of programmed strategies on cooperation in the prisoner's dilemma and other mixed-motive games. *Journal of Conflict Resolution*, 15, 225–59.

Patchen, M. (1989). *Resolving disputes between nations: Coercion or conciliation?* Durham, NC: Duke University Press.

Peachey, D. E. (1989). What people want from mediation. In K. Kressel and D. G. Pruitt (eds), *Mediation research*, pp. 300–21. San Francisco: Jossey-Bass.

Peirce, R. S. (1990). Conditions that influence managerial strategies in resolving conflict. Unpublished manuscript, Department of Psychology, State University of New York at Buffalo.

Peirce, R. S., Pruitt, D. G. and Czaja, S. J. (1991). Complainant–respondent differences in procedural choice. Unpublished manuscript, Department of Psychology, State University of New York at Buffalo.

Perin, C. T. (1943). A quantitative investigation of the delay-of-reinforcement gradient. *Journal of Experimental Psychology*, 32, 37–51.

Peters, E. (1952). *Conciliation in action*. New London, CT: National Foremen's Institute.

Petty, R. E. and Cacioppo, J. T. (1981). *Attitudes and persuasion: Classic and contemporary approaches*. Dubuque, IA: William C. Brown.

Pilisuk, M., Kiritz, S. and Clampitt, S. (1971). Undoing deadlocks of distrust: Hip Berkeley students and the ROTC. *Journal of Conflict Resolution*, 15, 81–95.

Pilisuk, M., Potter, P., Rapoport, A. and Winter, J. (1965). War hawks and peace doves: Alternate resolution of experimental conflicts. *Journal of Conflict Resolution*, 9, 491–508.

Pinkley, R. (1990). Dimensions of conflict frame. *Journal of Applied Psychology*, 75, 117–26.

Plous, S. (1985). Perceptual illusions and military realities: A social psychological analysis of the nuclear arms race. *Journal of Conflict Resolution*, 29, 363–89.

Poole, M. S., Holmes, M. and DeSanctis, G. (1991). Conflict management in a computer-supported meeting environment. *Management Science*, 37, 926–53.

Prein, H. (1984). A contingency approach for conflict intervention. *Group and Organization Studies*, 9, 81–102.

Pruitt, D. G. (1964). *Problem solving in the Department of State*. Denver, CO: University of Denver.

Pruitt, D. G. (1967). Reward structure and cooperation: The decomposed prisoner's dilemma. *Journal of Personality and Social Psychology*, 7, 21–7.

Pruitt, D. G. (1970). Motivational processes in the decomposed prisoner's dilemma game. *Journal of Personality and Social Psychology*, 14, 227–38.

Pruitt, D. G. (1981). *Negotiation behavior*. New York: Academic Press.

Pruitt, D. G. (1986). Trends in the scientific study of negotiation and mediation. *Negotiation Journal*, 2, 237–44.

Pruitt, D. G. (1990). Organizational negotiators as intermediaries. Presented at the Third Annual Meeting of the International Association for Conflict Management, Vancouver, British Columbia.

Pruitt, D. G. (1991). Strategy in negotiation. In V. Kremenyuk (ed.), *International negotiation: Analysis, approaches, issues*. San Francisco: Jossey-Bass.

Pruitt, D. G. (1992). Comments on flexibility in inter-organizational negotiation. Presented at IIASA Meeting, Vienna, Austria, March.

Pruitt, D. G., Carnevale, P. J., Ben-Yoav, O., Nochajski, T. H. and Van Slyck, M. (1983). Incentives for cooperation in integrative bargaining. In R. Tietz (ed.), *Aspiration levels in bargaining and economic decision making*. Berlin: Springer.

Pruitt, D. G., Carnevale, P. J., Forcey, B. and Van Slyck, M. (1986). Gender effects in negotiation: Constituent surveillance and contentious behavior. *Journal of Experimental Social Psychology*, 22, 264–75.

Pruitt, D. G., Crocker, J. and Hanes, D. L. (1987). Matching in social influence. In D. Druckman and J. Swets (eds), *Enhancing human performance: Issues, theories, and techniques*. Washington, DC: National Academy Press.

Pruitt, D. G. and Drews, J. L. (1969). The effect of time pressure, time elapsed, and the opponent's concession rate on behavior in negotiation. *Journal of Experimental Social Psychology*, 5, 43–60.

Pruitt, D. G. and Johnson, D. F. (1970). Mediation as an aid to face-saving in negotiation. *Journal of Personality and Social Psychology*, 14, 239–46.

Pruitt, D. G. and Kimmel, M. J. (1977). Twenty years of experimental gaming: Critique, synthesis, and suggestions for the future. *Annual Review of Psychology*, 28, 363–92.

Pruitt, D. G., Kimmel, M., Britton, S., Carnevale, P. J., Magenau, J., Peragallo, J. and Engram, P. (1978). The effect of accountability and surveillance on integrative bargaining. In H. Sauermann (ed.), *Bargaining behavior*. Tübingen: Mohr.

Pruitt, D. G. and Lewis, S. A. (1975). Development of integrative solutions in bilateral negotiation. *Journal of Personality and Social Psychology*, 31, 621–33.

Pruitt, D. G., Mikolic, J. M., Peirce, R. S. and Keating, M. (1992a). Aggression as a struggle tactic in social conflict. In R. Felson and J. T. Tedeschi (eds), *Aggression and violence: Social interactionist perspectives*. Washington, DC: American Psychological Association.

Pruitt, D. G., Peirce, R. S., McGillicuddy, N. B., Welton, G. L. and Castrianno, L. M. (1992b). Long-term success in mediation. *Law and Social Behavior*, (in press).

Pruitt, D. G. and Rubin, J. Z. (1986). *Social conflict: Escalation, stalemate, and settlement*. New York: McGraw-Hill.

Pruitt, D. G. and Syna, H. (1985). Mismatching the opponent's offers in negotiation. *Journal of Experimental Social Psychology*, 21, 103–13.

Pruitt, D. G., Welton, G. L., Fry, W. R., McGillicuddy, N. B., Castrianno, L. and Zubek, J. M. (1989). The process of mediation: Caucusing, control, and problem solving. In M. A. Rahim (ed.), *Managing conflict: An interdisciplinary approach*. New York: Praeger.

Putnam, L. L. (1990). Reframing integrative and distributive bargaining: A process perspective. In B. H. Sheppard, M. H. Bazerman and

R. J. Lewicki (eds), *Research on negotiation in organizations, Vol. 2,* pp. 3–30. Greenwich, CN: JAI.

Putnam, L. L. and Holmes, M. (1992). Framing, reframing and issue development. In L. L. Putnam and M. E. Roloff (eds), *Communication perspectives on negotiation.* Newbury Park, CA: Sage.

Putnam, L. L. and Jones, T. S. (1982). Reciprocity in negotiations: An analysis of bargaining interaction. *Communication Monographs,* **49,** 171–91.

Putnam, L. L. and Wilson, S. R. (1989). Argumentation and bargaining strategies as discriminators of integrative outcomes. In M. A. Rahim (ed.), *Managing conflict: An interdisciplinary approach.* New York: Praeger.

Quirk, P. (1989). The cooperative resolution of policy conflict. *American Political Science Review,* **3,** 905–20.

Rabbie, J. M. (1982). The effects of intergroup competition and co-operation on intragroup and intergroup relations. In V. J. Derlega and J. Grzelak (eds), *Cooperation and helping behavior: Theories and research,* pp. 123–49. New York: Academic Press.

Rafaeli, A. and Sutton, R. I. (1991). Emotional contrast strategies as means of social influence: Lessons from criminal interrogators and bill collectors. *Academy of Management Journal,* **34,** 749–75.

Rahim, M. A. (ed.) (1986). *Managing conflict in organizations.* New York: Praeger.

Raiffa, H. (1982). *The art and science of negotiation.* Cambridge, MA: Harvard University Press.

Raiffa, H. (1983). Mediation of conflicts. *American Behavioral Scientist,* **27,** 195–210.

Rapoport, A. (1960). *Fights, games and debates.* Ann Arbor: University of Michigan Press.

Rapoport, A. and Chammah, A. (1965). *Prisoner's dilemma: A study in conflict and cooperation.* Ann Arbor: University of Michigan Press.

Rapoport, A. and Guyer, M. (1966). A taxonomy of 2 × 2 games. *General Systems,* **11,** 203–14.

Regan, D. T., Straus, E. and Fazio, R. (1974). Liking and the attribution process. *Journal of Experimental Social Psychology,* **10,** 385–97.

Roehl, J. A. and Cook, R. F. (1989). Mediation in interpersonal disputes: Effectiveness and limitations. In K. Kressel and D. G. Pruitt (eds), *Mediation research,* pp. 31–52. San Francisco: Jossey-Bass.

Roloff, M. E. and Campion, D. E. (1987). On alleviating the debilitating effects of accountability on bargaining: Authority and self-monitoring. *Communication Monographs,* **54,** 1455–64.

Rosenthal, R. and Jacobson, L. F. (1968). *Pygmalion in the classroom.* New York: Holt, Rinehart and Winston.

Ross, L. and Nisbett, R. E. (1991). *The person and the situation: Perspectives of social psychology.* New York: McGraw-Hill.

Ross, W. H. Jr, Conlon, D. E. and Lind, E. A. (1990). The mediator as leader: Effects of behavioral style and deadline certainty on negotiator behavior. *Group and Organization Studies*, 15, 105–24.

Roth, A. E. (ed.) (1985). *Game-theoretic models of bargaining*. Cambridge: Cambridge University Press.

Roth, A. E., Prasnikar, V., Okuno-Fujiwara, M. and Zamir, S. (1991). Bargaining and market behavior in Jerusalem, Ljubljana, Pittsburgh, and Tokyo: An experimental study. *American Economic Review* (in the press).

Rothbart, M. and Hallmark, W. (1988). Ingroup–outgroup differences in the perceived efficacy of coercion and conciliation in resolving social conflict. *Journal of Personality and Social Psychology*, 55, 248–57.

Rubin, J. Z. (1980). Experimental research on third-party intervention in conflict: Toward some generalizations. *Psychological Bulletin*, 87, 379–91.

Rubin, J. Z. (1981). Introduction. In J. Z. Rubin (ed.), *Dynamics of third party intervention: Kissinger in the Middle East*, pp. 3–43. New York: Praeger.

Rubin, J. Z. (1985). Third party intervention in family conflict. *Negotiation Journal*, 1, 363–72.

Rubin, J. Z. and Brown, B. (1975). *The social psychology of bargaining and negotiations*. New York: Academic Press.

Rubin, J. Z., Kim, S. H. and Peretz, N. M. (1990). Expectancy effects and negotiation. *Journal of Social Issues*, 46, 125–39.

Rubin, J. Z. and Lewicki, R. (1973). A three-factor experimental analysis of promises and threats. *Journal of Applied Social Psychology*, 3, 240–57.

Rubin, J. Z. and Sander, E. A. F. (1988). When should we use agents? Direct vs. representative negotiation. *Negotiation Journal*, 4, 395–401.

Ruble, T. L. and Thomas, K. W. (1976). Support for a two-dimensional model of conflict behavior. *Organizational Behavior and Human Performance*, 16, 143–55.

Rusbult, C. E., Verette, J., Whitney, G. A., Slovik, L. F. and Lipkus, I. (1991). Accommodation processes in close relationships: Theory and preliminary empirical evidence. *Journal of Personality and Social Psychology*, 60, 53–78.

Rutte, C. G., Wilke, H. A. M. and Messick, D. M. (1987). Scarcity or abundance caused by people or the environment as determinants of behavior in the resource dilemma. *Journal of Experimental Social Psychology*, 23, 208–16.

Samuelson, C. D., Messick, D. M., Rutte, C. G. and Wilke, H. (1984). Individual and structural solutions to resources dilemmas in two cultures. *Journal of Personality and Social Psychology*, 47, 94–104.

Sarat, A. (1976). Alternatives in dispute processing: Litigation is a small claims court. *Law and Society*, 10, 339–75.

Sato, K. (1987). Distribution of the cost of maintaining common resources. *Journal of Experimental and Social Psychology*, 23, 19–31.

Sato, K. (1988). Trust and group size in a social dilemma. *Japanese Psychological Research*, 30, 88–93.

Sato, K. (1989). Trust and feedback in a social dilemma. *Japanese Journal of Experimental Social Psychology*, 29, 123–8.

Saunders, H. (1985). We need a larger theory of negotiation. *Negotiation Journal*, 3, 249–62.

Schelling, T. (1960). *The strategy of conflict*. Cambridge: Harvard University Press.

Schlenker, B. R., Bonoma, T. V., Tedeschi, J. T. and Pivnick, W. P. (1970). Compliance to threats as a function of the wording of the threat and the exploitativeness of the threatener. *Sociometry*, 33, 394–408.

Schlenker, B. R., Helm, B. and Tedeschi, J. T. (1973). The effects of personality and situational variables on behavioral trust. *Journal of Personality and Social Psychology*, 25, 419–27.

Schoeninger, D. W. and Wood, W. D. (1969). Comparison of married and ad hoc mixed-sex dyads negotiating the division of a reward. *Journal of Experimental Social Psychology*, 5, 483–99.

Schopler, J., Insko, C. A., Graetz, K. A., Drigotas, S. M. and Smith, V. A. (1991). The generality of the individual-group discontinuity effect: Variations in positivity–negativity of outcomes, players' relative power, and magnitude of outcomes. *Personality and Social Psychology Bulletin*, 17, 612–24.

Schulz, J. W. and Pruitt, D. G. (1978). The effects of mutual concern on joint welfare. *Journal of Experimental Social Psychology*, 14, 480–91.

Sermat, V. (1964). Cooperative behavior in a mixed-motive game. *Journal of Social Psychology*, 62, 217–39.

Sermat, V. (1967). The effect of an initial cooperative or competitive treatment upon a subject's response to conditional cooperation. *Behavioral Science*, 12, 301–13.

Shapira, Z. (1990). Discussant comments on decision making in competitive contexts. Presented at the Annual Meeting of the Society for Judgment and Decision Making, New Orleans, November.

Shapiro, D. L. and Bies, R. J. (1991). Threats, bluffs, and disclaimers in negotiations. Unpublished manuscript, Department of Business Administration, University of North Carolina, Chapel Hill, North Carolina.

Shapiro, D., Driegh, R. and Brett, J. M. (1985). Mediator behavior and the outcome of mediation. *Journal of Social Issues*, 41, 101–14.

Sharma, A., Shapiro, D. and Kesner, I. F. (1991). Targets of mergers: Applying a negotiation perspective to predict degree of resistance. *International Journal of Conflict Management*, 2, 117–38.

Shaw, J. I., Fischer, C. S. and Kelley, H. H. (1973). Decision making by third parties in settling disputes. *Journal of Applied Social Psychology*, 3, 197–218.

Sheppard, B. H. (1984). Third party conflict intervention: A procedural framework. In B. M. Staw and L. L. Cummings (eds), *Research in organizational behavior*, Vol. 6, pp. 141–90. Greenwich, CT: JAI.

Sheppard, B. H., Blumenfeld-Jones, K. and Roth, J. (1989). Informal thirdpartyship: Studies of everyday conflict intervention. In K. Kressel and D. G. Pruitt (eds), *Mediation research*, pp. 166–89. San Francisco: Jossey-Bass.

Sherif, M. (1967). *Group conflict and cooperation*. London: Routledge & Kegan Paul.

Sherif, M. and Sherif, C. W. (1953). *Groups in harmony and tension*. New York: Harper and Row.

Siegel, S. and Fouraker, L. E. (1960). *Bargaining and group decision making: Experiments in bilateral monopoly*. New York: McGraw-Hill.

Sillars, A. L. (1981). Attributions and interpersonal conflict resolution. In J. H. Harvey, W. Ickes and R. F. Kidd (eds), *New directions in attribution research*, Vol. 3, pp. 279–305. Hillsdale, NJ: Lawrence Erlbaum.

Sjostedt, G. (1991). Trade talks. In V. A. Kremenyuk (ed.), *International negotiation: Analysis, approaches, issues*, pp. 315–30. San Francisco: Jossey-Bass.

Skinner, B. F. (1938). *The behavior of organisms*. New York: Appleton.

Smith, D. L., Pruitt, D. G. and Carnevale, P. J. (1982). Matching and mismatching: The effect of own limit, other's toughness, and time pressure on concession rate in negotiation. *Journal of Personality and Social Psychology*, 42, 876–83.

Smith, W. P. (1985). Effectiveness of the biased mediator. *Negotiation Journal*, 1, 363–72.

Smith, W. P. (1987). Conflict and negotiation: Trends and emerging issues. *Journal of Applied Social Psychology*, 17, 641–77.

Smith, W. P. and Anderson, A. J. (1975). Threats, communication, and bargaining. *Journal of Personality and Social Psychology*, 32, 76–82.

Snyder, G. H. and Diesing, P. (1977). *Conflict among nations: Bargaining, decision making, and system structure in international crises*. Princeton, NJ: Princeton University Press.

Snyder, M. and Swann, W. B. Jr (1978). Behavioral confirmation in social interaction: From social perception to social reality. *Journal of Experimental Social Psychology*, 14, 148–62.

Snyder, M., Tanke, E. D. and Berscheid, E. (1977). Social perception and interpersonal behavior: On the self-fulfilling nature of social stereotypes. *Journal of Personality and Social Psychology*, 9, 656–66.

Solomon, L. (1960). The influence of some types of power relationships and game strategies upon the development of interpersonal trust. *Journal of Abnormal and Social Psychology*, 61, 223–60.

Stephenson, G. M. (1981). Intergroup bargaining and negotiation. In J. C. Turner and H. Giles (eds), *The social psychology of intergroup behavior*, pp. 168–98. Oxford: Blackwell.

Stevens, C. M. (1963). *Strategy and collective bargaining negotiation*. New York: McGraw-Hill.

Stillinger, C., Epelbaum, M., Keltner, D. and Ross, L. (1991). The reactive devaluation barrier to conflict resolution. Unpublished manuscript.

Stoll, R. J. and McAndrew, W. (1986). Negotiating strategic arms control, 1969–1979. *Journal of Conflict Resolution*, 30, 315–26.

Susskind, L. and Ozawa, C. (1985). Mediating public disputes: Obstacles and possibilities. *Journal of Social Issues*, 41, 145–59.

Syna, H. (1984). Couples in conflict: Conflict resolution strategies, perceptions about sources of conflict and relationship adjustment. Doctoral dissertation, State University of New York at Buffalo.

Tajfel, H., Flament, C., Billig, M. G. and Bundy, R. F. (1971). Social categorisation and intergroup behavior. *European Journal of Social Psychology*, 1, 149–77.

Tajfel, H. and Turner, J. C. (1986). The social identity theory of intergroup behavior. In S. Worchel and W. G. Austin (eds), *Psychology of intergroup relations*. Chicago: Nelson-Hall.

Taylor, S. E. (1991). Asymmetrical effects of positive and negative events: The mobilization–minimization hypothesis. *Psychological Bulletin*, 110, 67–85.

Taylor, S. E. and Crocker, J. (1981). Schematic bases of social information processing. In E. T. Higgins, C. P. Heiman and M. P. Zanna (eds), *Social cognition: The Ontario symposium*, pp. 89–134. Hillsdale, NJ: Erlbaum.

Tedeschi, J. T. and Bonoma, T. V. (1977). Measures of last resort: Coercion and aggression in bargaining. In D. Druckman (ed.), *Negotiations: social psychological perspectives*. Beverly Hills, CA: Sage.

Tedeschi, J. T., Schlenker, B. R. and Bonoma, T. V. (1973). *Conflict, power, and games*. Chicago: Aldine.

Terhune, K. W. (1974). "Wash-in," "wash-out," and systematic effects in extended prisoner's dilemma. *Journal of Conflict Resolution*, 18, 656–85.

Thibaut, J. W. and Kelley, H. H. (1959). *The social psychology of groups*. New York: Wiley.

Thibaut, J. and Walker, L. (1975). *Procedural justice: A psychological analysis*. Hillsdale, NJ: Erlbaum.

Thibaut, J., Walker, L., LaTour, S. and Houlden, P. (1974). Procedural justice as fairness. *Stanford Law Review*, 26, 1271–89.

Thomas, K. W. (1976). Conflict and conflict management. In M. Dunnette (ed.), *Handbook of industrial and organizational psychology*, pp. 889–935. Chicago: Rand McNally.

Thomas, K. W. (1982). Manager and mediator: A comparison of third-party roles based upon conflict-management goals. In G. B. J. Bomers and R. B. Peterson (eds), *Conflict management and industrial relations*, pp. 141–57. Boston: Kluwer Nijhoff.

Thompson, L. L. (1990a). The influence of experience on negotiation performance. *Journal of Experimental Social Psychology*, 26, 528–44.

Thompson, L. L. (1990b). Negotiation behavior and outcomes: Empirical evidence and theoretical issues. *Psychological Bulletin*, 108, 515–32.

Thompson, L. L. (1990c). An examination of naive and experienced negotiators. *Journal of Personality and Social Psychology*, 59, 82–90.

Thompson, L. L. (1991a). Information exchange in negotiation. *Journal of Experimental Social Psychology*, 27, 161–79.

Thompson, L. L. (1991b). Perceptions of negotiation: Observers' and participants' points of view. Presented at Annual Meeting Midwestern Psychological Association, Chicago.

Thompson, L. L. and Hastie, R. (1990). Social perception in negotiation. *Organizational Behavior and Human Decision Processes*, 47, 98–123.

Thompson, L. and Loewenstein, G. (1992). Egocentric interpretations of fairness and interpersonal conflict. *Organizational Behavior and Human Decision Processes*, 51, 176–97.

Tietz, R. and Weber, H. J. (1978). Decision behavior in multivariable negotiations. In H. Sauermann (ed.), *Bargaining behavior*. Tübingen: Mohr.

Tjosvold, D. (1977). Commitment to justice in conflict between unequal persons. *Journal of Applied Social Psychology*, 7, 149–62.

Tjosvold, D., Johnson, D. W. and Fabrey, L. J. (1980). Effects of controversy and defensiveness on cognitive perspective-taking. *Psychological Report*, 47, 1043–53.

Tjosvold, D. and Okun, M. A. (1976). Corrupting effects of unequal power: Cognitive perspective-taking and cooperation. Paper presented at the American Psychological Association Annual Convention, Washington, D.C.

Touval, S. (1975). Biased intermediaries: Theoretical and historical considerations. *Jerusalem Journal of International Relations*, 1, 51–69.

Touval, S. (1985). The context of mediation. *Negotiation Journal*, 1, 373–8.

Touval, S. (1989). Multilateral negotiation: An analytic approach. *Negotiation Journal*, April, 159–73.

Touval, S. and Zartman, I. W. (1985). *International mediation in theory and practice*. Boulder, CO: Westview Press.

Touval, S. and Zartman, I. W. (1989). Mediation in international conflicts. In K. Kressel and D. G. Pruitt (eds), *Mediation research*, pp. 115–37. San Francisco: Jossey-Bass.

Touzard, H. (1977). *La mediation et la resolution des conflicts* (Mediation and the resolution of conflicts). Paris: PUF.

Triandis, H. C. (1989). The self and social behavior in different cultural contexts. *Psychological Review*, 96, 506–20.

Turner, J. C. and Giles, H. (eds) (1981). *Intergroup behavior*. Chicago: University of Chicago Press.

Turner, J. C., Hogg, M. A., Oakes, P. J. and Smith, P. M. (1984). Failure and defeat as determinants of group cohesiveness. *British Journal of Social Psychology*, 23, 97–111.

Tversky, A. and Kahneman, D. (1974). Judgment under uncertainty: Heuristics and biases. *Science*, 185, 1124–31.

Tversky, A. and Kahneman, D. (1992). Loss aversion in riskless choice: a reference dependent model. *Quarterly Journal of Economics* (in the press).

Tyler, T. R. (1984). The role of perceived injustice in defendants' evaluations of their courtroom experience. *Law and Society Review*, 18, 51–74.

Tyler, T. R. (1987a). Conditions leading to value expressive effects in judgments of procedural justice: A test of four models. *Journal of Personality and Social Psychology*, 52, 333–44.

Tyler, T. R. (1987b). The psychology of disputant concerns in mediation. *Negotiation Journal*, 3, 367–74.

Ury, W. L., Brett, J. M. and Goldberg, S. B. (1988). *Getting disputes resolved: Designing systems to cut the costs of conflict*. San Francisco: Jossey-Bass.

Valley, K. L. (1990). Rank and relationship effects on formality in conflict management. Paper presented at the meeting of the International Association of Conflict Management, Vancouver, British Columbia, June.

Vallone, R. P., Ross, L. and Lepper, M. R. (1985). The hostile media phenomenon: Biased perception and perceptions of media bias in coverage of the Beirut massacre. *Journal of Personality and Social Psychology*, 49, 577–85.

van de Vliert, E. (1981). Siding and other reactions to a conflict: A theory of escalation toward outsiders. *Journal of Conflict Resolution*, 25, 495–520.

van de Vliert, E. (1990). Positive effects of conflict: A field assessment. *The International Journal of Conflict Management*, 1, 69–80.

van de Vliert, E. (1992). Questions about the strategic choice model of negotiation. *Negotiation Journal* (in press).

van de Vliert, E. and Prein, H. C. M. (1989). The difference in the meaning of forcing in the conflict management of actors and observers. In M. A. Rahim (ed.), *Managing conflict: An interdisciplinary approach*. New York: Praeger.

Vitz, P. C. and Kite, W. R. (1970). Factors affecting conflict and negotiation within an alliance. *Journal of Experimental Social Psychology*, 5, 233–47.

Voissem, N. H. and Sistrunk, F. (1971). Communication schedule and cooperative game behavior. *Journal of Personality and Social Psychology*, 19, 160–7.

Wall, J. A. Jr (1975). Effects of constituent trust and representative bargaining orientation on intergroup bargaining. *Journal of Personality and Social Psychology*, 31, 1004–12.

Wall, J. A. Jr (1977a). Intergroup bargaining: Effects of opposing constituents' stance, opposing representative's bargaining, and representatives' locus of control. *Journal of Conflict Resolution*, 21, 459–74.

Wall, J. A. Jr (1977b). Operantly conditioning a bargainer's concession making. *Journal of Experimental Social Psychology*, 13, 431–40.

Wall, J. A. Jr (1981). Mediation: An analysis, review, and proposed research. *Journal of Conflict Resolution*, 25, 157–80.

Wall, J. A. Jr (1985). *Negotiation: Theory and practice*. Glenview, IL: Scott, Foresman.

Wall, J. A. Jr and Blum, M. (1991). Community mediation in the People's Republic of China. *Journal of Conflict Resolution*, 35, 3–20.

Wall, J. A. Jr and Lynn, A. (1992). Mediation: A current review. *Journal of Confict Resolution*.

Wall, J. A. Jr and Rude, D. E. (1989). Judicial mediation of settlement negotiations. In K. Kressel and D. G. Pruitt (eds), *Mediation research*, pp. 190–212. San Francisco: Jossey-Bass.

Wall, J. A. Jr and Rude, D. E. (1991). The judge as mediator. *Journal of Applied Psychology*, 76, 54–9.

Walster, E. H., Walster, G. W. and Berscheid, E. (1978). *Equity: Theory and research*. Boston: Allyn & Bacon.

Walton, R. E. (1969). *Interpersonal peacemaking: Confrontations and third-party consultation*. Reading, MA: Addison-Wesley.

Walton, R. E. and McKersie, R. (1965). *A behavioral theory of labor negotiations: An analysis of a social interaction system*. New York: McGraw-Hill.

Weingart, L. R., Bennett, R. and Brett, J. (1993). The impact of consideration of issues and motivational orientation on group negotiation processes and outcome. *Journal of Applied Psychology* (in press).

Weingart, L. R., Thompson, L. L., Bazerman, M. H. and Carroll, J. S. (1990). Tactical behavior and negotiation outcomes. *International Journal of Conflict Management*, 1, 7–31.

Weiss, S. E. and Stripp, W. (1985). *Negotiating with foreign businesspersons: An introduction for Americans with propositions of six cultures*. Working paper series, New York University, Faculty of Business Administration.

Welton, G. L. and Pruitt, D. G. (1987). The mediation process: The effects of mediator bias and disputant power. *Personality and Social Psychology Bulletin*, 13, 123–33.

Welton, G. L., Pruitt, D. G. and McGillicuddy, N. B. (1988). The role of caucusing in community mediation. *Journal of Conflict Resolution*, 32, 181–202.

White, R. K. (1984). *Fearful warriors: A psychological Profile of US–Soviet relations*. New York: The Free Press.

Wichman, H. (1972). Effects of communication on cooperation in a 2-person game. In L. Wrightsman, J. O'Connor and N. Baker (eds), *Cooperation and competition*. Belmont, CA: Brooks/Cole.

Wilder, D. A. (1986). Social categorization: Implications for creation and reduction of intergroup bias. In L. Berkowitz (ed.), *Advances in experimental social psychology*, Vol. 19, pp. 291–355. New York: Academic Press.

Williams, D. L. and Lewis, S. A. (1976). The effects of sex-role attitudes on integrative bargaining. Presented at the Eighty-fourth Annual Meeting of the American Psychological Association, Washington, DC.

Winham, G. R. (1979). Practitioner's views of international negotiation. *World Politics*, 32, 111–35.

Winham, G. R. (1991). Simulation for teaching and analysis. In V. A. Kremenyuk (ed.), *International negotiation: Analysis, approaches, issues*, pp. 409–23. San Francisco: Jossey-Bass.

Witty, C. J. (1980). *Mediation in society: Conflict management in Lebanon*. New York: Academic Press.

Worchel, S. (1979). Cooperation and the reduction of intergroup conflict: Some determining factors. In W. G. Austin and S. Worchel (eds), *The social psychology of intergroup relations*, pp. 262–73. Monterey, CA: Brooks/Cole.

Yamagishi, T. (1986). The provision of a sanctioning system as a public good. *Journal of Personality and Social Psychology*, 51, 110–16.

Yamagishi, T. and Sato, K. (1986). Motivational bases of the public goods problem. *Journal of Personality and Social Psychology*, 50, 67–73.

Young, O. R. (1972). Intermediaries: Additional thoughts on third parties. *Journal of Conflict Resolution*, 16, 51–65.

Young, O. R. (ed.) (1975). *Bargaining: Formal theories of negotiation*. Urbana: University of Illinois Press.

Yukl, G. A. (1974a). The effects of situational variables and opponent concessions on a bargainer's perception, aspirations, and concessions. *Journal of Personality and Social Psychology*, 29, 227–36.

Yukl, G. A. (1974b). Effects of opponents initial offer, concession magnitude, and concession frequency on bargaining behavior. *Journal of Personality and Social Psychology*, 30, 332–5.

Yukl, G. A., Malone, M. P., Hayslip, B. and Pamin, T. A. (1976). The effects of time pressure and issue settlement order on integrative bargaining. *Sociometry*, 39, 277–81.

Zadney, J. and Gerard, H. B. (1974). Attributed intentions and informational selectivity. *Journal of Experimental Social Psychology*, 10, 34–52.

Zajonc, R. B. (1968). Attitudinal effects of mere exposure. *Journal of Personality and Social Psychology. Monograph Supplement*, 9 (2, Part 2), 2–27.

Zartman, I. W. (1977). Negotiation as a joint decision-making process. *Journal of Conflict Resolution*, 21, 619–38.

Zartman, I. W. and Berman, M. R. (1982). *The practical negotiator*. New Haven, CT: Yale University Press.

Zartman, I. W. and Touval, S. (1985). International mediation: Techniques, strategies, and situational effects. *Journal of Social Issues*, 41, 27–45.

Zartman, I. W., Antrim, L., Bonham, M., Druckman, D., Jensen, L., Pruitt, D. G. and Young, H. R. (1990). The many faces of fairness in negotiated decisions. Unpublished manuscript.

Zubek, J. M., Pruitt, D. G., Peirce, R. S., McGillicuddy, N. B. and Syna, H. (1992). Short-term success in mediation: Its relationship to disputant and mediator behaviors and prior conditions. *Journal of Conflict Resolution*, 36, 546–72.

NAME INDEX

SUBJECT INDEX